JAZZ AND THE WHITE AMERICANS

JAZZ

JAZZ AND THE WHITE AMERICANS

AND THE
WHITE AMERICANS

THE ACCEPTANCE OF A NEW ART FORM

NEIL LEONARD

THE UNIVERSITY OF CHICAGO PRESS

Library of Congress Catalog Card Number: 62-19626

The University of Chicago Press, Chicago & London

The University of Toronto Press, Toronto 5, Canada

© 1962 by The University of Chicago. All rights reserved

Published 1962. Printed in the United States of America

To My Father and Mother

CONTENTS

INTRODUCTION

DURING the long history of disputes over esthetic forms and styles, perhaps the most heated arguments have been those between defenders of the old and advocates of the new. Although wise observers have probably always been aware of the continuity between the old and new, extremists on both the traditionalist and the modernist sides have persistently asserted the absolute virtue of their own points of view. In 1477, Johannes Tinctoris, the Belgian authority on music, declared, "There is no music worth hearing save only in the last forty years."[1] And in 1912, after listening to Schoenberg's *Pierrot Lunaire*, traditionalist critic Otto Taubmann exclaimed, "If this is music of the future, then I pray my Creator not to let me live to hear it again."[2]

The controversy between modernist and traditionalist in all the arts has been particularly violent in recent times. By the last part of the nineteenth century, most artists, critics, and laymen in the music audience were traditionalists, who concentrated on the art of the past and regarded esthetic feeling as something quite apart from the rest of contemporary life. Artists who dealt with pressing human concerns and who expressed themselves in unconventional ways often found their work misunderstood or ignored. By the first part of the twentieth century only a few people saw positive meaning in the work of such modern artists as Picasso, Bartók, and Frank Lloyd Wright. In effect, a wide gap had opened between the sensibilities of the advanced artist and those of his potential audience.

Since the 1890's a series of controversies over jazz have provided dramatic illustrations of the gap between artist and audience. So far the most heated and, in many ways, the most significant controversy took place between the two world wars. It started in 1917, when phonograph records and a growing number of bands introduced collectively improvised jazz to the general public. Before long the new music became a public issue. Both the music and the non-music press reported vehement views on jazz and discussed it in their editorials. Musicians argued violently about it. Intellectuals, artists, and patrons of the arts took sides. Clergymen preached sermons about "the jazz problem." Educators offered their opinions. Legislators and civic officials debated the problem and now and again tried to regulate its supposed evils.

At first almost all the statements reported in the press condemned jazz. They called it distasteful and charged that it provoked immoral behavior. The few articulate advocates of the new music maintained that it was an exciting expression of the dynamic aspects of American life. Between the opposing camps stood people who found jazz puzzling and who leaned toward the anti-jazz side, or who were as yet uncommitted. Other Americans, less aware of the issues of the controversy, had their preferences decided by a variety of tastemakers who were emotionally, and sometimes financially, involved in the jazz dispute.

Because the new music sounded wildly unconventional, the

widespread and intense opposition it aroused is not surprising, but the speed with which the opposition declined is extraordinary. In two decades the mean of public opinion shifted from puzzlement and dislike to tolerance and acceptance of jazz. By the late 1930's only a few Americans still denounced it publicly. More and more of them (including some of the same ones who had condemned it in the 1920's) now regarded it not merely as respectable popular music but as art. Forward-looking academic musicians increasingly viewed it with interest. Composers borrowed its techniques and sometimes tried to capture its spirit. It entered the sanctums of the concert hall and the conservatory. Music critics and historians wrote books analyzing its elements and describing its evolution. It began to find its way into high school and college classrooms, and occasionally society matrons used it in concerts to benefit charity. A growing number of Americans took pride in what some of them believed to be their country's greatest contribution to the arts.

This book is a study of the rapid change of taste for jazz in America between the two world wars. My starting point was Morroe Berger's article, "Jazz: Resistance to the Diffusion of a Culture-Pattern."[3] Berger outlined the opposition to jazz and suggested several questions for future research. I have sought answers to five of his questions (sometimes altering them slightly to fit my needs): Why did jazz evoke such intense opposition? Why did jazz continue to spread in the face of this opposition? What kinds of jazz were acceptable to whom? What changes did it undergo as it gathered supporters? What were the public's feelings about it as it gained a relatively large audience? I limited these questions to acceptance of jazz among whites because acceptance by Negroes involves special problems too numerous and complex for examination here.

In order to give further direction to the study I subsumed the five questions under one: Did the events involved in the acceptance of jazz fall into any pattern? After a preliminary investigation of the evidence, I found that they seemed to fit a pattern of Hegelian derivation with a thesis, antithesis, and synthesis. The thesis included traditional music and the values connected with it; the antithesis comprised jazz and associated values; and the synthesis involved a compromise between the opposing sides. This theory formed the basis of a working hypothesis which guided the research on, and the presentation of, the material. Upon finishing the study, I had to alter some particulars of the hypothesis, but its basic outline remained intact. The detailed, revised version appears in the Conclusion of this book.

The book has two main purposes. First, it is an effort to throw light upon some of the questions raised by the jazz controversy and still unsettled in the minds of many Americans: Is jazz art music or tawdry popular music? What does it do to the sensibilities, especially of young people? Does it provoke vice or violence? If not, why is it frequently associated with them? Is it a reversion to savagery? Does it need refinement? Can it be blended successfully with academic music, and if it can, which of its elements should be kept, which discarded? Does it accurately reflect life in the United States? Whether or not it does, what does it say about our civilization? We inherit these questions and most of our answers to them from the 1918–40 jazz controversy. I hope that an examination of the dispute will help to illuminate the proper place of jazz both in American life and in the world of art.

Second, this book is an effort to show something of the nature of the artist-audience gap. Because it offers a clear pattern of rejection and then acceptance of music, the jazz controversy provides good material for investigating the dynamics of taste changes. Such an investigation may reveal some of the causes of the artist-audience gap and suggest ways of narrowing it. Because it has existed so long, we tend to accept it as a normal condition. In my judgment, it is not. Some differences between the sensibilities of artists and of their potential audience are inevitable, but the great breach that has separated them in recent years is, I believe, harmful and should not be ignored. One function of art is to provide emotional symbols for contemporary experience. In so far as we fail to know contemporary art, we surrender a vital tool in our attempts to understand, express, extend, and reform human experience. I hope this study will help to call attention to this problem and to suggest ways of making relatively full use of the tool.

CHAPTER ONE

BACKGROUND

THE ROOTS of the jazz controversy go back to the first part of the nineteenth century. At that time folk and popular music dominated the musical interests of most Americans. People sang or played instruments at home, school, church, work, and in theaters, outdoor concerts, and parades. Secular popular songs such as those by Stephen Foster or Dan Emmett were in great demand, but the favorites were religious popular songs such as those by Lowell Mason. In seventeen years shortly before the Civil War, his collection of hymns, *Carmina Sacra*, sold 500,000 copies.[1]

Although religious popular music remained profitable after the Civil War, an increasing number of Americans preferred secular music. A whole industry, which came to be called Tin Pan Alley, grew up to fill the demand for it. By the nineties the sale of popular songs had become a complicated and expensive business. Sometimes composers and publishers paid

a singer or a band leader to perform a prospective hit at a theater or restaurant. At other times song-sellers distributed lyrics so
that the audience could accompany a vaudeville singer. And in
some instances they planted performers in audiences to sing a
chorus at a strategic moment or to encourage patrons to sing
along with the orchestra. After 1911 music and five-and-ten
cent stores sold sheet music and sometimes employed a pianist,
singer, or player piano to demonstrate the product. The dance
craze preceding World War I contributed to the boom in popular music, which was now available on records as well as on
piano rolls and sheet music. By the twenties a commercial
success like Irving Berlin's "All by Myself" in seventy-five
weeks might sell a million copies of sheet music, over 150,000
piano rolls, and a million and a quarter records.[2]

While Tin Pan Alley was still young, the popular musical
theater catered to a wide audience. Minstrelsy, featuring blackface imitations of Negro life in songs and dances, as well as
other kinds of popular music, dominated the popular stage
through the Civil War and into the nineties. During the same
years assorted waltzes, jigs, froelichs, ballads, and dialect,
comic, and other songs were heard in saloons, honky tonks,
theaters of ethnic minorities and on the popular variety stage.
After 1890 acts from all these sources and from minstrelsy were
combined into vaudeville, which by 1900 became the most
profitable type of popular entertainment. Some form of music
accompanied most vaudeville acts, only a piano in small theaters, small and medium-sized orchestras in larger ones. Musicians performed on stage in many novelty acts; musical saws,
water glasses, and musical clowns of all sorts pleased audiences.
One well-known act of Field and Hanson featured a cornetist
who played the "Anvil Chorus" while his partner beat time on
the cornetist's seat with a slapstick.[3] More earnest musical acts,
such as ragtime pianist Ben Harney, brass bands, and eventually jazz bands of varying quality occupied prominent places in
vaudeville billing.

During the eighties Americans filled gaslit opera houses to enjoy the productions of Gilbert and Sullivan, but native composers, borrowing heavily from the Viennese, shortly won audiences away. Victor Herbert, the most successful of these composers, wrote thirty-five operettas between 1894 and 1917.[4] His rich melodies and adept orchestrations have kept his best productions fresh for years, and some of his songs like "Kiss Me Again," "Ah, Sweet Mystery of Life," and "I'm Falling in Love with Someone" are still familiar to most Americans. Reginald DeKoven, who wrote during the same years also earned acclaim, particularly with his *Robin Hood*, which contained the well-known "Oh Promise Me" and which some critics consider the best comic opera ever written by an American. Herbert's light operas and to a lesser extent DeKoven's are as durable as those of the most applauded Europeans, Franz von Suppé and Jacques Offenbach.

March music was also popular after the Civil War, and the United States Marine Band led the field. In 1892 its conductor, John Philip Sousa, resigned from the service to lead his own band, which quickly became the most famous organization of its kind. It made several European trips and even a world tour. Sousa composed nearly a hundred marches, many still played today, including "Semper Fidelis," "The Washington Post March," and "The Stars and Stripes Forever."[5] During his heyday, hometown bands were prominent in parades and political rallies. In many towns hexagonal bandstands were built in parks for concerts by local bands during the warm months.

Until the nineties popular music in the United States can be classified as what we shall call traditional music, whose elements came from Europe. Sousa marches, ballads such as "Silver Threads among the Gold," waltzes such as "After the Ball," novelty or dialect songs such as "Down Went McGinty," hymns such as "From Greenland's Icy Mountains," and the various types of music found in early vaudeville and light opera were dominated by Europe's traditional rhythmic, melodic, and harmonic elements. These elements characterized minstrel music, too, but some minstrel songs contained non-traditional elements of rhythm and tonality, like syncopation and microtones (blue notes), which Americans first associated with Negro music. For example, syncopation appears in "Ole Dan Tucker" at the words "git out de way," and there is a blue note (in this case a "flattened" seventh) in Dan Emmett's "My Aunt Sally." [6]

Such non-traditional elements were forerunners of a later trend. After the nineties American popular music increasingly availed itself of various characteristics later connected with jazz. In its dying days minstrelsy offered ragtime as a special attraction. Later, vaudeville, and the various musical revues and musical comedies, presented jazz or imitations of it. By the twenties, jazz characteristics had filtered into popular music to such an extent that Tin Pan Alley sold most of its sheet music, piano rolls, and phonograph records under the name of jazz.

II

A form of art music (i.e., music of high esthetic value), jazz emerged from folk and popular music. Jazz reached its first wide public as ragtime, initially a written syncopated piano music, invariably happy in mood, and rondo-like in form.[7] Ragtime developed chiefly under the hands of Scott Joplin, about 1896 in Sedalia, Missouri. The new music spread quickly to St. Louis and Chicago, and from there its various forms traveled across the country. By 1900 its commercial possibilities were apparent, and Tin Pan Alley composers and arrangers and other popular musicians diluted it with traditional musical elements, usually in the form of Tin Pan Alley clichés, lowering its esthetic content, and thus changing it from art music to a type of popular music known as commercial jazz. Commercial ragtime proved palatable to a growing number of people. Publishers systematically distributed and plugged it in music and ten-cent stores and paid performers to include it in their programs. Almost every tune available was "ragged" for recording cylinders or piano rolls. Teachers offered simplified ragtime lessons, and dealers in inexpensive instruction books did a large store and mail-order business.

By 1917, as public interest in ragtime was subsiding, its exploiters discovered profit in the blues. At first the blues were primarily vocal, folk music. W. C. Handy, whose shop was to become one of the most famous in Tin Pan Alley, was the first to recognize that something of the blues could be written down and sold. He took part of their form and melody to make his first commercial hit, "Memphis Blues." The response was gratifying. Minstrel, concert, vaudeville, and even military bands played versions of Handy's tunes. After 1917, commercial blues had saturated much of our popular music; however, it was not until the twenties that phonograph companies began to exploit the Negro market for real blues by issuing a series of so-called race records on which such jazz artists as Bessie Smith and Louis Armstrong first recorded.

In 1917 Tin Pan Alley began to exploit collectively improvised, instrumental jazz, which, like ragtime and the blues, had existed some time before it was diluted for a wide market. Although the history of collectively improvised jazz is not fully clear, it is patent that by 1900 New Orleans was the center for collectively improvising bands. Jazz in New Orleans reflected the different cultural and racial backgrounds of the city's population. Speaking of piano players, pianist Jelly Roll Morton explained, "We had Spanish, we had colored, we had white, we had Frenchmens [sic], we had Americans, we had them from all parts of the world . . . we had so many different styles."[8] In New Orleans, and elsewhere in the South, musical ideas from different sources jostled one another constantly. There was an easy exchange of material according to the whims and tastes of the performer and his audience. Developing in this environment, jazz borrowed from, among other things, Protestant hymns, British ballads, Spanish songs and Afro-Spanish rhythms, French quadrilles and marches, various

West African rhythms, and melodic elements found in spirituals, the blues, work songs, and field hollers.[9]

Much of the collectively improvised jazz came first from the brass bands of the New Orleans Negroes that played for parades, picnics, concerts, riverboat excursions, and dances. Gradually, New Orleans whites began to imitate the collective improvisation of Negroes. At first, the playing of jazz by both blacks and whites was an avocation, and the distinction between performer and audience was not always clear. Many early jazz men were part-time musicians called "fakers" because they lacked formal training. Louis Armstrong has observed that at first jazz came mostly from the type of person "who doesn't know anything about [music] — who is just plain ignorant, but has a great deal of feeling he's got to express in some way, and has got to find that way out of himself."[10] By 1910 jazz had become a full-time profession for most of the musicians who played in cabarets, brothels, taxi-dance halls, honky tonks, barrel houses, and gambling joints, in New Orleans and elsewhere in the South.

In 1917 a group of five white New Orleans musicians, the Original Dixieland Jass Band, consisting of a trumpet, trombone, clarinet, piano, and drums, achieved a resounding success in New York and, in effect, first introduced collectively improvised jazz to the general public. At first their music sounded so strange that the audience had to be told it was "jass" music and might be danced to. The band's drummer Tony Sbarbaro recalled, "We sweated it out for two weeks and then we hit solid, the place [Reisenweber's Cafe] was jammed."[11] More important for the acceptance of jazz were the Dixieland Band's first phonograph records, made in 1917. These sides were the first made by a real jazz band and their appeal, chiefly as novelties, was enormous. They broke the sales figures of Caruso and the Sousa Band by selling in the millions.[12]

Once a profit could be realized, commercial interests quickly altered collectively improvised jazz for wider distribution. The commercializing process took two lines of development.[13] One, which resulted in so-called nut jazz, sought to entertain the public by reducing jazz elements to absurdity. For instance, nut jazz men consciously distorted blue notes so that they lost their positive meaning in grossly exaggerated groans, growls, moans, and laughs. Often they purposely played squeakily or out of tune, and although many jazz men found it necessary to joke with the audience in order to hold its interest, nut jazz men indulged in excessive physical and musical horseplay. The Ted Lewis band stood out as an early nut jazz group.

Far more prevalent and significant, the second kind of commercial jazz developed through dilution (already applied to ragtime and the blues) resulting in so-called refined jazz. Whereas nut jazz men exaggerated jazz elements, refined jazz men reduced them in quality and quantity in favor of traditional elements. They de-emphasized, for example, those blue notes with particularly savage and poignant effects or substituted notes of conventional tonality. To most Americans refined jazz sounded less barbarous — sweeter and smoother — than real jazz. Yet, diluting reduced not only the technical elements but also the esthetic significance; the result was no longer art but popular music. The best-known refined jazz band was Paul Whiteman's. In 1922 Whiteman controlled over twenty-eight such bands, which brought him an income of over a million dollars annually.[14] Refined jazz had become so profitable by that time that even the Original Dixieland Band began to play it.[15]

While commercial (nut and refined) jazz abounded in New York, the focus of real jazz had moved from New Orleans to Chicago. In 1920 many outstanding New Orleans jazz men found a sympathetic audience among Negroes on Chicago's crowded South Side. At first, the best-known performer was King Oliver, a Negro cornetist from New Orleans, but he was soon overshadowed by Louis Armstrong, who arrived from New Orleans in 1922 and became the most influential jazz figure of this period. Also working in Chicago were the white New Orleans Rhythm Kings, who in 1922 inspired the so-called Chicago style of white jazz men, Bix Beiderbecke, the Wolverines, and the Austin High Gang.

III

In the meantime, development had occurred in the field of academic music (sometimes called classical or serious music) which are highly relevant to the jazz controversy. To understand their relevance a relatively full discussion of them is necessary.

Academic music of modern Western civilization is a community undertaking requiring, among other things, expensive instruments, concert halls, adequate communications, and large urban centers with cultivated inhabitants enjoying enough leisure and social opportunities to take advantage of it. Colonial and post-Revolutionary America moved slowly, if at all, to satisfy these requirements. People preoccupied with earning a livelihood in the wilderness, on the sea, or in market and mill towns had little time to perform or listen to an abstract tonal art. Concerts of academic music were few and there was little incentive to take the time and effort to become an academic musician.[16] By 1850 only twenty-six hundred men were occupied as musicians, academic and popular.[17] Except for a few individuals, such as certain members of the Handel and Haydn Choral Society, founded in Boston in 1815, and the New York Philharmonic Society, founded in 1842, academic musicians were amateurs.

After the Civil War changing social and economic conditions fostered rapid development of artistic interests in the United States. Impressed by what they felt to be the emptiness of their esthetic heritage, Americans turned increasingly to Europe for art. In 1859 the editor of *Harper's Magazine* expressed the idea of many Americans when he declared, "What is fine in the buildings of the old countries we can borrow; their statues and pictures we will be able in good time to buy."[18] Traditional academic music could also be imported from Europe. Summing up academic musical advances during the post–Civil War period, the well-known conductor and tastemaker, Walter Damrosch, wrote that "instead of growing upward from the masses [music] was carefully introduced and nurtured by an aristocratic and cultural community. . . . Its original impulse sprang perhaps more strongly from the head than the heart."[19]

Growing interest in academic music created attractive opportunities which drew foreign musicians to America. These immigrants who shaped our concert life were largely the products of the Germanic music tradition. They were inspired by the philosophical idealism of romantic critics and artists who had divided the universe into two realms. One was the material world, comprehensible and adjustable by means of the tools of science, observation and reason. The other was the supernatural, which, according to the Platonic, Christian, and other cosmic philosophies, was approachable only through art and religion. The fine arts encompassed man's vision of an infinite that only the genius could to some extent create. Of all the arts, music in its proper form was the most spiritual, the farthest removed from the material world. Traditional academic music, particularly symphonic, which was the purest sort, had a social mission. German immigrants, such as Walter Damrosch and Theodore Thomas, were gripped by an evangelical zeal to bring uplifting symphonic music to the people, and these men often insisted on uncompromising programs in the face of often indifferent, or even hostile, audiences.[20] Upon hearing that American audiences did not like Wagner, conductors Theodore Thomas and Karl Breggman are reported at different times to have said, "Then they must hear him till they do."[21]

Most European-born arbiters of musical taste and their American disciples reacted strongly against the supposed evils of popular music. Thomas summed up their position as follows: "A symphony orchestra shows the culture of a community. . . .

The man who does not understand Beethoven and has not been under his spell has not half lived his life. The master works of instrumental music are the language of the soul and express more than those of any other art. Light music, 'popular' so-called, is the sensual side of the art and has more or less devil in it."[22] The rulers of musical taste frowned most of all on popular music associated with the Negro. As early as 1853 the influential Germanophile critic, John S. Dwight, in his *Journal of Music*, condemned popular tunes like "Old Folks at Home." He admitted that such songs were on everybody's lips but charged that they "are not popular in the sense of musically inspiring" and explained that such a melody "*breaks out* now and then, like a morbid irritation of the skin."[23]

These European values shaped the standards of academic music circles in the United States. Members of the new upper classes, who were in search of fixed standards in the arts and who were largely responsible for the presence of the foreign musicians, readily embraced the European, or traditional, academic ideals. While some Americans of lower status dismissed traditional academic music as a luxurious affectation, a growing number of people in small towns and urban communities, in search of cultivation or attracted by the glamour of the concert hall, accepted and supported traditional musical values.[24]

Education served to introduce and buttress these standards. In 1838 the Boston Board of Education, after considerable prodding by Lowell Mason, inaugurated vocal instruction in the city's public schools. The success of the Boston experiment led an increasing number of cities and towns to follow its example. Mason had pioneered in the teacher-training movement, starting summer courses for teachers at his Boston Academy of Music in 1834. His educational programs stressed choral singing and the rudiments of traditional music. The efforts of Mason and other educators were so effective that by 1900 music education in public schools had spread to large and small communities throughout the country. Gradually, courses in instrumental training and in music appreciation appeared in public school curriculums, and the number of school bands and orchestras increased.

Music education in colleges and universities developed more slowly than in the public schools. In 1837 Oberlin gave the first college music course in America. Following Oberlin's example, other colleges gradually established courses or departments of music. Harvard organized a notable department in 1862, and eventually schools of music opened at Baylor, Boston University, Yale, and other schools. Conservatories of music also sprang up after the war. The New England Conservatory, the first and most famous of its kind, came into existence in 1867. The same year marked the founding of the New York and Chicago Colleges of Music, and in 1868 the Peabody Conservatory opened in Baltimore. The most influential teachers at these and similar institutions — John Knowles Paine at Harvard and George Chadwick at the New England Conservatory (to name two of the most prominent) — had studied in Europe and taught their pupils traditional academic music standards.

Composers and performers actively sought European training or experience and came home to support traditional academic musical norms. Of the Boston Classicists, a distinguished group of American composers in the last part of the nineteenth and first part of the twentieth century, all save one studied abroad. A European stamp of approval and sometimes a Europeanized name were also important to a successful concert or operatic career in the United States. In the early 1900's the leading concert-master in the United States told Texas-born pianist Olga Hickenlooper — before she changed her last name to Samaroff — "If you played like Liszt and Rubenstein rolled into one, I could do nothing for you without European notices."[25]

A growing school of musical journalism also supported traditional academic values. *Dwight's Journal* founded in 1852, *The Musical Courier* in 1880, *Etude* in 1883, *The Musician* in

1895, *Musical America* in 1898, *The Musical-Leader* in 1900, and *The Musical Quarterly* in 1915, as well as articles about music in leading newspapers, almost invariably gave an important place to foreign-born musicians, who were accepted as the most capable composers and performers, and the final authorities on musical subjects.

Of the different kinds of traditional academic music, choral music was at first most acceptable to Americans. Even before the Civil War there had been a good deal of choral activity in the United States. Indeed, many Americans heard oratorios before they heard symphonies or quartets. Notable choral organizations after the Civil War were the Chorus of the Handel and Haydn Society of Boston, the Oratorio Society of New York, and the Apollo Club of Chicago. Less famous local groups were also much in evidence. In 1873, during the first Music Festival held in Cincinnati, Theodore Thomas conducted a thousand singers from thirty-six local choral societies. Nine years later he led three thousand voices at a festival in New York. In 1886 Philadelphia had at least fifty-nine choral societies, the vast majority of them *Männerchor*, *Sängerbund*, or *Gesangverein*.[26]

Opera was heard less frequently, although it had been sung sporadically in the larger American cities before 1865, notably at the New York Academy of Music, built in 1854. The center of operatic activity in Manhattan moved uptown when the Metropolitan Opera Company began its distinguished operations in 1883. By the early 1900's a group of musical organizations loosely known as the Chicago Opera Company had joined the Metropolitan as a mounter of first-rate performances.

Like opera, symphonic and chamber music had slow beginnings in the United States. Before the Civil War there were amateur and semiprofessional concerts, but little in the way of professional performance. The first eminent chamber group in America, the Kneisel Quartet, was organized in 1885. By that time there were three professional symphony orchestras in the United States. Only one of these, the Boston Symphony, generously supported by Henry Lee Higginson, was a "permanent" organization, in other words, had a full season contract and regular rehearsals and could devote itself exclusively to symphonic music. The other two, the New York Symphony and Philharmonic, played but a small number of symphony concerts, for which they averaged three rehearsals. Their members were forced to supplement their earnings from the theater, opera, and various odd jobs. By the turn of the century, interest in symphonic music had steadily increased. Despite a high mortality rate among symphony orchestras, thirteen had achieved "permanent" status.[27]

The phonograph became a powerful factor in the diffusion of traditional academic music after 1903, when Victor and Columbia began to record singers, instrumentalists, and later full symphony orchestras. Gradually, the "victrola" came to be a standard piece of furniture in the parlors of refined Americans, and a collection of Red Seal recordings identified the owner as a person of taste and property.[28] During the twenties, the radio joined the phonograph in the American parlor for the diffusion of, among other things, traditional academic music.

After World War I the migration of European musicians to America was larger than ever before. The prosperity of the twenties brought new life to traditional academic music organizations. Fifty new major orchestras appeared, 150 per cent more than in the preceding decade.[29] Thousands of semiprofessional community orchestras sprang up in cities and small towns. For the most part, the quality of these groups rose with the quantity. Some of the music they played was what we shall call modern academic music, by such composers as Bartók and Stravinsky, whose compositions were heard increasingly in America in the twenties. Yet, the unconventional sounds of modern academic music were alien to most Americans, and traditional academic music continued to dominate our academic musical taste and institutions.

IV

In spite of this domination of official musical circles, traditional academic music had difficulty in taking root in the United States. Most of the public was little interested in supporting academic music, particularly its absolute forms. The difficult struggle of the privately subsidized Kneisel Quartet in attracting audiences in the last part of the nineteenth and early twentieth century testifies to the lack of public concern for chamber music.[30] By 1921, America's major symphony orchestras and two eminent opera companies operated at a loss. A few wealthy citizens had to make up the deficits.[31]

Moreover, the level of appreciation of those people who did support the music was often low. In the middle of the nineteenth century many were attracted to the concert hall not primarily by an interest in art music but by the hope of finding novel entertainment. The entrepreneurs and performers who drew the largest crowds relied heavily on showmanship both on and off the stage. In 1850 P. T. Barnum exploited the talents of Jenny Lind with the same type of publicity he used for his carnival attractions.[32] Three years later the enormously popular conductor Louis Jullien employed similar devices. For example, he advertised that his repertoire consisted of twelve hundred pieces including an "American Quadrille," "which will contain all the NATIONAL AIRS and embrace no less than TWENTY SOLOS AND VARIATIONS."[33] Other, less money-minded, artists sometimes found it necessary to include showmanship in their programs. In 1854, after five years of study in Europe, Lowell Mason's son, concert pianist William Mason returned to the United States determined to spread the gospel of good music. At one recital a member of the audience asked him to play "Old Hundred" and "Yankee Doodle" simultaneously. The performance was so successful that for a time thereafter Mason offered to play simultaneously any two tunes the audience might suggest.[34] By 1900 such tricks had largely disappeared, but the presence of a glamorous or an electrifying personality was still an important drawing card, as is evidenced by the cult of the conductor or artist. In the twenties the name of the conductor or performer was often more important than the music to be played. Ticket agencies advertised, "Tickets for Farrar for tonight." Deems Taylor wryly suggested that Rachmaninoff could fill Carnegie Hall equally well by playing a program of Czerny's "Exercises for the Beginner" or an all-Chopin concert.[35]

Two polls taken after 1900 for all-request programs indicate the failure of American audiences to appreciate the best of traditional academic music. The first, held in New York, showed that such pieces as Von Suppé's "Poet and Peasant Overture" and Rubenstein's "Melody in F" were most in demand. No symphony or overture was chosen, nor anything by Bach, Mozart, Haydn, Brahms, or Wagner. In the other poll, a St. Louis audience showed similar taste by selecting no symphony before the twenty-eighth choice, which was Beethoven's Fifth; it received forty-four out of two thousand votes.[36]

The development of traditional academic music was hampered not only by the inability of most Americans to find high esthetic meaning in it but also by prejudice. Music was considered an enjoyable avocation, but a musical career was thought to be unfit for a gentleman. In Georgia, Sidney Lanier's father, a lawyer, opposed his son's hope of becoming a musician. In Massachusetts, George Chadwick's father, a businessman, disapproved of his son's decision to study music abroad. Yet each parent encouraged musical and other esthetic pursuits as leisure activities.[37] Some people viewed academic musical activities as women's work, while others associated academic music with effeminacy. "A strong feeling existed," wrote Walter Damrosch, "that music was essentially an effeminate art, and that its cultivation by a man took that much away from his manliness."[38] Such prejudice helps to explain why the professional playing and teaching of music was frequently left to women in the last part of the nineteenth and first part of the twentieth century. In 1900 there were 52,000 women and 39,000 men occupied as musicians and music teachers in the United States. By 1910 the figures had risen to 84,000 women and 54,000 men,[39] roughly an eight to five ratio.

The scarcity of important compositions by American artists is further evidence that traditional academic music took root in America with difficulty. After the Civil War the United States produced a number of competent and sometimes inspired writers of traditional academic music. These included John Knowles Paine, Dudley Buck, Frederick Gleason, Silas Pratt, Edward MacDowell, George Chadwick, Horatio Parker, Daniel Gregory Mason (a grandson of Lowell Mason), Frederick Converse, and a number of others. For all their distinction, none of them created anything comparable in esthetic value to the greatest works of their European contemporaries. Nor, with the possible exception of MacDowell and Parker, did any of them write a major work of lasting interest to the American musical audience.

American concert-goers had been largely indifferent to works by native composers since before the Civil War. The constitution of the New York Philharmonic (founded in 1842) contained a clause offering to play "any grand orchestral composition such as overtures or symphonies composed in this country," but only three works (two of them short pieces), by native-born Americans were played during the orchestra's first eleven years.[40] In spite of later efforts by such figures as Theodore Thomas, Walter Damrosch, and Franz van der Stucken to encourage American composers (within the framework of traditional academic standards), native artists continued to have difficulty in getting a sympathetic hearing; their works usually met with boredom, if not hostility. Another indication of this lack of positive interest is that no opera by an American composer reached the stage of the Metropolitan between its founding, in 1883, and 1910. From 1910 to 1942 the Metropolitan staged only eleven operas by native-born Americans. The most successful of these works was Deems Taylor's *The King's Henchman* (1927), which had fourteen Metropolitan performances in three seasons.[41] Orchestral works fared no better. For example, in the 1924–25 season only 4 per cent of the works played by our five best-known symphony orchestras were by American artists.[42]

V

The reasons for the shortcomings of our traditional academic composers are not always clear. Certain important aspects of the question will probably remain moot. Still, it is significant that in the 1920's many knowledgeable musicians thought American composers were adhering too closely to European models. As the composer, critic, and teacher Daniel Gregory Mason declared, "The dominance of foreign models seems to paralyze personal feeling."[43] His colleague Deems Taylor argued that American composers from Paine to MacDowell had come home from Europe to write "good honest square-toed Kapellmeistermusik" which had little to do with America.[44]

The idea of escaping from European models was not new. Shortly after the founding of the Republic, American artists hoped to match America's political independence and other successes with indigenous artistic development. In the first half of the nineteenth century these hopes took shape in esthetic chauvinism. Among the earliest musicians with patriotic interests was the Bohemian Anton Philip Heinrich, who came to America in 1818. Inspired by American history, landscapes, and Indian music, he sought to become the great American composer and was even called "the Beethoven of America." He wrote such things as "The Columbiad," "Yankee Dooliad," and

"Jubilee"; this last he described as "a grand national song of triumph, composed and arranged for a full orchestra and a vocal chorus — in two parts, commemorative of the events from the landing of the Pilgrim fathers to the consummation of American liberty."[45] Such ambitious work, however, did not fulfil the expectations of the audience, and observers began to take note of the disappointing showing of American musicians. In 1852 the native composer William Fry, disappointed by the lack of attention given American composers by the New York Philharmonic, called on them to make a "Declaration of Independence in art." He urged composers to stop genuflecting before European masters and to open up new musical worlds by using only nature and their own inspiration as guides. Fry believed that only an "American school" could end our esthetic provincialism.[46] His bold plan for throwing off the European yoke cannot be taken too seriously, for his own work remained almost totally subservient to foreign models. Fry was only one of a number of nineteenth-century Americans who demanded independence yet imitated the spirit and letter of European composition.

The American visit of Anton Dvořák, 1892–95, gave great impetus to musical nationalism in the United States. This manifestation of romanticism put a high value on the use of folk material. Dvořák was fascinated by what he called "plantation melodies" which partly inspired his *New World Symphony*. "These beautiful and varied themes," he told Americans, "are the product of the soil. They are the folk songs of America, and your composers must turn to them. In the Negro melodies of America I discover all that is needed for a great and noble school of music."[47] In its day this was a provocative statement. Musical authorities had hitherto considered America peculiarly barren of such folk music as might inspire a national school. Implying that music associated with the Negro was particularly without merit, Edward MacDowell seemed to speak for most traditional academic musicians when he laughed at the "American national musical costume" advocated by "the Bohemian Dvořák" and demanded to know what Negro music had to do with "Americanism in art."[48]

Gilbert Chase has suggested that the most important result of Dvořák's visit was the encouragement he gave to a break with the European hegemony. Of the several native artists to take Dvořák's advice, the most influential was Arthur Farwell. In 1901 he founded the Wa-Wan Press in an attempt to launch what he described as "a progressive movement for American music, including a definite acceptance of Dvořák's challenge to go after our folk music."[49] The Wa-Wan Press was a publisher and rallying point for such men as Henry F. B. Gilbert, Arthur Shepard, Edward B. Hill, and Edward Stillman Kelley. Farwell, the chief spokesman of the group, declared in 1903, "The first correction we must bring to our musical vision is to cease to see everything through German spectacles, however wonderful, however sublime those spectacles may be in themselves!"[50] Farwell advocated an enlightened eclecticism, for he felt that imitation of all forms together with the dynamic influence of the American environment would lead to a characteristically native music, taking its inspiration from "ragtime, Negro songs, Indian songs, Cowboy songs, and, of the utmost, importance, new and daring expressions of our own composers, sound-speech previously unheard."[51]

However, these efforts to take folk, popular, and early jazz music earnestly were unacceptable to many. Ragtime seemed particularly objectionable. Rupert Hughes (apparently the first academically trained music critic to believe that ragtime would play an important role in American musical development) noted in 1899 that ragtime received almost no encouragement among academic musicians. "It has two classes of enemies: the green-eyed, blue-goggled fogy who sees all in popular music a diminution of the attention due Bach's works; and the most modern scholar who thinks he has dismissed the whole musical activity of the Negro" by calling it a "reminiscence" of Scottish or Spanish music.[52] Furthermore, the technical problems of ragtime embarrassed traditional academic musicians and heightened their opposition to the new music. Hughes recalled, "It was so strangely difficult to master. It required a new technique in rhythm and fingering, and I saw many a snooty conservatory-trained expert get his fingers all tangled up as he tried to do what thousands of Negroes and their imitators did naturally and with ease."[53] Mainly for these reasons traditional academic musicians in America usually opposed the spread of the new music. At its Denver convention in 1901 the American Federation of Musicians condemned ragtime and recommended that its members refrain from playing it. The president of the federation declared, "The musicians know what is good, and if the people don't, we will have to teach them"[54] — a statement worthy of Theodore Thomas. Lampooning the federation's opposition to ragtime, the Cincinnati *Post* declared, "If you hear music and like it, be sure that somebody will explain to you that it is popular, and therefore immoral; that it lacks soul."[55]

The ragtime dancing rage that began to sweep the nation in 1911 aroused a more general indignation. Respectable citizens looked aghast at the frenzied movements the new music seemed to provoke. Now and then people found doing the Turkey Trot were taken to court or dismissed from their jobs. In 1914 Edward Bok, editor of the proper *Ladies' Home Journal*, began a series of articles to help reform dancing, but pictures of Vernon and Irene Castle demonstrating "correct" dancing positions brought such expressions of moral outrage from readers that Bok felt obliged to abandon his efforts.[56]

During World War I the argument over ragtime engaged more thoughtful Americans. The most articulate spokesman in the pro-ragtime camp was the critic Hiram K. Moderwell, who observed that advocates of traditional academic music generally ignored the new music. He argued that the "native-born, foreign-educated musician" insulates himself from the public taste and deplores ragtime as vulgar, but "the art of the *vulgus*, the people, is the material for national expression."[57] The American composer could solve his dilemma by opening his ear to ragtime. Moderwell loved "the delicacy of its inner rhythms and the largeness of its rhythmic sweeps. I like to think that it is the perfect expression of the American city with its restless bustling and motion, its multitude of unrelated details. . . . Its [ragtime's] technical resourcefulness continually surprises and its melodies at their best, delight me."[58] He believed that ragtime "songs appeal to a people who expect to sing them, a people who have no national and no grand opera tradition. . . . This is American. It is our lives, and it helps to form our character and condition, our modes of action. It should have expression in art, simply because any people must express itself if it is to know itself. No European music can or possibly could express this American personality."[59] In ragtime and "nowhere else are the beginnings of American music if America is to be anything but a pleasant reflection of Europe."[60]

Daniel Gregory Mason, the most eloquent spokesman for the anti-ragtime group, deplored the notion that ragtime was a significant outgrowth of American culture. Noting that the war had intensified consciousness of nationality, he argued that the issue was drawn between the proponents of ragtime, whose patriotic ardor had blunted their powers of discrimination, and its opponents, who judged music by its intrinsic value alone. He found the "jerk and rattle" of ragtime ugly and without possibilities for academic composition.[61] Mason conceded that ragtime was the music of the common people, but he argued that they lacked discrimination. Although ragtime might be characteristically American, it represented not our virtues but our vices: our restlessness, fondness for hustling and our "thoughtless, superficial 'optimism.'"[62] Ragtime had vitality, but it resembled the vitality of the comic strip. The new music was a local idiom, a trick of speech, a carica-

ture rather than a portrait. "No folk music . . . no individual composer, no school of composers," Mason concluded,
"can 'express' America."[63]

These argumentative skirmishes preceded the jazz battle
of the twenties. By the end of the war other kinds of jazz
were superseding ragtime and the dispute over the proper
place of the new music in our civilization was fully under
way.

CHAPTER TWO

TRADITIONALIST
OPPOSITION

IN 1922, when the jazz controversy was coming to a head, J. Hartley Manners' play *The National Anthem* opened on Broadway. The plot depicted naïve young people ignoring the counsel of a wise traditionalist parent and debauching themselves into decadence. Manners dramatized the way jazz stimulated the youth's downfall, and in his Foreword argued that the new music was "modern man's saturnalia."[1] Throughout the play jazz not only undermined the morality of susceptible young people, but also threatened all civilization, which, if the jazz age continued unchecked, seemed doomed to barbarism. Many people who saw *The National Anthem* shared Manners' fears about jazz. Journalist Bruce Bliven described the audience at one performance as resembling a group of indignantly wide-eyed members of "the Ladies' Auxiliary of Flushing, L. I. assembled to hear a lecture on the white slave traffic." He further reported that jazz had become a burning issue among many middle-class people in New York and its suburbs.[2]

The National Anthem and the fears it helped to provoke indicate the nature and the amount of agitation aroused by the jazz dispute. Such excitement over music on the part of so many Americans was extraordinary. Previously music had caused relatively little excitement because it seemed largely irrelevant to practical matters. Most Americans thought of it in terms of entertainment, often pleasant but of minor importance. Even traditional academic music, which the arbiters of musical taste urged upon the public as a strong social and moral force, seemed to have little to do with the pressing concerns of most people. But after World War I many Americans began to take music more seriously, when they found that jazz was strongly connected with social and moral problems which could not be ignored. These social and moral implications made the jazz controversy part of the bitter conflict between the relative norms which were gaining currency and traditional, absolute values.

Upheld chiefly by Protestant, middle-class Americans of Anglo-Saxon ancestry, traditional values demanded among other things belief in moral and metaphysical idealism, confidence in the individual's capacity for self-directed growth toward intelligence and high purpose, and faith in the progress of civilization.[3] For some time, traditionalists were becoming increasingly alarmed at the threats to their values posed by relative norms that were fast making inroads into American society. After the Armistice traditionalists were fully aroused for a militant counter-attack on what they saw as a rising tide of degeneration. Many of them regarded jazz, along with intemperance and unconventional sexual behavior, as a sign or a cause of the advancing degeneration and assailed the new music as a major vice.

To understand these assaults, it is important first to know

what traditionalists meant by the word jazz. After the Armistice few of them differentiated between real and commercial jazz. Anything that sounded even faintly like jazz (in other words, that had one or more of a variety of recognizable jazz characteristics) they called "jazz." Therefore it seems best to refer to this jazzlike music as "jazz" — surrounding the word with quotation marks, as traditionalists often did.

II

The statuses of the opponents of "jazz" depended, in varying degrees, on traditional values. There were two groups of opponents.[4] The first included guardians of traditional morals and manners: clergymen, educators, and other community leaders, certain business and professional men, and politicians. The second group embraced people economically dependent upon, or esthetically committed to, traditional music: musicians, music critics, music teachers, dancing teachers, patrons, and lovers of traditional music. These and others influenced by them disliked "jazz" for several reasons.

To begin with, it seemed grossly to violate traditional musical values, particularly those of academic music, which defined for many of the cultivated and their emulators what music should be. D. G. Mason summed up the musical criteria of such traditionalists: "The truth is, our whole view of music was based on the style of classic and romantic symphonists beginning with Haydn and Mozart and ending with Mendelssohn and Schumann."[5] The traditionalists' esthetic principles grew out of the romantic philosophy of art described in the preceding chapter. Howard Mumford Jones has conveniently summarized them: Art was the expression of the highest idealism, which might be interpreted as purposefulness in the life of the cosmos, soul, or state. Art of both the classic and romantic schools was acceptable in so far as it expressed the highest morality, which was nobility. However, the danger of the romantic school was that it could lead to excess or formlessness.

The notion of art as a discipline demanding restraint and craftsmanship was central.[6]

Upholders of these values found "jazz" so strange that it could scarcely be called music. Dr. Henry Van Dyke, a prominent Presbyterian clergyman and a professor at Princeton, declared "As I understand ["jazz"], it is not music at all."[7] For many it seemed full of wild excesses and formlessness, totally lacking in restraint and discipline. Music critic Sigmund Spaeth called it "merely a raucous and inarticulate shouting of hoarse-throated instruments, with each player trying to outdo his fellows, in fantastic cacophony."[8] In an article entitled "Back to Pre-War Morals," in the Ladies' Home Journal, journalist John R. McMahon wrote, "If Beethoven should return to earth and witness the doings of [a "jazz"] orchestra, he would thank heaven for his deafness. . . . All this music had a droning, jerky incoherence interrupted with a spasmodic 'blah!! blah!!' that reminded me of the way that live sheep are turned into mutton."[9] Thomas A. Edison was quoted as saying he preferred to play "jazz" records backward because they sounded better that way.[10]

Most traditionalists seem to have agreed with concert pianist Ashley Pettis that "jazz is nothing more or less than the distortion of every esthetic principle."[11] Walter R. Spaulding, a professor of music at Harvard, observed that "jazz" was "exciting" but good music "must surely have many other qualities such as . . . sublimity and ideality."[12] Frequently traditionalists complained that "jazz" lacked soul or purposefulness in the life of the soul. Walter Damrosch charged, "Jazz . . . is rhythm without . . . soul."[13] A New York Times writer was more explicit about the traditionalist spiritual feelings which jazz failed to evoke.

> With music of the old style, even the most moving, the listener was seldom upset from his dignified posture. When listening to Tchaikovsky's "March Slav," perhaps, he might feel a tingling starting at his heels and lifting the roof of his head clear

up to the ceiling, as though his ectoplasm — as the spiritualists call the spirit substance — had suddenly broken free from its mortal container and was up in the open spaces of the auditorium looping the loop and nose-diving. Yet the bodily anchor remained intact. The listener behaved as impassively as the radio's microphone. Nothing in his manner indicated either a struggle for self-control or an absence of decorum. The perturbation spent itself internally.[14]

III

Far from spending itself in the life of the soul or the spirit, jazz seemed to provoke man's "lower nature," the carnal. John Philip Sousa objected that "jazz" "employs primitive rhythms which excite the basic human instincts." Others complained that the new music had the same effect on the brain as alcohol: A New York physician, Dr. E. Elliot Rawlings, explained, "Jazz music causes drunkenness . . . [by sending] a continuous whirl of impressionable stimulations to the brain, producing thoughts and imaginations which overpower the will. Reason and reflection are lost and the actions of the persons are directed by the stronger animal passions."[15]

The bodily movements which "jazz" elicited seemed to be further evidence of the way the intoxicating sounds of the new music brought out man's lower nature — in ways that reminded traditionalists of the behavior of "inferior" races. H. O. Osgood, an editor of *The Musical Courier*, described the movements of the Ted Lewis Band as a kind of savage rite with "all the players jolting up and down and writhing about in simulated ecstasy, in the manner of Negroes at a Southern camp-meeting afflicted with religious frenzy."[16] A New Jersey Supreme Court Justice J. F. Minturn charged that, "In response to ["jazz's"] call there ensues a series of snake-like gyrations and weird contortions of seemingly agonized bodies and limbs, resembling an Asiatic *pot pourri* which . . . is called a dance."[17]

The sensual appeal of "jazz" collided with traditionalist

ideas of sex. In *Race and Nationality in American Life* Oscar Handlin summarized these ideas: The spiritual union of married adults for purposes of procreation was the only acceptable occasion for sexual intercourse. Frequent indulgence or masturbation, the results of animal passion, were said to bring on illness, shorten life, and breed degenerate progeny. Furthermore, most people in the government, the medical profession, and the clergy viewed birth control and abortion as crimes against the state, nature, and God. The law in sexual matters was self-restraint.[18]

Jazz seemed to fly in the face of this repression. Fenton T. Bott, head of the traditionalist National Association of Masters of Dancing, charged in 1921, "those moaning saxophones and the rest of the instruments with their broken, jerky rhythm make a purely sensual appeal. They call out the low and rowdy instincts. All of us dancing teachers know this to be a fact. . . . Jazz is the very foundation and essence of salacious dancing."[19] *The Catholic Telegraph* of Cincinnati complained, "the music is sensuous, the embracing of partners . . . is absolutely indecent; and the motions — they are such that as may not be described with any respect for propriety in a family newspaper. Suffice it to say that there are certain houses appropriate for such dances but those houses have been closed by law." Other religious periodicals denounced "jazz" dances as "impure," "polluting," and "debasing."[20]

Moreover, traditionalists often believed that the feelings "jazz" evoked were not confined to the dance hall. Miss Alice Barrow, who had worked for a number of educational and welfare institutions as a teacher and investigator, made a study of the evil results of "jazz" in mid-Western towns and she warned parents that

> The nature of the music and the crowd psychology working together bring to many individuals an unwholesome excitement. Boy-and-girl couples leave the hall in a state of dangerous dis-

turbance. Any worker who has gone into the night to gather
the facts of activities outside the dance hall is appalled, first
of all perhaps, by the blatant disregard of even the elementary
rules of civilization. . . . We must expect a few casualties in
social intercourse, but the modern dance is producing little short
of holocaust. The statistics of illegitimacy in this country show
a great increase in recent years.[21]

Other traditionalists delivered still darker warnings. A New
York Episcopal rector, Percy Grant, cautioned his congrega-
tion about the evils of "jazz" by reading from a leaflet which
said that 65,000 girls had disappeared from the United States
in 1921 "without leaving a trace."[22] The rector told his pa-
rishioners to remember this if they forgot everything else he
had said. A report of the Illinois Vigilance Association, led
by the Reverend Phillip Yarrow, was equally disturbing. Its
agents found that in 1921–22 jazz had caused the downfall of
1,000 girls in Chicago alone.[23]

Objections raised against words of "jazz" songs supported
complaints that the music was vulgar and sensual. Fenton T.
Bott, the dancing teacher, who charged that "jazz" music had
a sensual appeal said, "The words also are very suggestive,
thinly veiling immoral ideas."[24] Other people went further,
avowing that the words were downright vulgar. In 1920 Mrs.
Marx Obendorfer, national music chairman of the General
Federation of Women's Clubs, told members of the federation
that "jazz" lyrics were "unspeakable" and that "ninety per cent
of [them] would not be allowed to go through the mails if [they]
were literature."[25] The following year in an article entitled,
"Does Jazz Put the Sin in Syncopation?" Mrs. Obendorfer reported that the music supervisor of a large urban high school
had examined the lyrics of over 2,000 "best selling" songs and
had deemed only forty "fit for boys and girls to sing together."[26]

Traditionalists found that the circumstances surrounding
"jazz" and the people who played it offered evidence of the

evil nature of the music. Insisting that "everything must be judged by the company it keeps and attracts," Will Earhart, music director of the School of Education at the University of Pittsburgh, observed that the works of traditional composers "are heard in certain places and received by a certain clientele gathered there. They seem to be appropriate to the places in which they are heard, and to the people who gather to hear them. So does 'Jazz.' "[27] An editorial in *Etude* declared, "Jazz, at its worst, is often associated with vile surroundings, filthy words, unmentionable dances and obscene plays with which respectable Americans are so disgusted that they turn with dismay at the mere mention of 'Jazz,' which they naturally blame for the whole fearful caravan of vice and near-vice."[28]

Probably the most damaging association of "jazz" was its identification with the brothel, usually the Negro brothel. The music critic of the *New York Herald Tribune*, H. E. Krehbiel, who had been interested in other types of music connected with the Negro, was disgusted by such a lewd association, and he feared that more "jazz" and foul dances were "soon to emanate from the Negro brothels of the South."[29] Jazz clarinetist Milton Mezzrow wrote that in the twenties, "Our music was called 'nigger music' and 'whorehouse music' and 'nice' people turned up their noses at it."[30]

The most disturbing thing about the new music was that it seemed to infect almost every part of American life. A. W. Beaven, a minister in Rochester, New York, explained, "It has gotten beyond the dance and the music and is now an attitude toward life in general. We are affliced with a moral and spiritual anemia."[31] Bringing out man's lower nature in a number of ways ranging from crime and suicide to the break-up of the home, jazz seemed to strike at the very heart of the traditional way of life. Dr. John R. Straton, a Baptist clergyman in New York and the chief spokesman for Fundamentalism after the death of William Jennings Bryan, argued, "I have no patience with this modern jazz tendency, whether it be in music, science, social life or religion. It is part of the lawless spirit which is being manifested in many departments of life, endangering our civilization in its general revolt against authority and established order."[32] Dr. Francis E. Clark, president of the Christian Endeavor Society, called jazz dancing "an offence against womanly purity, the very fountainhead of our family and civil life."[33]

Traditionalists were particularly disturbed at the way "jazz" was infecting the minds of children. Sherwood Boblitz in *The Musician* warned of "one fact, which is too vile and too glaring to longer go unnoticed and uncommented upon: the only music that many children and adults are ever able to hear . . . [is] generally rag-time and tawdry at that."[34] And Mrs. Elise F. White, a musician, writer, and active New England clubwoman, observed that generally children had little interest in academic music. They preferred "rag-time" and demanded, "What good is all this high-class music, anyhow, except just to harrow up your feelings? Let's play something lively."[35]

It was difficult to arrest this tendency, for young people appeared particularly susceptible to "jazz." In 1925 the author of the *Etude* editorial, "Is Jazz the Pilot of Disaster?" cautioned, "Jazz is doing a vast amount of harm to young minds and bodies not yet developed to resist evil temptation."[36] The orchestra leader of the state hospital at Napa, California, declared, "I can say from my own knowledge that about fifty per cent of our young boys and girls from the age 16 to 25 that land in the insane asylum these days are jazz-crazy dope fiends and public dance hall patrons. Jazz combinations — dope fiends and public dance halls — are all the same, 'one.' Where you find one you will find the other."[37] The extent to which some people feared the corruption of untrained minds by "jazz" is illustrated in the brief of the Salvation Army of Cincinnati, which in 1926 obtained a temporary court injunction, preventing construction of a movie theater next to one of its homes for expectant mothers. The plaintiff argued, "We are loathe to believe that babies born in the maternity hospital are to be legally subjected to the implanting of jazz emotions by such enforced proximity to a theater and jazz palace."[38]

Traditionalist concepts of race bore strongly upon the opposition to jazz. Many traditionalists seem to have agreed with well-known actress Laurette Taylor (who played a lead in her husband's play, *The National Anthem*) when she said, "Jazz, the impulse for wildness that has undoubtedly come over many things besides the music of this country, is traceable to the negro influence."[39]

In a summary of traditionalist racial ideas, Oscar Handlin shows that the findings of scientists such as Darwin and Weismann were taken to confirm the belief that sexual behavior determined the nature of the race. These findings made the need for self-restraint and purity all the more obvious. Continence except for procreative purposes not only limited births but also ensured a breed fit for the struggle for existence. Yet there was a constant threat. Through miscegenation, "inferior" races, like Negroes and orientals, endangered the purity of the blood. Sensual rather than spiritual by nature, these peoples offered a steady temptation to whites. Furthermore, whereas such aliens were child-like and irresponsible at best, their brute passions sometimes burst into dreadful acts. And there was still another disquieting problem: it was feared that the savage passions of the vicious might nullify the careful abstinence or repression of the virtuous. As early as the 1860's doctors began to notice that the birth rate of the "better" native, white, Protestant families was declining while that of the poorer, alien groups was rising. People were frightened to think of growing numbers of "inferiors" eventually overwhelming the "superior" stock. The strong few would not be able to support the great mass of degenerates and the result would be the decline of civilization. To counteract these dangers, the well-intentioned favored tight restraints in sexual matters, and sought to suppress anything harmful to purity.[40]

Traditionalist notions about the origins of jazz provided fuel for these racial fears. Whereas some traditionalists believed that jazz was born in the Negro brothel, others traced the origins of the music to the jungle and believed that the African roots of "jazz" explained its association with violence. Mrs. Marx Obendorfer argued that, "Jazz originally was the accompaniment of the voodoo dancer, stimulating the half-crazed barbarian to the vilest deeds. . . . [It] has also been employed by other barbaric people to stimulate brutality and sensuality."[41] Such notions helped spread fears that Negroes under the influence of "jazz" would become violent. Negro jazz clarinetist Buster Bailey pointed out that during the years when he first played professionally, whites were afraid "we'd go after their women."[42]

Many traditionalists found that the African origins of "jazz" held even more frightening implications. "The consensus of opinion of leading medical and other scientific authorities," wrote Dr. Florence Richards, medical director of a Philadelphia high school for girls, "is that its influence is as harmful and degrading to civilized races as it always has been among savages from whom we borrowed it." She warned that continued exposure to this evil influence "may tear to pieces our whole social fabric."[43] Others believed that "jazz," the music of the jungle, was a form of retrogression that was returning American society to an age of barbarism.[44] Not only science but history as well lent credence to such fears. Appalled at the prospect of Americans "reduced to the low state of inferior races now on this planet," a biologist exhorted, "better extinction than a decline to the savage past. Jazz is a signboard on the road that was travelled by Greece and Rome. Orgies of lewd dancing preceded the downfall of those nations."[45] Either as a cause or as a symbol, Negro jazz threatened to turn back the clock of civilized progress.

IV

Just as "jazz" was objectionable because it conflicted with the standards of traditional music, the jazz man was disturbing because he did not conform to the pattern followed by the traditional musician.

The traditionalist concept of idealism, interpreted to mean purposefulness in the life of the cosmos, implied God's guidance in the esthetic expression of universal truths. Part of the artist's proper inspiration was a kind of emotion, which traditionalists called "passion," the longing for the ideal world of perfection. In the attainment of this ideal the discipline of restraint and craftsmanship was basic. A music teacher's monthly magazine like *The Musician* printed numerous articles which reiterated the "success" pattern and held up for emulation by the young student the early strivings of famous musicians. Such examples showed that to become an artist required pluck, diligence, and persistence during years of patient training in the established tradition of the concert stage.

Traditionalists worried because jazz men ignored or flouted these ideas. Walter Damrosch felt that jazz men lacked proper inspiration, "real emotion which . . . might give life to their music."[46] Far too many young musicians seemed little concerned with the discipline that accompanied "real emotion," or "passion." Mrs Elise F. White argued that the coming generation, preoccupied as it was, with such baubles as "rag-time," failed to concern itself with "real" music, "which demands much time and thought; the music of artistic cultivation, of humble ambitions, prayerfully and earnestly followed; of obedience to teachers; of self-denial, renunciation and sacrifice; of the worship of beauty, and the passionate desire to express it."[47]

Because jazz men had not been trained in traditional discipline, traditionalists called them incompetent. The "Topics of the [New York] *Times*" column compared "jazz" with the "new poetry," and concluded "both are the products, not of innovators, but of incompetents. The maker of jazz would compose music if he could . . . and had something to say."[48] And what could be more indicative of the jazz musician's incompetence than the fact that he frequently turned to academic music for his material. Walter Damrosch's brother, Frank, an influential musician in his own right, charged that jazzing the classics was "not only an outrage on beautiful music, but also a confession of poverty, of inability to compose music of any value."[49]

Moreover, "jazz" threatened the growth of traditional music by spoiling the musician's desire for "proper" training and performance. Walter Damrosch argued, "Undoubtedly it stifles the true musical instinct, turning away many of our talented young people from the persistent, continued study and execution of good music."[50] In addition, "jazz" spoiled the prospective musician's technique. "To become an artist on any wind instrument is work of a lifetime," explained bandmaster Edwin Franko Goldman. He warned that the "grotesque effects" of the new music ruined the player's intonation.[51] H. E. Krehbiel complained that "the principal characteristic of jazz is a vulgar sliding from tone to tone [which caused an] . . . unnatural contortion of the lips and forcing of the breath," thus unfitting the performer for playing academic music.[52]

V

Although traditionalists took great pain to point to the evil "jazz" was working in American moral and musical development, few of them specified precisely what characteristics of the music were causing the trouble. It seems safe to say, however that some traditionalists found virtually any non-traditional jazz element or practice to be offensive.

Twentieth-century academic musicians seldom, if ever, improvised, and many of them condemned improvisation, which flourished in jazz. Frank Patterson, an editor of *The Musical*

Courier, polled a number of academic musicians and reported that "They all agreed that the 'ad libbing' or 'jazzing' of a piece is thoroughly objectionable, and several of them advanced the opinion that this Bolshevistic smashing of the rules and tenets of decorous music, this excessive freedom of interpretation, tended to a similar letting down on the part of the dancers, a similar disregard for the self-contained and self-restrained attitude that has been prescribed by the makers of the rules of dignified social intercourse."[53]

The rhythm of jazz was disturbing also. Daniel Gregory Mason called it "formally inane" and "mechanically repeated."[54] Will Earhart charged that jazz "represents, in its convulsive, twitching, hiccoughing rhythms, the abdication of control by the central nervous system — the brain."[55]

Equally objectionable were the strange "staccato tempi," "curlicues," "rasps," "cries," and "laughs" and the sounds of such "nerve-wracking devices" as "cow bells, rattles, and fog horns" which seemed conducive to immorality.[56] The "plaintive and pleading notes of the violin and clarinet, the imploring tones of the saxophone" seemed to lead to drunkenness and the overpowering of the will. The "moaning" saxophones were said to increase the "sensual appeal" of jazz and to bring out "low and rowdy instincts."[57] Some elements of "jazz" were even said to impair health. The Health Commissioner of Milwaukee, Dr. George C. Ruhland, maintained that they excited "the nervous system until a veritable hysterical frenzy is reached. It is easy to see that such a frenzy is damaging to the nervous system and will undermine the health in no time."[58]

VI

Traditionalists combatted the evils of "jazz" in several ways. First, a number of persons associated with traditional music and dance joined what a *New York Times* article called "The Conspiracy of Silence against Jazz." The conspirators worked on the theory that the "least said soonest mended."[59] Their policy was to fight evil with good. For example, the superintendent of the Des Moines, Iowa, schools noted that his music department said "practically nothing about jazz. Instead there is a carefully planned program . . . and definite music appreciation instruction which seems to offset the crudities of the jazz madness."[60]

Another tactic was to describe "jazz" as a dying fad. The author of *In His Steps*, Charles M. Sheldon, was one of those who assured lovers of "good" music that "jazz" had lost its appeal.[61] Still others dismissed "jazz" as a burlesque of "real" music. Violinist Fritz Kreisler, then living in New York, explained, "We do not think of pen and ink caricatures as art. Jazz has the same relationship to music."[62] Traditionalists also tried to tarnish the popularity of the new music by ridicule. For instance, the *New York Times* printed articles headed "Jazz Frightens Bears" and "Cornetist to Queen Victoria Falls Dead on Hearing Coney Island Jazz Band."[63]

Still other traditionalists took organized action. In 1919 the National Association of Dancing Masters opened a campaign to reform dancing in America. At its convention in New York the association passed a resolution urging members not to "permit vulgar dancing and cheap jazz music to be played. . . . After all what is dancing but an interpretation of the music." The association sought the co-operation of churches and it printed booklets condemning "jazz," as well as a chart illustrating the approved dance steps. This material went to schools, dancing teachers, and dance halls with the commendation of the United States Public Health Service, which distributed it to thousands of welfare agencies.[64]

In 1921 the music section of the General Federation of Women's Clubs launched a crusade against "jazz." The president of the musical section of the General Federation urged that never before had America so needed the help and inspiration of "good" music and concluded, "Let us carry out this motto in every home in America firmly, steadfastly, until all the music in our land becomes an influence for the good." Two years later at its national convention delegates of the 2,000,000-member federation voted to "annihilate" the new music.[65]

The Federal Interdepartmental Social Hygiene Board issued reports on the evils "jazz" was working in small towns. The board co-operated with the dancing masters and women's clubs and planned to enlarge the Public Welfare Department of Illinois in order to check the "jazz" cancer where it was spreading most rapidly.[66]

In 1922 the Ninth Recreational Congress convened at Atlantic City and resolved to war on "jazz" with better songs which would embody "the finer ideals of American life." Professor Peter Dykeman, of the University of Wisconsin, a well-known authority on music, led the reform committee, which included music critic Sigmund Spaeth as well as the director of the Philadelphia Music League, and an official of the Bureau of Community Music of the Community Services.[67] Three years later Henry Ford opened a drive against the new music by sponsoring a series of traditional folk dances which he hoped would counteract the evils of "jazz" dancing.[68] A group of influential Episcopal churchwomen in New York, including Mrs. J. P. Morgan, Mrs. Borden Harriman, Mrs. Henry Phipps, Mrs. James Roosevelt, and Mrs. E. H. Harriman, proposed an organization to discourage "excess of nudity" and "improper ways of dancing."[69]

Some traditionalists suggested government prohibition. In a speech before 1,000 teachers, the superintendent of schools in Kansas City, Missouri, warned "This nation has been fighting booze for a long time. I am just wondering whether jazz isn't going to have to be legislated against as well."[70] In 1922 the New York State Legislature passed the Cotillo Bill, which empowered the Commissioner of Licenses of New York City to regulate "jazz" and dancing. He promptly banned both on Broadway after midnight.[71] By 1929, at least sixty communities, including Cleveland, Detroit, Kansas City, Omaha, and Philadelphia, had regulations prohibiting "jazz" in public dance halls.[72]

In other areas members of women's clubs chaperoned municipal dance halls to insure that no "jazz" was played. Authorities at a number of high schools, colleges, and universities considered prohibiting or regulating "jazz" at student social gatherings. Certain country clubs disallowed "jazz" dancing. Finally, a number of industries which had introduced music into their plants banned "jazz" as a "demoralizing" influence upon the workers.[73]

By the mid-twenties it was becoming increasingly clear that the appeal of "jazz" was growing in spite of traditionalist opposition. In the face of this realization, and in view of growing evidence that the evil elements of the music were being refined or filtered out, the frontal attack which sought to banish "jazz" lost strength. At the same time there emerged an effort to restrict the development and popularity of the new music. Morroe Berger points out that opponents of "jazz" attempted to fix its esthetic value and social prestige below the worth and position of academic music.[74] This policy resulted in tolerance of the new music as long as it remained in its "proper place." Dean Smith of the Yale Music School spoke for those traditionalists who sought not to kill "jazz" but to confine it to its "proper" sphere. In an article, "Putting Jazz in Its Place," he argued that "Any criticism of its music or of its composers is academic and uncalled for — provided jazz holds to its original purpose of entertaining people in their times of recreation."[75] This meant that "jazz" in any form was to stay out of the concert hall. "The development of art music," explained Ashley Pettis, "is separate and distinct from the work of so-called jazz exponents. . . . It is all right in its place — the cabaret and the dance hall — but it should not be allowed to invade the sacred precinct of our concert halls."[76]

Furthermore, jazz men were to leave "classical" music alone. In 1927 the 400,000 women organized in the National Federation of Music Clubs launched an effort to fight "jazzing of the noble compositions of the great composers."[77] Commenting on this move, an editorial in the *New York Times* pointed out that one purpose of the clubs was "to keep modern music in its place." It was permissible, the editorial continued, for "jazz" "to snort and jangle in night clubs, dance halls and on the musical comedy stage. But it must keep its brassy hands off the classics, or walking delegates from the music clubs will do something official."[78]

An examination of the traditionalists' response to jazz suggests that values primarily esthetic are interrelated with those chiefly social or moral, that groups of people with different manners and morals tend to associate themselves with different styles or forms of art, and that any attempt to introduce the musical values of one group into the musical life of a different group is a difficult or impossible operation. Since the musical and non-musical values of supporters of jazz differed from those of traditionalists, it is not surprising that traditionalists rejected jazz. The strongest opposition came from those whose status depended most heavily on conventional values, people like the Reverend Mr. Straton, Mr. Bott, and Mrs. Obendorfer. Their values were so deeply rooted and so inflexible that an esthetic novelty like jazz aroused distaste and fear that forced strong opposition. Ironically the intense opposition to jazz unified its supporters and ultimately helped it gain a firm place in the sensibilities of many American.

CHAPTER THREE

ACCEPTANCE OF JAZZ
IN THE TWENTIES

CONNECTIONS between esthetic, social, and moral values manifest themselves in the acceptance of, as well as in the opposition to, "jazz." Whereas the extent to which one opposed "jazz" usually corresponded to the degree to which one affirmed traditional values, the extent to which one accepted it tended to tally with the degree to which one rejected traditional standards.

In the years after 1918 a growing number of Americans found many traditional norms inadequate for the problems and challenges of the twentieth century. The decline of faith in these values was a complex matter. Some of the historical events leading to the decline were: the disappearance of the frontier in the nineties; the rising tide of immigrants (until 1914) who were often unaccustomed to, or unsympathetic toward, traditional values; the growth of cities and of their socially unabsorbed populations; the rise of science and industry; and the growing influence of Darwinism, socialism, and Freudianism. Although many changes had occurred before 1914, World War I and the failure of the peace dramatized the breakdown of traditional values in ways that helped to bring about an even broader revolution in manners and morals.

Among the traditional values to lose support most rapidly were those governing the use of leisure time. In the nineteenth century because of long working hours and moral and religious strictures against "idleness," there was little desire for avocational activities. Gradually, however, technological advances and labor agitation shortened the working day and the moral strictures lost much of their effectiveness. A consumption ethic tended to replace the traditional production ethic, and, as it did, Americans of every social class began to believe that they had a right to, and a need for, increased relaxation. They devoted much of their newly acquired leisure time to entertainment and art.

The revolution in values manifested itself in the arts. Works of advanced artists reflected and supported the breakdown of traditional values. Writers interested in naturalism and in fiction's attack on "puritanism" described social ills caused by adherence to traditional values. Especially after the Armory Show in 1913, many of our painters and sculptors abandoned traditionalist cliches for realism or abstraction. Architects such as Sullivan and Wright ignored many traditional forms in attempts to create new ones more consonant with American environment and experience. And growing discontent with traditional academic music led to efforts to find other sources of musical inspiration.

Sensibilities of audiences as well as of artists changed. Particularly in metropolitan areas, members of different social classes had previously associated themselves with art or entertainment which they believed to befit their respective statuses. For example, well-to-do and fashionable people and their emulators were the chief supporters of the opera and symphony. Usually such people upheld the dominant traditional culture (culture defined as learned behavior and attitudes) and many of them looked down on popular music. On the other hand, members of lower-income groups made up the audience of vaudeville and Tin Pan Alley. Generally they adhered to one of the non-traditional subcultures and thought of the opera and symphony as luxuries available only to the refined and well-to-do. In effect, a well-defined line often separated upper from lower class art or entertainment.

The breakdown of traditional values led to an exchange of norms between these classes which tended to blur the line.[1] Many of the well-to-do became dissatisfied with traditional esthetic norms and grew increasingly interested in art and entertainment usually associated with the subcultures. At the same time upholders of the subcultures found the art of the traditionalist, upper classes more and more accessible.

The reasons for upper-class interest in lower-class art and entertainment are not always clear. Oscar Handlin seems to have been right, however, in suggesting that as upper-class people lost faith in traditional standards, they were left with a vacuum in their lives. In an effort to fill it they sought exposure to the values of the subcultures which seemed to offer fun, excitement, romance, a more genuine contact with reality, and identification with art.[2]

Art provided the most respectable kind of exposure to the subcultures. Since the 1890's American artists had been introducing audiences to standards and seamy experiences of the lower classes. Muckrakers and naturalists had written about urban and rural slums. Painters of the "Ash Can School" and photographers such as Stieglitz and Steichen portrayed life in the poorer sections of town. Composers such as Farwell and Gilbert wrote music inspired by that of Negroes and American Indians.

Many well-to-do Americans had sought exposure to lower-class entertainment as well as art. In search of informal, noisy, and exciting amusement they patronized lower-class cafes, cabarets, and speakeasies to mix with the regular customers. Jazz clarinetist Milton Mezzrow recalled that while playing in such a place, "It struck me funny how the top and bottom crusts in society were always getting together during the Prohibition era. In this swanky club, which was run by members of the notorious Purple Gang, Detroit's bluebloods used to congregate — the Grosse Pointe mob on the slumming kick, rubbing elbows with Louis the Wop's mob. That Purple Gang was a hard lot of guys . . . and Detroit's snooty set used to feel it was really living to talk to them hoodlums."[3] For upper-class customers such places, expensive or not, provided a view of what seemed to be raw life, unspoiled by the rules and pretensions of sophisticated society. The floor shows at lower-class clubs were as fascinating as the regular patrons. Music publisher Edward B. Marks recalls the appeal of one Bowery performer of the twenties as follows: "Tommy Lyman of the pasty pallor, the nervous hands, the limpid, wicked eyes, was the unhealthy but exciting essence of a time. . . . He talked his songs in a husky whisper which . . . breathed of a blasted life and delightful depths of depraved degradation . . . he was the pet of the classes who had never experienced real trouble, and who found his ditties particularly fascinating."[4]

Upper-class interest in lower-class entertainment did not necessarily represent an understanding of the life of the poor. Often it was seen only in terms of the wants of well-to-do visitors. Langston Hughes wrote of an episode at a fashionable party, where Paul Haakon, whom somebody had "discovered," danced. Everybody "Oh'd and Ah'd," and said ,"what a beautiful young artist!" But later Haakon confided to Hughes, "Some baloney — I'm no artist. I'm in vaudeville." Similarly, at a *bon voyage* party in the Prince of Wales Suite of a Cunard liner the guests drank champagne while a Negro entertainer sang the ribald "My Daddy Rocks Me with One Steady Roll." After she had finished, a well-known society matron rushed up to her and exclaimed ecstatically, "My dear! Oh, my dear, how beautifully you sing Negro spirituals"[5]

While upper-class people went to the poorer sections of town for stimulation, people from the poorer sections went to more fashionable parts of town. Guests from the extremes of social class mixed at parties. Not only did members of "Society" dance in cabarets, but cabaret dancers like the Castles became social lions. A showgirl could marry asbestos heir Tommy Manville. And the song-writer and former singing waiter at Nigger Mike's, Irving Berlin, brought up as Israel Baline on New York's Lower East Side, married socialite Ellin Mackay, daughter of the head of Postal Telegraph.[6]

The twenties were the years of Manhattan's "Black Renaissance." Whites wrote about, and bought books by, Negroes more frequently than ever before. Wealthy patrons adopted colored artists. Whites invaded the Negro clubs and bars in Harlem and Chicago's South Side. Shows with all-Negro casts played on Broadway.

Other people and standards associated with the subcultures also permeated the "legitimate" stage. Vaudeville and burlesque were made more elegant and taken to legitimate theaters in such revues as George White's Scandals and the Ziegfeld Follies, which competed with the opera for the attention of the fashionable. An increasing number of Rabelaisian farces and other shows accented sex or some form of moral disintegration and shocked or titillated the audience.

The radio and phonograph further tended to break down the line between traditional values and those of the subcultures. It became possible for the upper classes to hear popular music and for the lower classes to hear academic music inexpensively and easily in their own homes. The movies, before the war considered a low form of amusement, drew an upper-class audience in the twenties. Nickelodeons gave way to sumptuous "movie palaces" and "cathedrals of cinema." In 1927, when the

Roxie opened in New York, patrons enjoyed luxurious surroundings and lavish entertainment not unlike the opera, including along with the film, a comfortable seat, a "symphonic"
orchestra, and a spectacular stage show.[7]

Nor were people with newly-acquired spending power to be
denied other kinds of refinement formerly the preserve of the
upper classes. The growing interest in art was partly satisfied by
books which compressed or popularized literature for lower-
and middle-class readers. *Collier's* advertised the Harvard
Classics and a program for reading them "fifteen minutes a
day." The mid-twenties saw the founding of the Literary Guild
and the Book-of-the-Month Club, two organizations which
publicized and sold books recommended by well-known critics
and authors to readers in search of refinement. In 1918 the Modern Library began offering cheap reprints of the classics. E.
Haldiman-Julius's ten-cent reprints and abridgements of the
classics, the Little Blue Books, sold one hundred million copies
between 1919 and 1929.[8]

II

The acceptance of "jazz" in the twenties followed the pattern in
other forms of art and entertainment. Members of the upper
classes went to the poorer parts of town to hear the new music,
and at the same time it was imported into upper- and middle-
class sections. Whether in the poor sections, where it came
from, or in a more fashionable environment, those who embraced its undiluted forms had broken wholeheartedly with a
large number of traditional values. Such people were mostly
adolescents revolting against convention.

Perhaps particularly in the United States adolescence is a
time for questioning established values. Most psychiatrists
seem to agree that chief among the causes of adolescent revolt
are the various psychological and physiological changes accompanied by increasingly strong sex drives and an aggressive
desire to be independent. Since the adolescent is often pre-

vented from expressing these, he frequently is confused and frustrated. As a result he protests against the forces of repression in any form.[9]

After World War I the rapid breakdown of traditional values helped to make the rebellion of young people more violent and extended than the revolts of earlier generations of Americans. A key in the breakdown of the older norms was the decline of the traditional role of the family, a decline which manifested itself in several ways. A growing number of marriages ended in divorce: one out of ten in 1910, one out of six in 1928.[10] Less and less tied to domestic drudgery, women gained more and more economic, social, and political freedom. Children also got more freedom as attitudes toward child-rearing changed. Traditionally, many parents and teachers had reared children with a strict discipline which implied that they could behave in an adult manner. Now the move was more and more toward treating children as organic individuals whose particular needs were important and whose development was to be measured in terms of age groups.[11] Furthermore, the school increasingly took from the family the responsibility of guiding older children. Between 1914 and 1926 high school enrolment jumped from 1,500,000 to 4,000,000. By 1927 one half of the people in the eligible age groups attended high school. Colleges and universities expanded rapidly also; 760,000 students were enrolled by 1926 — one-eighth of the population in the eligible age group.[12]

Young people growing up after World War I did not view the world as adolescents in earlier generations had. Whereas their parents and grandparents had had limited schooling and had gone to work early in life, young people in the 1920's spent more time in school, thus extending their adolescence and postponing adult responsibilities. Preoccupied with earning a living in accordance with the production ethic and the ideal of "success," earlier generations had been willing to abide by traditionalist restrictions, but members of the younger generation often found them unnecessary or false. World War I and the failure of the peace dramatized the shortcomings of traditional standards and further widened the gap between the older and younger generation. One young man, who spoke for many in his generation, explained the gap as follows:

> The older generation has certainly pretty well ruined this world before passing it on to us. They give us this Thing, knocked to pieces, leaky, red-hot, threatening to blow up; and then they are surprised that we don't accept it with the same attitude of pretty, decorous enthusiasm with which they received it, way back in the eighteen-nineties. . . .
> Now my generation is disillusioned, and, I think, to a certain extent, brutalized, by the cataclysm which their complacent folly engendered. The acceleration of life for us has been so great that into the last few years have been crowded the experiences and the ideas of a normal lifetime. We have in our unregenerate youth learned the practicality and cynicism that is safe only in unregenerate old age. We have been forced to become realists overnight, instead of idealists, as was our birthright.[13]

Jazz had a strong appeal for those with such rebellious inclinations. Two psychiatrists, Aaron Esman and Norman Margolis, have helped to explain why. Esman argues that it interests people seeking liberation and individuality: adolescents, intellectuals, and Negroes. "The unspoken protest, the kinesthetic release, the stimulation of repressed erotic drives — all these strike a responsive chord in the spirits of those members of society who regard themselves at once its outcasts and its prisoners."[14] Supplementing Esman's hypothesis, Margolis maintains that jazz appeals for several reasons to those (of whatever age) with adolescent psychology. First, the jazz group is a protest group rejected by the general culture. By membership in this group the young person can assert his independence from his parents and conventional society. Second, jazz symbolizes the instincts with which the adolescent is grappling, the normal sexual and aggressive feelings. Third, with its loose structure and emphasis on improvisation, jazz provides that medium of free expression which the adolescent needs. Finally, the jazz group offers possibility of dependence formerly found in the family relationship. All members of the group are together dealing with some inner need for protest, self-expression or self-realization.[15] If true, these formulations illuminate the acceptance of jazz among adolescents in the 1920's, but they should be qualified in at least two respects: for one thing, jazz enthusiasts with different racial and cultural backgrounds respond differently to the music. And, as the following chapters will show, groups of jazz enthusiasts behave differently depending on their age, on the historical period, and on the reception of jazz in the larger society.

III

Among those young whites of the twenties who either ignored or were in open revolt against traditional values, the new jazz musicians were the most rebellious. Take, for example, the best-known group of white midwestern jazz men whom we shall loosely call Chicagoans. Four of them have written autobiographies which reflect four gradations of repudiation of traditional norms. The most rebellious was clarinetist Milton (Mezz) Mezzrow. For him jazz was sacred, and his rejection of traditional standards was so vehement that he self-consciously gave up his ties with the white world and moved into a Negro community. At the other extreme was clarinetist Benny Goodman, who learned to play jazz in a poor section of town but at the same time mastered traditional musical techniques and disciplines and maintained an air of respectability. Between these two extremes were guitarist Eddie Condon and pianist Hoagy Carmichael. Goodman's book is largely anecdotal and deals only briefly with his early experiences in Chicago. But the books of Mezzrow, Carmichael, and Condon,[16] in spite of naïveté, exaggeration, and occasional foolishness, clarify the thoughts and feelings of the white jazz men of the twenties.

For young white jazz men like the Chicagoans, jazz was a voice of rebellion. As Hoagy Carmichael explained, "The first World War had been fought, and in the back-wash conventions had tumbled. There was rebellion then, against the accepted, and the proper and the old. . . . The shooting war was over but the rebellion was just getting started. And for us jazz articulated. . . . It said what we wanted to say though what that was we might not know."[17] Members of the "Austin High Gang," who came from comfortable middle-class families in Chicago's West Side (all but one of them had discarded a violin for an instrument more appropriate in a jazz band), considered their music parallel to criticism they found in Mencken's *American Mercury*. Mezz Mezzrow, who frequently played with them, described their feelings as follows: "Their jazz was . . . collectively improvised nose-thumbing at all pillars of all communities, one big syncopated Bronx cheer for the righteous squares everywhere. Jazz was the only language they could find to preach their fire-eating message."[18]

While the Chicagoans accorded composers of academic music — particularly modern ones — respectful silence or outright admiration, most of them rebelled against the formal techniques, procedures, and discipline they associated with traditional academic music. "When you come right down to it," argued Mezzrow extravagantly, "what brought about the whole change in American music? What spread the gospel of jazz far and wide across the country, pulling at least one part of our native music free at last from European influences? It was the rebel in us. Our rebel instincts broke music away from what I'd call the handcuff-and-straitjacket discipline of the classical school, so creative artists could get up on the stand and speak out in their own honest and self-inspired language again."[19] Although academic musical training did not necessarily ruin a jazz musician, it often did him no good. Jazz requires the ability to improvise, but many academic and commercial jazz men either could not improvise at all or failed to equal the accomplishments of the true jazz man when they tried. Benny Goodman showed the jazz man's disdain for traditionalists' inability to improvise and for the importance they gave to reading music: "If a fellow happened to be a good legitimate [traditionally trained] trumpet man or a swell straight clarinet player, he might get credit for being a fine musician who could read a part upside down at sight, but we didn't pay much attention to them [sic]."[20] Other Chicagoans joked about traditional musical norms. When Eddie Condon was teaching himself to play the banjo, his father told him, "You are terrible and you can't read music." Condon replied, "What's that got to do with being a musician?"[21] And when one member of a group of Chicagoans known as the "Wolverines" (only two of their original eight members could read music) suggested that the band use written arrangements, another member disposed of the idea by asking, "What would we do if the lights went out?"[22]

The Chicagoans first found jazz on records, and some of these men indiscriminately received the commercial outpourings of, say, Ted Lewis, with the same enthusiasm they did real jazz. But their preferences soon galvanized around bands such as the Original Dixieland Jazz Band or the New Orleans Rhythm Kings, bands made up of whites whose style was close to that of the Negro jazz men. The trail eventually led to Negroes. The Chicagoans learned of colored artists through records and went to the South Side to hear or to play with them. Elsewhere, young musicians, who would later join the Chicagoans, also imbibed jazz and its esthetic values. In Indianapolis, having been expelled from high school, Hoagy Carmichael learned to play the piano by listening to a Negro pianist, Reggie Duval. Carmichael recalls the following conversation:

What are you doing there?
I bring my thumb down, like that, [explained Duval] I dunno it just makes it.
You bring your thumb down on the chord right after you've hit it with your right hand [Carmichael said].

Yeah, [answered Duval], I want that harmony to *holler.* . . .
[Italics Carmichael's throughout].
I want it so it sounds right to *me.* And that is the way it sounds
rightest.
It's wonderful [declared Carmichael].
Naw but it's *right* [Duval answered]. Never play anything that
ain't *right.* You may not make any money but you'll never get
hostile with yourself.[23]

The young Chicago musicians and their future associates
found in jazz not only a voice of rebellion but also a rich esthetic experience which helped fill the vacuum left by the
rejection of traditional or other values inherited from their parents. Eddie Condon wrote of the first time he heard the Negro
cornetists, King Oliver and Louis Armstrong, play together on
Chicago's South Side: "It was hypnosis at first hearing. Every-
one was playing what he wanted to play and it was all mixed together as if someone had planned it with a set of micrometer
calipers; notes I had never heard were peeling off the edges and
dropping through the middle; there was a tone from the trumpets like warm rain on a cold day. Freeman and McPartland
[two other Chicagoans] and I were immobilized; the music
poured into us like daylight down a dark hole."[24] Hoagy Carmichael recalls upon hearing Bix Beiderbecke and the Wolverines, "Boy, he took it! Just four notes. . . . But he didn't blow
them — he hit'em like a mallet hits a chime — and his tone, the
richness. . . . Whatever it was he ruined me. I got up from
the piano and staggered over and fell on the davenport."[25]
Such experiences created a strong fraternal understanding
among young jazz men. They felt that they had something important that the rest of the world should recognize. Carmichael
recalls the following reaction upon first hearing Louis Armstrong: "'Why,' I moaned, 'why isn't everybody in the world
here to hear that?' I meant it. Something as unutterably stirring
as that should be heard by the world."[26] But other Americans
did not hear jazz this way. Some resisted its diffusion — some-

times vehemently — and others who had partially or half-heartedly strayed from orthodox norms accepted traditional popular music or the commercial dilutions of jazz but ignored or disliked jazz itself. It was, in short, a musician's music, which had only a handful of lay enthusiasts.

As a result of public scorn or lack of interest white jazz men took a pessimistic view of their audience. Cornetist Jimmy McPartland showed this pessimism in speaking about a recording session, "We started kidding around and playing corny. Out comes the recording manager from his booth, and he says, 'That's it. You gotta do that'. So we sort of used the 'St. Louis' chord progressions and blew all this cod [sic] Dixie, and we called the number 'Shirt Tail Stomp.' It sold more than any of the others; or I should say it sold the rest of the sides because it was corny. It shows the taste of people; still the same, I guess, the world over."[27] Other Chicagoans were more disturbed. "What's the use, Milton?" Mezzrow recalls clarinetist Frank Teschmacher saying, "You knock yourself out making a great new music for the people, and they treat you like some kind of plague or blight, like you were offering them leprosy instead of art, and you wind up in the poor house or the asylum."[28]

The fact that not only jazz but its practitioners were rejected or not recognized by the respectable world heightened their sense of brotherhood. "The result of this [rejection]," explained Benny Goodman, "was that musicians who played hot [real jazz] were pretty much of a clique by themselves. They hung around in the same places, made the same spots after work, drank together and worked together whenever they had the chance. . . . None of us had much use for what was known then, and probably always will be, as 'commercial' musicians."[29] Mezzrow wrote, "If you could catch a couple of cats [jazz musicians or enthusiasts] that just met each other talking about certain musicians they know or humming a riff or two

to each other, before you could call a preacher they'd be practically married. . . . Jazz musicians were looked down on by
the so-called respectable citizens as though they were toads
that crawled out from under a rock, bent on doing evil. We
could roam around town for weeks without digging [seeing]
another human who even knew what we were talking about."[30]
And drummer Dave Tough said, "We jazz players are supposed
to be vulgarians beyond the moral as well as the musical pale; I
guess we might as well live up to what is expected of us."[31]

At the heart of the jazz musician's behavior was an absorption
in esthetic experience which made the new music their main
source of happiness and morality.[32] Speaking of the time he
first heard Bix Beiderbecke, Hoagy Carmichael wrote, "Those
four notes that Bix played meant more to me than everything
else in the books. When Bix opened his soul to me that day, I
learned and experienced one of life's innermost secrets to happiness — pleasure that it had taken a whole lifetime of living
and conduct to achieve in full."[33] Mezzrow declared, "Every
time I got in trouble, it was because I strayed away from the
music. Whenever I latched on solid to the music, I flew right.
I was beginning to sense a heap of moral in all this."[34]

Jazz men lived primarily for "kicks" in music but by extension also in other activities. While the stereotype of the jazz man
as a drunkard or dope addict was and is false, the incidence of
indulgence in drink and drugs among jazz men was higher than
among most Americans in their sex and age group.[35] For those
who indulged, dope and liquor removed inhibitions and provided stimulation, confidence, and ease helpful to the creation
of jazz. Carmichael describes the influence of marijuana and
liquor on him while listening to Louis Armstrong: "Then the
muggles [marijuana] took effect and my body got light. Every
note Louis hit was perfection. I ran to the piano and took the
place of Louis's wife. They swung into 'Royal Garden Blues.'
I had never heard the tune before but somehow I knew every

note. I couldn't miss. I was floating in a strange deep-blue whirlpool of jazz. It wasn't the marijuana. The muggles and gin were, in a way, stage props. It was the music. The music took me and had me and it made me right."[36] Mezzrow's first taste of marijuana affected him in much the same way. "I found I was slurring much better and putting just the right feeling into my phrases — I was really coming on. All the notes came easing out of my horn like they'd already been made up, greased and stuffed into the bell, so all I had to do was blow a little and send them on their way. . . . I felt I could go on playing for years without running out of ideas and energy. . . . I began to feel very happy and sure of myself."[37]

Autobiographies of white jazz men in the twenties are full of examples of living for "kicks." Sometimes kicks took the form of normal adolescent pranks. Benny Goodman tells about an incident in the Ben Pollack band: "For a while . . . we had been trying to cook up a gag on Ben, and finally somebody got the idea of smearing limburger cheese on the inside of Pollack's megaphone. Harry [Goodman] was delegated to do the job. . . . When the time came, Pollack picked up his megaphone and put it up to his face, then suddenly got a whiff of this stuff. He made a horrible face. . . . Everybody thought Harry had done a wonderful job, until we picked up our megaphones to sing, and discovered that he had given the same dose to us."[38] Sometimes kicks went beyond this sort of horseplay as the following quotation from Mezzrow indicates:

> I brought the record [Louis Armstrong's "Heebie Jeebies"] home to play for the gang, and man, they all fell through the ceiling. Bud, Dave and Tesch almost wore it out by playing it over and over until we knew the whole thing by heart. Suddenly, about two in the A.M., Tesch jumped to his feet, his sad pan all lit up for once, and yelled, "Hey, listen you guys, I got an idea! This is something Bix should hear right away! Let's go out to Hudson Lake and give him the thrill of his life!"
> A scramble was on, and it was most mad, old man. Bix was

fifty miles away, but we were all half-way down the stairs before Tesch's chops got together again. We drove every which-away in that green monster of mine (that's what the boys called my chariot) and started off like gangbusters for Hudson Lake, a summer resort where Bix, Pee Wee Russell and Frankie Trumbauer were playing with Gene Goldkette's Greystone Dance Orchestra. All the way there we kept chanting Louis' weird riffs, while I kept the car zigzagging like a roller-coaster to mark the explosions. . . .

It was three in the morning when we busted into the yard-dog's stash that Bix and Pee Wee used for a cottage. Jim, the funk [stench] in that dommy was so thick you could cut it with a butterknife, and them cats had the whole insect population of Indiana for their roommates. . . .

Pee Wee and Bix shared a small room off the kitchen that would have made any self-respecting porker turn up his snout and walk away. They slept in their clothes most of the time. . . . The first thing they did when they unglued their lamps each day was to reach for the gallon of corn that always leaned against the bedpost and wash out their mouths. Those cats used corn mash like it was Lavoris. Whenever you tipped into their room you had to pile through big stacks of empty sardine and baked-bean cans; those two canned delicacies made up the whole menu of this establishment. The backporch was loaded with thirty or forty quarts of milk, some of them over a month old. . . .

That morning, as soon as we grabbed those cats out of their pads and played *Heebie Jeebies* for them, they all fractured their wigs. "Ha! Ha! Ha!" Bix kept chuckling as the record played over and over, and his long bony arms beat out the breaks, flailing through the air like the blades of a threshing machine. He never did get over Louis' masterpiece. Soon as it was over he grabbed it from the machine and tore out of the house, to wake up everybody he knew around Hudson Lake and make them listen to it. . . .

Anyhow, on this particular night, like all the other times we visited him, Bix sat at that beat-up piano for hours, sometimes making our kind of music and sometimes drifting off into queer harmony patterns that the rest of us couldn't dig. The rest of the world melted away; we were the last men left on earth, skidding on a giant billiard-ball across a green felt vacuum with no side-pockets, while Bix crouched over his keyboard in a trance, barleycorned and brooding, tickling bizarre music out of the ivories.[39]

Despite apparent exaggerations, this account illustrates the musician's single-minded interest in their music and their tendency to ignore or affront considerations that concerned traditionalists; it shows their habit of living for kicks both in music and in unusual experiences; and it demonstrates their willingness to tolerate almost anything in an environment that did not interfere with playing or listening to jazz. The sharing of all these inclinations helped to unify the jazz fraternity.

Jazz men's unconventional use of language further tended to bind them together and separate them from traditional values. They employed a private or semi-private slang in everyday speech. This included words or phrases like "get off," "change," "lick," "cut," "ride," "sock," "solid," "jam," "fake" — all with unorthodox meanings.[40] Another unconventional type of language was scat vocal which contained nonsense syllables that had no meaning for people outside of the jazz fraternity. Take, for example, the second chorus of "Heebie Jeebies" by Louis Armstrong.

> Eef, gaff, mmff, dee-bo, dee-la-bahm,
> Rip-rip, de-do-de-da-do, do-de-da-de-da-doe,
> Ba-dode-do-do, ba-ro-be-do-be-do,
> Geef-gaf, gee-bap-be-da-de-do, d-da-do,
> Rip-dip-do-dum, so come on down, do that dance,
> They call the heebie jeebies dance, sweet mammo,
> Poppa's got to do the heebie jeebies dance.[41]

Still another sort of language of the jazz men resembled Dada usage. For example, the following quatrain by Hoagy Carmichael's fellow-musician, Bill Moenkhaus:

> If castor oil removes a boil
> And Oscar rows a goat
> Don't use your feet on shredded wheat
> Inhale it through a boat.[42]

Or, the first lines of a story by the same author: "Once upon a time, during an extra horse, Silo McRunt, age thirteen, tried to count up to his mother. His actions were noticed by his wet neighbor (a mere bacon fanner by trade) who had just defeated his breakfast."[43]

While these utterances said little or nothing to most people, they held meaning for the initiated and played a part in the jazz men's rebellion against the traditional culture. Mezzrow considered the musician's slang a form of protest,[44] and Carmichael thought of Moenkhaus' Dada-like expressions as compaints against conventional society.[45]

Moreover, unconventional language served as part of a ritual and a means of identification within the brotherhood. As Louis Armstrong would later say of both white and Negro jazz men, "They have a language of their own, and I don't think anything could better show how much they feel they are apart from 'regular' musicians and have a world of their own that they believe in and that most people have not understood."[46] According to Mezzrow, when outsiders began to adopt fragments of their private vocabulary, such phrases and words were dropped for new terms and usages unfamiliar to the public. Commenting on the word "swing," he explained, "This word was cooked up after the unhip public took over the expression 'hot' and made it corny by getting up in front of a band and snapping their fingers in a childish way, yelling 'Get hot! Yeah man, get hot!' . . . This happened all the time. . . . It used to grate on our nerves because it was usually slung in our faces when we were playing our hottest numbers. . . . That's the reason we hot musicians are always making up new lingo for ourselves."[47]

The language of the jazz man was also a source of kicks. When Louis Armstrong's recording of "Heebie Jeebies" was first issued, Chicago jazz men began to greet each other with Armstrong's scat phrases. Carmichael wrote that Armstrong's "blubbering, strangely cannibalistic sounds, tickled me to the marrow."[48] Upon still another occasion a white vocalist scatting his lyrics drove Carmichael and his companions into hysterics: "Off-color inanities, in staccato baffled the chaperones. Do-dada-la, corupbutgrabuptitandslugupashot . . . are dimly remembered samples. . . . When the dance was over Monk [Moenkhaus] composed one of his greatest lines for Bix [Beiderbecke] 'One by one a cow goes by.' Bix's eyes popped, he turned his head a little to the side as he did on the bandstand, when great things were coming from his horn, and murmured happily, once again, his entire vocabulary of praise and admiration. 'I am not a swan.' The great days were upon me once more. Music, friends, happiness and poverty. The good life. No pleadings except to plead with Bix 'do that again' on his horn. To Monk to 'say that line again.'"[49]

The jazz man was a specialist in one type of musical communication, but since he was usually untutored in traditional esthetics he was, as William Cameron suggests,[50] unable to translate his feelings into conventional symbols and he could communicate his musical, and to a lesser extent his verbal, sentiments only to persons who already understood his esthetic world. He resorted to unconventional language because he knew no other words to express his feelings. The language helped cement the unity of the jazz fraternity in the face of an indifferent or hostile world.

The fraternity of white jazz men was strengthened also by the role of its hero, Bix Beiderbecke, and the image of him that began to emerge while he was still alive. As with many another heroic image, the stories associated with Beiderbecke frequently have a factual basis glossed by the wants of the story teller. In spite of the efforts of jazz scholars who have sought to separate fact from fancy, the behavior and characteristics attributed to Beiderbecke often represent as much the ideals of the jazz fraternity as they do a true picture of him.

Beiderbecke repudiated much of the traditional rearing he received from his well-to-do middle-class parents and was cynical about, and bored by, many conventional standards. As

Mezzrow said, "what got most people worked up left him completely cold . . . it took something really stirring, something
really good, to get a rise out of him. . . . Music was the one
thing that really brought him to life."[51] Having never had a
lesson on the cornet, he largely ignored academic techniques
and discipline. He never became a good reader, his fingering
was unconventional, and he thought of his B-flat instrument as
being a whole tone higher, in the key of C. Joe Gustat, a well-
known symphony trumpeter and teacher, was reported to have
said that Beiderbecke would have to begin all over again and
learn the traditional method if he ever wanted to be a cornetist.[52] But with his "wrong" technique Beiderbecke developed
a unique style with a full tone, sharp attack, and rapid execution which amazed fellow jazz men.

For them Beiderbecke was the incarnation of the esthetic
morality. "Nothing which has been invented about him," Condon's book states, "is as accurately symbolical as the everyday
things he did. Without effort he personified jazz; by natural
selection he devoted himself to the outstanding characteristics
of the music he loved. He was obsessed with it . . . he drove
away all other things — food, sleep, women, ambition, vanity,
desire."[53] Cornetist Jimmy McPartland recalls, "His main interest in life was music, period. It seemed as if he just existed
outside of that."[54]

Beiderbecke's music and image provided less gifted jazz men
with a feeling of direction and inspiration. What they had difficulty in communicating, he said for them, or helped them to
say for themselves. "The thing about Bix's music," explained
clarinetist Pee Wee Russell, "is that he drove a band. He more
or less made you play whether you wanted to or not. If you had
any talent at all he made you play better."[55] Beiderbecke's
leadership also gave his colleagues a feeling of identification
and security which were imperative for a group misunderstood
and frowned upon by the outside world. "When you're a kid
and your first millennium falls on you," explained Mezzrow,

"when you get in a groove that you know is *right* for you, find a way of expressing something deep down and know its *your* way — it makes you bubble inside. But it's hard to tell outsiders about it. It's all locked up inside you, in a kind of mental prison. Then, once in a million years, somebody like Bix comes along and you know the same millennium is upon him too. . . . That gives you the courage of your convictions — all of a sudden you know you aren't plodding around in circles in a wilderness."[56]

There was something charismatic in Beiderbecke's personality, something mysterious or otherworldly about his genius, Paul Whiteman said that Beiderbecke's "continual searching for some sort of ultimate created an almost mystic halo about him."[57] Carmichael thought of him as a "vessel of immortal music."[58] And as a fellow bandsman, Russ Morgan, declared, "The guy didn't have an enemy in the world. But he was *out of this world* [italics Morgan's] most of the time."[59]

When Beiderbecke died at the age of 28, he was still seeking new ways of expression. His premature death and his apparently-unfulfilled genius did much to enhance the romantic image of him in the minds of jazz enthusiasts, who circulated melodramatic stories about what many felt to be his martyrdom. Some spoke of gangsters' tortures that "really caused his death." Others claimed that he died because he gave too much of himself to friends who took advantage of his kindness. Another version was that the traditional technical requirements of Paul Whiteman's commercial arrangements broke him down.[60]

By the mid-thirties numerous stories, some factual, others imaginative embroidery of half-recalled events, and still others mere hearsay, had built up a sentimental image which the growing jazz following took to its heart. Suddenly, everybody connected with jazz seemed to have known him or have a story to tell.[61] Remembrances of Beiderbecke were published, and music journals brought out editions devoted to his life and music. There were tales of pilgrimages to sacred spots, such as, how, "some of the boys went out to Davenport one August Seventh, on the anniversary of Beiderbecke's death [actually he died August 6, 1931], and played jazz over his grave." Accounts of his musical prowess appeared. For example, musicians told about "the night Bix and Louis [Armstrong] were having a battle of horns. When Armstrong heard Bix, he broke down and cried, then admitted that he could never play as well as that."[62]

Reacting to the scorn or indifference of the traditional culture, jazz men sometimes behaved childishly or negatively. Yet, in spite of its shortcomings their unconventional behavior had the positive function of strengthening the brotherhood of the jazz fraternity, and by doing so, it helped to protect the new music from the assaults of those who could not appreciate it.

IV

Aside from the musicians there were other young whites who accepted jazz in the 1920's. As Louis Armstrong pointed out, "the people who liked [jazz] bands best at that time, and followed them were the people who didn't know much about the older music, mostly the young people in high schools and colleges."[63] The most avid of these enthusiasts repudiated or ignored traditional values almost as thoroughly as did the jazz men themselves. Condon's and Mezzrow's friend, Josh Billings, and Carmichael's fraternity brothers at Indiana University were typical of non-playing jazz zealots. There were also advocates in the student bodies of Harvard, Yale, Princeton, and other schools. They were among the first jazz record-collectors[64] and some of them later helped to define and formalize jazz esthetics.

Such avid enthusiasts were few. Most supporters of jazz in the 1920's were high school and college students whose rebellious spirit was temporary or lukewarm. André Hodeir has suggested that appreciation of jazz requires fresh, unsatisfied sensibilities found in young people, especially boys, who are overflowing with energy and seeking an outlet for it.[65] As students, many young Americans had such sensibilities and energies, but once out of school most people lost the qualities of adolescence. In order to earn a living, many found it necessary to conform to or accept traditional values. At the same time even those who had been most zealous in their enthusiasm for jazz lost interest in it. As Carmichael (Indiana, '24) observed of himself and his friends who had returned to Bloomington for the 1928 Commencement, "Rebellion was dying in us. Jazz was dying too."[66]

A group that we can loosely characterize as young intellectuals also supported jazz in the twenties. In general, these were artists, writers, critics, and others, often residents of bohemian communities. There were important similarities between the way of life of jazz men and that of many young intellectuals. Finding themselves no longer at home with traditional values of middle and upper-middle class communities, young intellectuals sought refuge or inspiration elsewhere. Whether they escaped to a place like Woodstock, New York, or exiled themselves in Europe, they adopted a strong esthetic morality which often amounted to a religion of art. For them as well as for jazz men life was full of poverty, good humor, and occasional wild antics. There was plenty of drink and sometimes stronger stimulants. Although the intellectuals fought among themselves over matters of esthetic principle and displayed strikingly different personalities, they tended to tolerate idiosyncrasies and to band together in places like Greenwich Village or Carmel.

Such persons accepted jazz, although they did not necessarily discriminate between the real thing and its commercial derivatives. They listened to it in Greenwich Village clubs and traveled to Harlem to hear it in clubs and places like the Savoy Ballroom. Among expatriates in Europe the new music also played a role. "Always, everywhere, there was jazz," wrote Malcolm Cowley of expatriate life in Paris in 1929, "everything that year was enveloped in the hard bright mist of it. There were black orchestras wailing in cafés and *boîtes de nuit*, radios carrying the music of the Savoy Ballroom in London, new phonograph records from Harlem and Tin Pan Alley played over and over again."[67]

Along with esthetic morality, what we may call "primitivism" — also a refuge from conventional standards — helped to quicken an interest in jazz among intellectuals and others. To many who had disowned orthodox norms the most oppressive aspect of American life was the disregard or outright suppression of supposedly natural instincts. The Negro offered an ideal subject for primitivist attentions because he seemed to manifest the direct virility suppressed in overcultivated whites. Interest in Negro art and entertainment soared. The music critic and esoteric novelist Carl Van Vechten was the chief white propagandist of New York's African cult, which he promulgated in his writing and at numerous parties he gave for his white and Negro friends. Van Vechten found in jazz an indigenous product which seemed to be the best hope of American music. He kept boxes of records by blues singer Bessie Smith which, as he said, "I played and played in the early twenties and everybody who came to my apartment was invited to hear them."[68] Langston Hughes wrote that Van Vechten's parties "were *so* [italics Hughes's] Negro that they were reported as a matter of course in the Harlem press."[69] At one such party Bessie Smith sang the blues after Margarita D'Alvarez of the Metropolitan Opera sang an aria. Van Vechten's description of the response to Bessie's performance that night illuminates the nature of the appeal of jazz for the primitivist: "I am quite certain that anybody who was present that night will never forget it. This was no actress; no imitator of a woman's woes; there was no pretence. It was the real thing — a woman cutting her heart open with a knife until it was exposed for us all to see, so that we suffered as she suffered, exposed with a rhythmic ferocity, indeed, which could hardly be borne."[70]

Eugene O'Neill, Theodore Dreiser, Dorothy Parker, Heywood Broun, Fanny Hurst, and Franklin P. Adams [71] were among the intellectuals who frequented Harlem night clubs like Small's Paradise, Connie's Inn, and the Cotton Club, which all offered jazz as a specialty. Fashionable people were also in attendance. "The clubs in Harlem stayed open all night," explained Louis Armstrong, "In the audience any old night would be famous actresses and critics and writers and publishers and rich Wall Street men and big people of all kinds, being gay and enjoying the hot swing music and fast-stepping floor shows. Everybody of course was in evening clothes."[72] The shows and patrons of the various bars and clubs which attracted white tourists seldom represented Harlem life. The most famous night club, the Cotton Club, catered almost exclusively to whites, usually gansters and fashionable people. A Negro was admitted only if he were a celebrity and then was seated at a back table. Much of the entertainment was a primitivist *pot pourri*. The jazz historian Marshall Stearns wrote, "I recall one [show] where a light-skinned and magnificently muscled Negro burst through a papier-mâché jungle onto the dance floor clad in an aviator's helmet, goggles, and shorts. He had obviously 'been forced down in darkest Africa,' and in the center of the floor he came upon a 'white' goddess clad in long tresses and being worshipped by a circle of cringing 'blacks.' Producing a bull whip from heaven knows where, the aviator rescued the blonde and they did an erotic dance. In the background, Bubber Miley, Tricky Sam Nanton, and other members of the [Duke] Ellington band growled, wheezed, and snorted obscenely."[73]

Not only in Harlem did the well-to-do associate jazz with the expression of natural instincts. At parties given in New York and Palm Beach by people such as Mrs. Graham Fair Vanderbilt, Mary Brown Warburton, George Preston Marshall, and Mrs. Woolworth Donahue, the all-white Mound City Blue Blowers made primitive-sounding music on a guitar, banjo, suitcase, and a piece of paper wrapped around a comb.[74] When Eddie Condon and a group of ex-Chicagoans played at a society ball at Newport, they made a resounding hit. Condon heard one matron exclaim, "extraordinary demonstration of the freed libido," and call him an "extraordinary creature!"[75]

Jazz fulfilled various esthetic needs for those who rejected traditional values. For the jazz men and their close followers it provided a voice of rebellion and a source of positive morality. For its less ardent young supporters jazz furnished accompaniment to their growing pains and adolescent enthusiasms. Intellectuals found it an exciting new form of art. Primitivists found in it an expression for their natural instincts. And in one way or another it titillated the sensibilities of well-to-do members of slumming parties. However differently people responded to jazz, it provided all of them with emotional symbols for the relative values that were replacing the standards of traditional idealism.

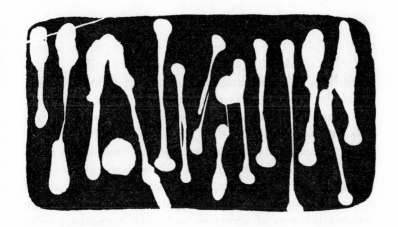

CHAPTER FOUR

THE BREAKTHROUGH
OF COMMERCIAL AND
SYMPHONIC JAZZ

IN today's musical terminology, the phrase, "the jazz age," is a misnomer when applied to the 1920's. This decade might more accurately be called "the commercial jazz age," since the relatively small amount of real jazz played during these years was all but lost in the volume of commercial jazz — usually refined — which popular musicians poured into American ears. People listened to and sang commercial jazz, but mainly they danced to it.

Americans had been dancing for a long time, of course, but in the twenties dancing to commercial jazz became a national craze which easily surpassed in popularity earlier dancing fads. People danced after the show in small-town movie theaters, at parties of fraternal and recreational associations, at suburban country clubs, at home to the radio or phonograph, and in various urban speakeasies, night clubs, and dance halls.

We have little knowledge of the kinds of people who preferred the different sorts of commercial jazz or reasons for their preference. It is helpful, however, to discuss briefly New York City dance halls and their patrons in order to suggest the nature of the acceptance of commercial jazz [1] among city dwellers. The number of licensed dance halls in New York City grew rapidly in the early twenties, from almost 500 in 1920 to almost 800 in 1925. In 1925 most of the patrons of these halls were between the ages of seventeen and forty. Approximately 10 per cent of the female and 14 per cent of the male population of New York attended once a week or oftener.[2]

A report made in the middle of the decade by investigators of the New York City Recreational Committee suggests that many of the patrons had no loyalty to the most restrictive traditional values. The report said that in clubs and restaurants, which presumably attracted middle- and upper-class patrons, young dancers "tend to let down the bars that restrict them in the environments where they usually move . . . they can make rather indiscriminate love, etc." Probably many of the middle-aged customers of such places were caught up in the vogue of the twenties of looking young and acting adolescent, and behaved much like the youngsters. As for patrons of the numerous lower-class dance halls, the report declared that their primary motivation for attending was the opportunity to meet people. It seems safe to say that many of them ignored traditional values because as members of Negro, Irish, Italian, or Jewish communities they had had non-traditional upbringings. To whatever extent dancers in New York revolted against, or ignored, the traditional standards, their interest in commercial jazz seems to have been temporary or lukewarm. The investigators agreed that most of the patrons interviewed in dance halls said that they were bored and that they only came to the place where the music was played because they had nothing better to do.[3]

Today's listeners find nut jazz of the twenties faintly amusing or simply tawdry and refined jazz of that period showy and sentimental. Yet despite their esthetic weaknesses, both played a significant role in advancing the ultimate acceptance of real jazz. By offering jazz elements confected into a palatable form of entertainment, commercial jazz helped Americans to become familiar with them. After hearing jazz characteristics (however altered) for several years, many listeners could begin to accept or tolerate jazz less as a wild-sounding novelty and more as a form of music to be judged not in terms of traditional musical standards but in terms of its own merits.

II

Aside from the numerous Americans who sang and danced to refined jazz and took it for granted as popular music, by the early twenties an influential minority had endorsed it for more sophisticated reasons. This minority was made up of moderates standing between the radicals who wholeheartedly embraced real jazz and the conservatives who rejected all jazz sounds. The moderates approved of refined jazz because it had been "purified" by traditional musical elements, and therefore seemed to be not only respectable popular music but also a step toward an American concert music which came to be called symphonic jazz. The logical extension of the refinement process, symphonic jazz further replaced jazz elements with traditional characteristics, particularly academic characteristics. Its compositions were usually extended works, concertos, operas, and ballets.

Symphonic jazz supporters had temperate reservations about the traditional culture. Men such as Paul Whiteman and H. O. Osgood complained about sanctimonious ministers and uplifters from women's clubs; and spoke disparagingly about "puritanism," smugness, and boosterism which seemed to grow out of adherence to anachronistic traditional standards.[4] More frequently they were dissatisfied with the static nature of traditional values. Paul Whiteman's experience illuminates the nature of such dissatisfaction. After a traditionalist upbringing he had been a violin player in the Denver and San Francisco symphony orchestras until he found something missing in his life. "You get to a place," he wrote, "where you wear out your interest in all the things you are used to doing and need something fresh. . . . If I stayed with the symphony, I was pretty sure to continue following the line of no resistance. . . . And I had such stores of vitality to be turned into some channel. . . . I was listless, dissatisfied, despondent."[5]

The restlessness of symphonic jazz advocates over traditional values led to no revolt. Instead their objections reflected attempts to compromise in terms of traditional norms. Like many others dissatisfied with conventional norms, symphonic jazz advocates looked to the subcultures for something fresh and vital. Yet, they were unwilling to go so far as to embrace real jazz. For that matter, they looked upon it almost as unfavorably as traditionalists. Most symphonic jazz exponents who had heard "jazz" after the war agreed with critic Alfred V. Frankenstein, who said that it "sounded like a crazy clarinetist broadcasting from a boiler factory on a night when the static was particularly bad. The melodic line . . . was all but non-existent. Its rhythm was not exactly syncopated, it was simply goofy. And so far as harmony was concerned, the wildest dissonant dream of a Francis Poulenc is as Schubert's unfinished symphony by comparison."[6] Critic Samuel Chotzinoff at first complained that jazz bands "erupted into climaxes of wailing trombones, shrieking whistles, and farmyard noises of a chromatic sort, which resembled nothing that had been heard before." He went on to speak of the "complete lack of restraint and frequent degeneration" connected with jazz.[7]

Before long, however, such people realized that refined jazz men like Whiteman, Vincent Lopez, and Isham Jones were filtering the "offensive" elements out. "There developed a 'sweet jazz,'" wrote critic Sigmund Spaeth, "which produced soft, dreamy, subtly exotic effects, often presenting real beauty of tonal coloring. The old, raucous noises . . . are now almost forgotten."[8] H. O. Osgood, a critic and associate editor of the *Musical Courier* and an opponent of real jazz, responded favorably when he first heard refined jazz performers: "Before the first sixteen bars were over the revelation of new jazz had descended upon me. By the end of the tune I was a happy convert. . . . These gentlemen made music, languishing, crooning music, rude neither in sound nor tempo, music that soothed and yet, with insinuating rhythms, ear-tickling melody and ingenious decorations, stirred me within. . . . While I had been going about, with my nose in the air with patronizing ignorance, somebody had put music into jazz."[9]

In their own moderate ways symphonic jazz advocates found in their music something of the same thing that real jazz enthusiasts found in theirs — an expression of revolt and a fresh source of morality. Paul Whiteman wrote: "In America, jazz is at once a revolt and a release. Through it, we get back to a simple, to a savage, if you like, joy in being alive. While we are dancing or singing or even listening to jazz, all the artificial restraints are gone. We are rhythmic, we are emotional, we are natural."[10] Gilbert Seldes felt much the same way about "jazz." In *The Seven Lively Arts* he asserted that the art of the Negro "has kept things alive without which our lives would be much meaner, paler, and nearer to atrophy and decay."[11]

Symphonic jazz advocates admitted the savage appeal of refined jazz; however, they were quick to show that its practitioners committed none of the "excesses" of real jazz men. "The music played by the ['jazz'] orchestra," Helen Lowry of the *New York Times* explained, "now is arranged and written as for a symphony — each player must be a trained musician, who would probably be a member of a symphony orchestra, save for

that God-given trick of being a master of syncopation. . . .
Each player does the part allotted to him — and no more." [12]
Refined jazz bands were conducted by recognizable leaders
who hired academically trained musicians possessing compe-
tence to read complex, exacting arrangements. Ernie Golden,
the nationally-known leader of one refined jazz band, declared:
"The best jazz orchestras use the services of men who are fully
equipped to play with the best symphony orchestras. I have
men in my organization who were educated in the best conservatories abroad." [13]

Symphonic jazz enthusiasts pointed further to the traditionalist credentials of composers and arrangers who were "putting
the music into jazz." Frank Patterson, an editor of the *Musical
Courier*, pointed proudly to refined jazz arrangers like J. B.
Lampe, George Trinkhaus, and Frank Barry, all of whom, Patterson assured his readers, had had thorough musical training
at universities like Yale and Northwestern, and later had become distinguished musicians. [14] Sigmund Spaeth shared Patterson's respect for these men: "The real artists of jazz in the
popular field have been the arrangers and masters of orchestra-
tion — men like Ferde Grofé, Bodenwald [*sic*] Lampe, Domen-
ico Savino, and Frank Black." [15]

III

Efforts to blend jazz and academic music were not without
precedent. Before the early twenties foreign-born musicians,
Debussy, Stravinsky, and Milhaud, had included jazz elements
in some of their compositions. As early as 1903 the American,
Scott Joplin, had written the ragtime opera *Treemonisha*, and
at approximately the same time Farwell and other American
composers had called for a concert music combining, among
other things, ragtime and academic elements. Interest in symphonic jazz grew so that by the early twenties some Americans
believed that symphonic jazz represented the culmination of a
truly indigenous art music worthy of a serious hearing.

In 1923 Carl Van Vechten and Maurice Ravel induced Eva
Gautier, a well-known singer of academic music, to include
several "jazz" songs in a recital at Aeolian Hall, an auditorium
hitherto connected with academic music. Deems Taylor reported that the concert attracted what he called a "brilliant
house" of sophisticated and artistically curious individuals. The
first part of the program consisted of songs by such modern
academic composers as Bartók and Hindemith. Taylor wrote
that the audience listened with "interest but without emotion."
The second part of the program consisted of George Gershwin
accompanying Miss Gautier in "jazz" songs like "Alexander's
Ragtime Band" and "Waiting for the Robert E. Lee," to which
the audience reacted far more enthusiastically. "Here was music they didn't have to intellectualize over or take solemnly
. . . [and] apparently it said something to them, touched some
hidden spring that evoked a response as genuine as it was a
little shame-faced. . . . That jazz group touched something
the other music didn't."[16] The Gautier concert stirred a brief
flurry of interest. It remained, however, for Paul Whiteman to
bring symphonic jazz to the serious attention of a large number
of Americans.

For some time Whiteman, whose refined jazz had been an
immense success on records and on dance floors in the United
States and in England, had considered symphonic jazz worthy
of the attention due art. "All the years I had been playing," he
wrote, "I never stopped wanting to go into the concert halls
and in some measure remove the stigma of barbaric strains and
jungle cacophony."[17] After the Gautier concert, to the surprise
of some and to the shock of others, he announced an all-"jazz"
concert at Aeolian Hall for February 12, 1924. "My idea for the
concert," he wrote, "was to show . . . skeptical people the advance which had been made in popular music from the day of
discordant early jazz to the melodious form of the present. I
believed that most of them had grown so accustomed to condemning the 'Livery Stable Blues' [a tune made popular by

the Original Dixieland Jazz Band] sort of thing, that they went on flaying modern [refined and symphonic] jazz without realizing that it was different from the crude early attempts. . . . My task was to reveal the change and try to show that jazz had come to stay and deserved recognition."[18]

Beside being a musician Whiteman was a promoter. By means of a series of statements, press luncheons, and rehearsals to which critics were invited and lectured about his objectives, Whiteman made his "Experiment in Modern Music" (he disliked the term "jazz" as did many other symphonic jazz advocates) the object of widespread interest. For concert patrons he got the musicians,— Damrosch, Godowsky, Heifitz, Kreisler, McCormack, Rachmaninoff, Stokowski, Alda, Galli-Curci, and Garden. Otto Kahn and Jules Glaenzer represented the patrons of the arts, and Fanny Hurst, Heywood Broun, Frank Crowninshield, S. J. Kaufman, Leonard Liebling, Pitts Sanborn, O. O. McIntyre, Deems Taylor, and Carl Van Vechten the critics and writers.[19]

On the day of the concert, those in charge of ticket sales estimated that they could have sold the house out several times over. The audience was a mixture of upper- and lower-class people, from academic composers and concert musicians to vaudevillians and Tin Pan Alley figures. The program began, with Whiteman's Palais Royal Orchestra playing imitations of real jazz and concluded with symphonic jazz selections played by the orchestra augmented to twenty-three men playing thirty-six instruments — including the hecklephone, basset horn, and octavian. The high point of the program was the first performance of George Gershwin's *Rhapsody in Blue*, which Whiteman had commissioned as "Something that would show that jazz had progressed. Something that would illustrate that it was a great deal more than savage rhythm from the jungle. Something that would give expression to what I was seeking to bring out."[20] Although the critics were much interested, they gave the concert a mixed reception. On the other hand, the audience which had grown restless in the middle of the poorly planned program, was most enthusiastic after the *Rhapsody* and returned the performers for five curtain calls. "It seemed as if people would never let us go," Whiteman wrote. "We played all the encores we knew and still they applauded."[21] The acclaim after the concert helped make Whiteman the "King of Jazz" and the most influential spokesman of the symphonic jazz movement.

In the wake of this acclaim Whiteman gave the same program three more times in New York in the spring of 1924, once in Carnegie Hall. Then he took his orchestra on a national and later a European tour on which he played the works of modern American composers Eastwood Lane, John Alden Carpenter, and Leo Sowerby, among others. When Harvard professor and composer Edward Burlingame Hill and Gilbert Seldes introduced the Vincent Lopez Orchestra to the New York concert of the League of Composers, symphonic jazz gained further approval in "official" quarters. Later in 1924 Lopez used forty musicians in a concert at the Metropolitan Opera House. His program included works by Emerson Whithorn, Vladimir Heifetz, and W. C. Handy.[22] The following year Walter Damrosch, who had been much impressed with the *Rhapsody in Blue,* commissioned Gershwin to write the *Concerto in F.* When Damrosch conducted the New York Symphony at Carnegie Hall in the first performance of the *Concerto* Gershwin himself was the piano soloist.

The seal of acceptance of many persons in official musical circles came in Damrosch's speech to the audience before this performance. Like others who had anticipated that jazz might be elevated to concert stature, Damrosch had hoped for some genius who "would pour into this very low form of art, some real emotion which, welling from the very heart of man, might give life to what is at present but a nervous excitement."[23] Speaking of the Concerto Damrosch said, "Lady Jazz . . . [previously] has encountered no knight who could lift her to a level that would enable her to be received as a respectable member of musical circles. George Gershwin seems to have accomplished this miracle."[24]

Gershwin later wrote *An American in Paris* (1928) and the *Second Rhapsody* (1931), neither of which achieved the popularity and critical interest accorded the first rhapsody. Other composers also attempted to combine refined jazz with academic forms. In 1926 the Metropolitan produced John Alden Carpenter's jazz ballet *Skyscrapers* and the Chicago Opera staged his *Light from St. Agnes*. Still other Americans to compose academic music with jazz elements were Aaron Copland, George Anthiel, Louis Gruenberg, and Walter Piston.

After the Whiteman concert and the events which followed, official musical circles began to examine refined and symphonic jazz earnestly — but often apologetically. Leading musical publications reflected the growing interest. The *Musical Courier* had become a convert as early as 1922 and slowly others followed. The die-hard *Etude* devoted the major part of its August 1924 issue to "The Jazz Problem." The lead editorial, "Where the *Etude* Stands on Jazz," stated that "The *Etude* reflects action in the music world. We . . . do most emphatically *not* [editor's italics] endorse jazz merely by discussing it. . . . In its original form it has no place in musical education and deserves none. . . . On the other hand, the melodious and rhythmic inventive skill of many composers of Jazz, such men as Berlin, Confrey, Gershwin, and Cohan is extraordinary." The editors added, "Serious musicians such as John Alden Carpenter, Percy Grainger and Leopold Stokowski, have predicted that Jazz will have an immense influence upon musical composition, not only of America, but of the world."[25] The *New York Times* also shifted its editorial policy and commented that there were two types of jazz and that the good type deserved serious study. It concluded that refined and symphonic jazz "arranged and played by experts has much about it of interest and even of value, and all unite in condemning the inexpert and overenthusiastic disturbers of the peace."[26] The scholarly *Musical Quarterly* for April, 1926, carried an article which illustrates the effort to split jazz into good and bad kinds. "It may seem a bit strange that Jazz should receive serious attention from music educators," began Edwin J. Stringham, "but the truth is, if one will be fair, there are two sides to the Jazz question. This form of music, as we shall call it for the time being, at least for sake of argument, has been denounced far and wide as being of immoral character and having within it the means of inducing immorality. . . . I have in mind only the better type of jazz; that which is composed by understanding musicians, that which is well conceived and written according to ordinary esthetical and technical standards . . . the bad types of Jazz are self-evident and carry within themselves their own swiftest and surest condemnation."[27]

In 1926 the first two books about "jazz" were published. *So This Is Jazz*, by H. O. Osgood, was a chatty effort to explain the elements of refined and symphonic jazz. More important was Paul Whiteman's *Jazz*[28] (written in collaboration with Mary Margaret McBride), which first appeared in instalments in the *Saturday Evening Post*. Despite the popular style of the writing and the publicity-stunt pictures — one depicted Whiteman and his band performing shoulder-deep in water — the book discusses such serious questions as the nature of art and the place of music in America.

Interest in symphonic jazz grew strong in the middle twenties but began to decline when the music failed to blossom into greatness as its advocates had predicted. By the Depression the issues of symphonic jazz no longer made headlines, and the talents of many of its practitioners were drained off by the growing radio and movie industries.

IV

Why did symphonic jazz composers for the most part fail to create music of enduring esthetic interest? There are several possible reasons, each of which deserves attention. Only one, however, is fully relevant to an explanation of the acceptance of jazz.

As the term "symphonic jazz" implies, the people who sought to write this music felt they were taking the substance of "jazz" and dressing it up for the concert stage. Walter Damrosch believed that Gershwin had succeeded because he clothed jazz in "the classic garb of the concerto" without detracting from the character of the new music. Yet today, the *Rhapsody* seems to be not so much symphonic jazz as jazzy symphonic music. Instead of jazz dressed in "classic garb," the *Rhapsody* seems to be traditional music dressed in jazz costume and coloring — Liszt, as it were, in blackface, a rented tuxedo, and battered top hat. In the uplifting process composers had been absorbed with some of the techniques of jazz but had neglected its essential character. As Aaron Copland later wrote, "What interested composers . . . was not so much the spirit, whatever it symbolized, as the more technical side of jazz — the rhythm, melody, harmony, timbre through which that spirit was expressed."[29] But as Osgood explained, "It is the spirit of the music, not the mechanics of its frame or the characteristics of the superstructure built upon that frame, that determines whether or not it is jazz."[30]

The dangers of "purifying" jazz did not go unnoticed in the twenties. Paul Whiteman acknowledged the problem when he wrote: "The demonaic energy, the fantastic riot of accents and the humorous moods have all had to be toned down. I hope in toning down we shall not, as some critics have predicted, take the life out of our music."[31] Gershwin shared this concern, "Certain types of it are in bad taste, but I do think it has certain elements which can be developed. I do not know whether it will be jazz when it is finished."[32] To a later generation such apprehensions seem to have been justified.

Symphonic jazz failed not only as jazz but also as academic music — apparently for the same reasons that most American traditional academic composers failed. Gradually it became clear that Gershwin and other symphonic jazz composers had, as the English critic Ernest Newman said in 1927, attempted to sit on two stools and had fallen between them.[33] America had not produced a composer with a sufficient grasp of jazz and academic music to effect a synthesis out of the two.

V

Like other Americans in one way or another dissatisfied with traditional values, symphonic jazz advocates engaged in what Van Wyck Brooks called "the search for a usable past." Digging into the history of American "popular" music, they interpreted the evolution of "jazz" to suit their assumptions about it. As heirs to the tradition of Dvořák and Farwell, they emphasized the value and the historical role of folk music, particularly that of the Negro, from which "jazz" had developed. "The great music of the past in other countries," explained George Gershwin, "has always been built on folk-music. This is the strongest source of musical fecundity. . . . It is not always recognized that America has folk music. . . . Jazz I regard as an American folk-music; not the only one, but a very powerful one which is probably in the blood and feeling of the American people."[34] Symphonic jazz advocates pointed out that Negro folk music had come to this country with the first slaves, that it had grown from spirituals, and that it had provided the basis for the work of song-writers like Irving Berlin and W. C. Handy and various orchestra leaders like Whiteman and Vincent Lopez. Either through ignorance or in attempts to gloss over the unsavory origins of "jazz," they left out the role of the New Orleans slums and other disreputable places or dismissed them in a contemptuous word along with other associations that seemed objectionable. Real jazz they treated as a rude upstart in the process of being disciplined.[35]

For symphonic jazz enthusiasts the music not only had its roots in the American past, but also it expressed the character of present-day American life. John Alden Carpenter, after

Gershwin the best-known composer of symphonic jazz, declared, "I am convinced that our contemporary popular music (please note that I avoid labelling it 'jazz') is by far the most spontaneous, the most personal, the most characteristic, and, by virtue of all these qualities, the most important musical expression that America has achieved."[36] He considered his ballet *Skyscrapers* "an attempt to picture American life in a rhythmic frame."[37] Gershwin asserted that "music should be a product of the time in which it was produced . . . the old masters reflected in their music the spirit of their ages; isn't it up to us to do the same?" He declared that "the originator uses material and ideas that occur around him and pass through him. And out of his experiences comes the original creation or work of art." Of his *Rhapsody* Gershwin wrote, "I hear it as a sort of musical kaleidoscope of America — of our vast melting pot, our blues, our Metropolitan madness."[38]

Most symphonic jazz enthusiasts were as vague or ingenuous as Gershwin in regard to the American character that "jazz" expressed. Paul Whiteman, the most articulate exponent of the movement believed that

> Jazz is the spirit of a new country. It catches up the underlying life motif of a continent and period, molding it into a form which expresses the fundamental emotion of the people, the place and time so authentically that it is immediately recognizable.
>
> At the same time, it evolves new forms, new colors, new technical methods, just as America constantly throws aside old machines for newer and more efficient ones.
>
> I think it is a mistake to call jazz cheerful. The optimism of jazz is the optimism of the pessimist who says, "Let us eat, drink, and be merry, for tomorrow we die."
>
> This cheerfulness of despair is deep in America. Our country is not the childishly jubilant nation that some people like to think it. Behind the rush of achievement is the restlessness of dissatisfaction, a vague nostalgia and yearning for something indefinable, beyond our grasp. . . . something beautiful, good, satisfying; and with our tremendous energy we keep

building and destroying and building again, in our passionate desire to have it — a desire never satisfied. That is the thing expressed by that wail, that longing, that pain, behind all the surface clamor and rhythm and energy of jazz. . . . It is the expression of the soul of America and America recognizes it.[39]

VI

Symphonic jazz enthusiasts were quite sensitive to traditionalist opposition to "jazz." They acknowledged the complaints of ministers, club women, educators, editors, "puritans," "professional reformers," "uplifters," traditionalist musicians, and others,[40] and many of the public utterances by symphonic jazz advocates between 1922 and 1929 were attempts to refute their charges.

The critical discussion about refined and symphonic jazz reached its peak in 1927, when Ernest Newman summed up in articles in the American press what he called "music's case against jazz."[41] Although much of this kind of opposition seemed to be in good faith, symphonic jazz adherents believed that too often the objections sprang from snobbery and narrow-mindedness.[42] Therefore, they attacked the views of esthetiically Europeanized traditionalists whose musical interest covered only traditional academic music and who considered art the exclusive property of the cultivated few.[43] Symphonic jazz adherents also condemned Americans who too closely imitated European composers. Carl Van Vechten made fun of the "Grieg-Schumann-Wagner sound" of MacDowell;[44] and Olin Downes had little interest in composers who could "only echo respectfully and with little force . . . foreign artistic influences."[45] On the other hand, enthusiasts of symphonic jazz eagerly pointed to prestigious European musicians such as Hindemith, who praised refined and symphonic jazz and the techniques of their practitioners.[46] Armed with this praise advocates of symphonic jazz repudiated the traditionalist accusation about "jazz" ruining Americans' taste for "good" music. They quoted Toscanini and Percy Grainger as saying that "jazz" did not detract from, but helped to stimulate, the development of academic music.[47] Others maintained that "jazzing the classics" did not profane or harm the appreciation of great music. As Otto Kahn, chairman of the Board of Directors of the Metropolitan Opera Company, argued "All the classics have been jazzed by now, and it has resulted in getting the people interested in them in their original form."[48]

Symphonic jazz enthusiasts also answered traditionalist complaints that the music spawned immorality. They admitted that it might at times have an intoxicating effect, but they added that life calls for stimulation of some sort, whether or not it comes from music, and that of the many kinds of stimulation, refined and symphonic jazz offered one of the best.[49] They ridiculed fears that the music stimulated indecent behavior. H. L. Mencken, whose *American Mercury* printed articles in support of symphonic jazz, wrote: "Among Christian workers and other intellectual cripples the delusion seems to persist that jazz is highly aphrodisiacal. I never encounter a sermon on the subject without finding it full of dark warnings to parents, urging them to keep their nubile daughters out of jazz palaces on the grounds that the voluptuous music will enflame their passions and so make them easy prey for bond salesmen, musicians and other such carnal fellows."[50] Nor were symphonic jazz enthusiasts bothered by apprehension that the music helped an "inferior" race to undermine American society. The concert pianist Percy Grainger, himself not without prejudice, assured people: "The seductive, exotic, desocializing elements imputed to jazz by musical ignoramuses have no musical basis. . . . As music it seems far less passionate or abandoned than music of many peoples. It is what one would expect from a solid, prosperous Nordic race."[51]

In general symphonic jazz adherents acknowledged that American society was changing, but they denied that the change meant decline — and even if it did, they argued that the music would not be responsible. Whiteman concluded: "The time was right to almost any explosion. . . . The war merely accelerated the spirit of the movement that was under way in 1915 and jazz merely expressed it."[52]

For some years people endorsing real jazz have viewed symphonic jazz disdainfully. They have regarded Paul Whiteman as an outsized clown, the ringmaster of a large musical circus. The work of symphonic jazz composers like Gershwin (apart from his music for the stage) has seemed sentimental, uninspired, and pretentious. Although these criticisms have been perhaps too harsh, their estimate of the esthetic content of symphonic jazz has been generally correct. Yet in pointing out these shortcomings, jazz enthusiasts have ignored the role of symphonic jazz exponents in the advancement of music in America. In spite of their esthetic blunders and occasionally ridiculous statements, symphonic jazz advocates helped greatly to overcome formalism and highbrowism that had done much to constrict the development of music in the United States. Symphonic jazz enthusiasts encouraged composition and performance of music that departed from the European tradition. They were the first Americans with any prestige in official musical circles to see that jazz (however much they wanted to change it) should not be dismissed as vulgar dance music, that something in it deserved the attention due art. By reason and ridicule they helped to brush aside many prejudices and misconceptions that blocked the way for this recognition. In large measure, it was through their efforts that the term "jazz" became in the twenties and thirties associated less with the brothel and more with the concert hall as a native product of which Americans could be proud. Real jazz enthusiasts have been too quick to point out the faults of symphonic jazz adherents and too slow to acknowledge the contributions of men like Whiteman and Gershwin to the acceptance of real jazz and to the growth of other types of art music in America.

CHAPTER FIVE

THE IMPACT OF MECHANIZATION

BEFORE 1917 Americans heard jazz "live," that is, played directly to them, in dance halls, saloons, barrel houses, brothels, lumber and turpentine camps, river boats and at minstrel and vaudeville shows, carnivals, parades, and funerals. After the war people still heard it "live," but more and more it reached them "canned," that is, through mechanical sound-reproducing devices: the player piano, the phonograph, the radio, and the film sound track. Conceived at the end of the nineteenth century, these devices were developed and widely marketed in the first part of the twentieth. They grew up with jazz and strongly influenced its diffusion and evolution.

The first instrument to reproduce canned music for a large audience was the player piano (or pianola). Shortly after 1900 its manufacturers marketed piano rolls which played a variety of music from Chopin to ragtime. At first the sound was poor.

As one listener wrote: "The notes were shot out like bullets. . . . In the overwhelming solos there was no recognition of the principles which underlie playing; no important or unimportant sounds, no increase or decrease in volume. Such crudeness soon gave place to machine-like imitation of light and shade, to sound emphasis of the melodic line, and variations of speed."[1] By World War I improved pianolas had become fashionable and sounded fragments of Beethoven's *Moonlight Sonata* or, more often, "Alexander's Ragtime Band," in many places of entertainment and in thousands of homes.

In the early 1900's the phonograph was no commercial rival to the pianola. The music of early records was often scarcely discernible from the surface scratch, squeaks, and snorts that came out of the horn. Before long, however, several improvements, notably the replacement of cylindrical records with flat disks, made the phonograph more marketable. Gradually, recordings of academic singers, instrumentalists, and eventually full orchestras helped the "victrola" to become more profitable than the player piano. So-called popular records sold well also, particularly after the onset of the dance rage. By the twenties popular musicians received as much for their records as did their academic counterparts, and from then on the biggest profits came from popular music.

In 1921 over 100,000,000 records were manufactured, and Americans spent more money for them than for any other form of recreation.[2] The depression of 1922 and the arrival of radio hit the phonograph industry hard. In the mid-twenties, when acoustical recording was abandoned in favor of electrical recording, business improved; but when the economy collapsed in 1929, the recording industry suffered, along with the rest of the country. In 1933 only 2,500,000 records were made. Gradually, the record business revived with the help of the juke box, which found its way into almost every restaurant and bar across the country. There were 350,000 juke boxes at work by 1940 and 44 per cent of the records sold went into them. By 1942 sales figures for records reached an unprecedented 127,000,000. The vast majority of these were popular records (mostly jazz and commercial jazz). In 1939 Americans bought 45,000,000 "popular" records and only 5,000,000 "classical," a ratio of 9:1.[3]

Following Marconi's experiments in the nineties, radio developed rapidly, particularly after De Forrest invented the vacuum tube in 1906. During World War I the government controlled the radio industry, but after 1918 it was thrown open to commercial exploitation and quickly attracted wide public interest. In 1922 the "radio boom" was well underway; over 200 stations and 3,000,000 sets were in operation. By 1926 there were 694 stations. The number of receivers in use grew to an estimated 15,000,000 in 1931 and reached 51,000,000 by the end of the decade.[4]

During the twenties music constituted three-fourths of the material heard on the radio.[5] At first broadcasters programed only a small amount of academic music because they believed it did not appeal to a mass audience and because many academic musicians were reluctant to broadcast. Some of them considered a radio performance — distorted by static and other disturbance, which they dubbed "De Forest's prime evil," — below their dignity.[6] In the twenties commercial jazz dominated radio. An editorial in *Etude* declared in 1924, " 'Listen in' on the radio any night. Tap America anywhere in the air and nine times out of ten Jazz will burst forth."[7] Four years later Charles Merz sampled for one week the content of radio programs from stations throughout the country. Of 357 hours broadcast by ten typical large stations, Merz found 259 devoted to popular "harmony and rhythm" and 42 to "serious music." Of 294 hours broadcast by ten typical smaller stations, 189 were given over to "syncopation" and 77 to "serious or partway serious" music.[8] The predominance of time allotted to "jazz" entertainers such as the Cliquot Club Eskimos, Ipana Troubadors, and A&P

Gypsies was more imposing than the figures indicated. Merz pointed out that the policy of large stations was to broadcast the serious part of the daily program, lectures on the Dawes Plan and academic music, early, and to leave the evenings, when the largest number of people tuned in, free for popular entertainment, mostly commercial jazz.[9]

In the thirties new types of programs were taking up some of the hours formerly devoted to music, but commercial jazz still dominated broadcasting by a wide margin. During 1933, "dance and light music" filled 43 per cent of the broadcasting time on the NBC and CBS networks combined, while "classical and semi-classical" took up 18 per cent. In 1939 the figures were 37 per cent for "dance and light" and 10 per cent for "classical and semi-classical."[10]

The development of motion pictures was also extraordinarily rapid. By the end of World War I they had come a long way from the peep show and nickelodeon. Flickering images had changed to distinct pictures, and multi-reel narratives were being shown in comfortable theaters. An estimated 35,000,000 Americans went to the movies at least once a week in 1920. At first the film shared the bill with vaudeville acts, but the arrival of talking pictures in 1927 gradually forced live entertainment out of the theater. By this time weekly movie attendance had jumped to 110,000,000, or four-fifths of the American population. The Depression reduced the film audience as it had the number of phonograph and radio listeners. Weekly attendance climbed to 77,000,000 by 1935, however, and once again approached 100,000,000 in 1939.[11]

Music played an important part in the movie industry. From the first, a piano or small orchestra accompanied the film intensifying the stereotyped dramatic situations with stereotyped dilutions of jazz or academic music. With the arrival of "talkies" a mixture of academic and popular music blared from the sound track. Hundreds of commercial jazz songs were written for film musicals, like the first of the "talkies," *The Jazz Singer*. Both in musicals and non-musicals syncopated *crescendi* and blue-toned *sforzandi* of symphonic and refined jazz helped to create atmosphere, to suggest unspoken thoughts or other implications, to provide continuity, and to build up or round off dramatic episodes.

Probably it is impossible to explain adequately the effect of the relentless projection of canned music, mostly commercial jazz, into American ears. Yet one result is clear: reproducing devices made music available cheaply and easily and consequently greatly speeded its diffusion. A leading radio performer reached more people in the course of a single program than a vaudeville headliner played before in an entire year. In little more than a week reproducing devices could make a song a hit across the nation.[12] On the other hand, their use exhausted material rapidly. Before the arrival of canned music, the commercial life of a song lasted months, sometimes a year or longer. Reproducing devices repeated a tune so often that the public tended to tire of it in sixty days. The market demanded more and more songs, and the public heard so many jazz tunes that, as music publisher Edward Marks pointed out, it had trouble in distinguishing between them.[13] The radio in particular saturated the public's sensibility with jazz sounds. Charles Merz declared:

> There are literally hundreds of bands, jazz orchestras and syncopated entertainers whose fame the radio has broadcast into millions of homes reaching all the way from city flats to the loneliest farms in the wheat country. . . . We tune in — on a mighty rhythm to which millions of people are marking time, the pulse beat of a nation. All over the country the trombones blare and the banjos whang and the clarinets pipe the rhythm. All over the country the same new tunes that will be generations old before the week is out are hammered home to the same vast audience from a hundred different places. . . . If it is true that from twenty to thirty million Americans are listening in on the

radio every evening, then for a large part of that evening they are listening in on the greatest single sweep of synchronized and syncopated rhythm that human ingenuity has yet conceived.[14]

By the end of the twenties reproducing devices had made jazz sounds exceedingly familiar to most people. No longer did syncopation, polyrhythm, *glissandi*, blue notes, and antiphonal effects sound completely barbarous, and indignant complaints about them grew scarce after 1928.

II

While commercial dilutions dominated the musical output of the phonograph, the radio, and the movies, real jazz remained on the fringes of the business. Jazz men seldom played on the radio or in films, and made relatively few recordings. Yet despite their comparatively small number, jazz records affected the growth of jazz significantly.

At first, most of the jazz diffused mechanically was on so-called race records, which were directed to Negroes. All of the King Oliver, Bessie Smith, early Duke Ellington, and Louis Armstrong, and even some of the Bix Beiderbecke disks came out as race records. Far from considering their contents to be art music, issuing companies regarded them as popular music and advertised them as "red hot," "guaranteed to put you in that dancing mood," or as "the latest hot stuff to tickle your toes." Race records were cheap to make. They required from one to ten musicians, who frequently earned no more than five dollars a side, ten dollars for the leader. Often the performers composed their own material inexpensively in the recording studio, and if there were any royalties, they were small.[15] And race records were as easy to market as they were cheap to make. They required no expensive, nationwide promotion or distribution since they could be sold readily in Negro areas.

Even though race and the few other real jazz records were but a trickle in the enormous tide of disks that came from the recording industry, they immeasurably speeded the acceptance of jazz. The phonograph, the first device to preserve the music of improvising bands, permitted a single performance to be heard simultaneously and repeatedly at different places throughout the country. The first few sides made by the Original Dixieland Band, selling as they did in the millions,[16] did more to facilitate the acceptance of jazz than hundreds of jazz bands playing "live" could have done. Furthermore, records served as devices of self-instruction. In 1916, when the Victor Talking Machine Company approached Freddie Keppard and his Original Creole Band with a recording offer, he is reported to have said to his musicians, "Nothin' doin', boys. We won't put our stuff on records for everybody to steal."[17] A few months later the recorded music of the Original Dixieland Jazz Band provided a model for aspiring jazz men everywhere to imitate. In such widely separated places as Boston, Chicago, and Spokane young musicians copied or learned to accompany their favorite performers on records.

The experience of cornetist Jimmy McPartland and his high school friends illustrates how young jazz men learned from records. One day in a local soda parlor they found a record of the New Orleans Rhythm Kings. "Boy, when we heard that — I'll tell you we went out of our minds," McPartland recalls. "Everybody flipped. It was wonderful." They replayed the record during the course of several days and "we decided we would get a band and play like these guys." In one way or another they obtained instruments and tried to accompany the record. "What we used to do was put the record on . . . play a few bars, and then all get our notes. We'd have to tune our instruments up to the record machine, to the pitch, and go ahead with a few notes. Then stop! A few more bars of the record, each guy would pick out his notes and boom! We would go on and play it. . . . It was a funny way to learn, but in three or four weeks we could finally play one tune all the way through."[18] Records permitted aspiring jazz men to learn music without bothering with the formalism, discipline, technique, and expense of traditional training.

III

Mechanical reproducing devices hastened the acceptance of jazz not only by familiarizing both listeners and musicians with non-traditional characteristics of the new music but also by helping to bring it into closer alignment with traditional values.

The widespread diffusion of canned music had an all-important part in bringing to a head traditional opposition to "jazz." Live performances of jazz before lower-class audiences in unsavory locations had caused traditionalists concern enough but when reproducing devices brought the music with astonishing frequency to the ears of the general public, traditionalists became alarmed. It was one thing to know about "jazz" played in brothels and other disreputable places patronized by supposedly disreputable people, yet it was quite another thing to hear sound tracks and records bring it to middle- and upper-class places of amusement and to find radios and phonographs blaring it into "respectable" homes. Sound-reproducing devices translated traditionalists' concern about "jazz" into demands to suppress it. One of the most powerful suppressive measures was the pressure on the music business to purify or eradicate "jazz."

The popular music industry has long sought to produce the lowest common denominator in its material: that music which will please as many and offend as few potential customers as possible. After 1917 the industry ignored complaints about "jazz" as long as they did not threaten profits. By the late twenties, however, creators and distributors of popular music had grown sensitive to traditionalist criticism about jazz, and many of them became concerned to clean it up for both business and ethical reasons.

As early as 1921 a group of Tin Pan Alley publishers organized the Music Publishers' Protective Association to censor popular songs. Citing the increasing use of mechanical, sound-reproducing devices, the chairman of the Executive Board, E. C. Mills, explained: "The publishers do not want to be sponsors of indecent material. These songs go into the homes of the country." Accordingly, the association began a "vigilant watch for such sentiments and expressions which are common to the suggestive." It adopted as its motto, "Just keep the words clean and the music will take care of itself," and proceeded to weed out any material which was indecent or which made fun of any law, sect, or race. Member publishers had to register all songs with the association and to post a bond as a pledge of obedience to the regulations. Mills, who was also chairman of the Administrative Committee of ASCAP (American Society of Composers, Authors, and Publishers), claimed the co-operation of certain vaudeville producers, sheet-music jobbers, phonograph and piano-roll companies, and interested laymen.[19]

By 1927 the demands to clean up popular songs had reached the proportions of an organized movement. A convention of fifty member-firms of the New York Piano Merchants' Association resolved not to sell any sheet music, records, or piano rolls with "lewd, lascivious, salacious, or suggestive" titles or lyrics. They sent a copy of their resolution to publishers and record companies.[20] Three months later the National Association of Orchestra Directors appointed a "czar" and a committee to investigate hotels, night clubs, and dance halls to determine "the kind of jazz that tends to create indecent dancing" and to instruct band leaders on "the correct rendition."[21] In June of the same year, the National Association of Music Merchants passed a resolution declaring that American music had been lowered by "smut words" and pledged to do nothing to make music unfit for American homes. They called on Congress to permit censorship of songs in order to maintain "a high standard of decency, morality, and fitness."[22]

Nor were the radio, film, and eventually the phonograph industries deaf to traditionalist objections about "jazz." Radio broadcasters were particularly sensitive to any complaints. In 1925 Carl Dreher wrote: "They are in a constant stew about 'adverse publicity.' A few letters from irate listeners give them the horrors. They run their stations for advertising or good will, and as soon as any one looks at them cross-eyed their knees shake. When in doubt, they wield the blue pencil, and any one who tries to please the whole world is in doubt most of the time."[23] Two years later the federal government began to encourage broadcasters' squeamishness about questionable material. In 1927 Congress passed the Radio Act creating a commission to allocate wave lengths, license stations, and generally oversee broadcasting. Section 26 of the Act declared that the commission had no powers of censorship, but added that "no person within the jurisdiction of the United States shall utter any obscene, indecent or profane language by means of radio communication." This section was written (as section 326) into the Federal Communications Act of 1934.[24]

The commissions created by both acts were bound to license only those broadcasters deemed to be "operating in the public interest, convenience, and necessity" and since licenses were granted for only a short time, censorship resulted in practice if not in theory. "Fear of disappproval," explained David Sarnoff, the head of R.K.O. (Radio-Keith-Orpheum), can blue-pencil a dozen programs for every one that an official censor might object to. . . . Few realize that post-program discipline by the government can be a form of censorship that is all the more severe because it is undefined."[25] Government vagueness obliged every station master to act as a censor in self-defense. The big networks developed internal censorship, euphemistically called "Continuity Acceptance" at N.B.C. and "Continuity Editing" at C.B.S.[26] In 1929 the National Association of Broadcasters adopted a code of ethics which proscribed broadcasting material that would be banned from the mails as "obscene or offensive."[27]

As a result of government and private regulation, anything

that seemed in the slightest degree "objectionable" was ruled off the air. Real jazz and certain lyrics associated with it were frequently unacceptable. By 1942 N.B.C. had blacklisted the words of 290 songs. Of these, 217 could not be sung at all, while the remainder could be performed only with cleaned-up lyrics.[28] The first known instance of radio censorship of any type occurred when Station WFFA banned the song "Little Red Riding Hood" because of the line "How could Little Red Riding Hood have been so very good and and still keep the wolf from the door?"[29] Later N.B.C. changed the words "Silk stockings thrown aside" to "Gloves thrown aside."[30] Offensive musical elements were also deleted or refined before they reached the microphone. During the twenties, one New York station disallowed "jazz" between certain hours while another, WRNY, dropped it altogether.[31] The FCC did not rule directly on "jazz" until 1938, when Chairman Frank McNinch answered a complaint of the Bach Society of New Jersey by urging station masters to use "a high degree of discrimination" in broadcasting the music.[32]

Long before McNinch's statement, broadcasters recognized the need for discretion in transmitting "jazz," yet most were reluctant to stop broadcasting a major attraction. Audience response assured them that support for the music outweighed opposition to it. For instance, when an organization called the "Keep-the-Air-Clean-on-Sunday-Society" tried to make WMCA, New York, stop broadcasting "jazz" on Sunday, letters from listeners favoring the music prevented its being dropped.[33] Broadcasters also knew that the general approval applied only to refined jazz. In 1927 Kingsley Welles stressed this point in his column, "The Listeners' Point of View," in *Radio Broadcast*. He quoted from a letter from a "typical listener" who had written that "the universal condemnation of jazz is contrary to the true feeling of a majority of radio listeners. . . . Would these objectors want to stop the broadcasting of such organizations as those of Paul Whiteman, Vincent Lopez,

Jean Goldkette, and many others," Decidedly not," answered Welles.[34]

Arguments of the proponents of symphonic jazz provided further reasons for broadcasters to support or tolerate the transmission of refined jazz. As the manager of musical programs for one western station declared in 1925, "Personally I feel that jazz is not all bad. . . . Lately, jazz has gathered to itself some notable defenders among the musically correct. Serious minded musicians have perceived under the battered and tattered appearance of jazz, evidence of a new vitality in music, a struggle after a new form of expression, crude as the hieroglyphics of Cubism, but genuine art, nevertheless. The moans, shrieks, catcalls and sobs of jazz will eventually disappear, but the vibrancy of its stimulating rhythms will remain to be caught some time by a master composer."[35]

Movie producers were sensitive to traditionalist criticism also. After the Armistice a series of suggestive films and Hollywood scandals aroused complaints from traditionalists; indignant clergymen, church organizations, women's clubs, and other guardians against vice demanded reform. By 1922 six states had passed legislation to censor films. To prevent further censorship from outside, the film industry appointed Will Hays head of the Motion Picture Producers and Distributors Association of America and overseer of Hollywood morals both on and off the screen. Among other steps, the association, better known as the Hays office, developed and enforced a production code. In general the code stipulated that no film could sympathetically portray manners and morals too contrary to those founded on traditional values. For example, the sanctity of the home and marriage was to be upheld and the treatment of sex was to be handled delicately. Obscenity in words, gesture, reference, song, joke, or suggestion was forbidden.[36]

The Hays office set a moral tone which helped keep real jazz out of films. There was always the danger that a movie offering the new music as a special attraction would not be acceptable. In 1929 when the uninhibited "Empress of the Blues," Bessie Smith, made a two-reel short *St. Louis Blues*, it was condemned for its bad taste and suppressed.[37] Other films starring jazz men were more fortunate, but generally real jazz found little favor in Hollywood until the thirties.

Although the radio and film industries tended to exclude real jazz, the phonograph companies were less obliged to do so. Like other producers of canned music, record-makers sought material that would please as many and offend as few people as possible. At the same time, however, because of the nature of records and the ways in which they were distributed, record-makers could still cater profitably to minority tastes. Records did not necessarily reach the general public, more often than not, individuals bought them to play for a limited audience. In any event, the sounds of distasteful records were easily kept out of public places and off the public air.

Race records, which covered most of the real jazz recordings of the twenties, seldom found their way into white neighborhoods, and therefore no formal organization like the F.C.C. or the Hays office emerged to censor their content. Still, record-makers could not completely ignore traditionalist rules of decency. In 1927, for example, Louis Armstrong made "S.O.L. Blues" (Okeh 8496), which the Okeh Company considered too offensive to market. Armstrong had to return to the studio the following day to remake the number ("Gully Low Blues" Okeh 8474) using a "clean" title and more appropriate lyrics.[38]

Growing centralization of the entertainment business had an important role in bringing jazz closer to traditional values. As technical improvements permitted increased commercial exploitation of sound-producing devices, show business became, more than ever, big business. By the twenties Wall Street had invested heavily in commercial entertainment and at the end of the decade radio and films were among the nation's leading industries. While the process of centralization may be said to have begun before World War I, not until the twenties and

thirties did the entertainment business fall under the control
of a handful of corporations. In 1926 N.B.C. marked the beginning of network broadcasting by linking 19 stations. In 1937 it
had 138. The Columbia Broadcasting System, which had
started in 1927 with 16 stations, was sending its programs to 110
in 1938.[39] As radio became centralized, it swallowed up the
leading phonograph companies. In January, 1929, the Victor
Talking Machine Company merged with R.C.A. (Radio Corporation of America). Nine years later C.B.S. bought the American Record Company, whose catalogue included Columbia,
Okeh, Vocalion, Brunswick, and some minor labels. The arrival of the talking picture brought about further concentration.
R.C.A. took over the Keith-Albee-Orpheum vaudeville circuit
and the Pathé film company, and formed R.K.O. (Radio-Keith-
Orpheum). Warner Brothers merged with the Stanley Corporation of America and First National Pictures.

To satisfy their unending need for songs, film companies
purchased the leading New York music-publishing firms or
created their own musical affiliates. Warner Brothers bought
the Tin Pan Alley houses of Harms, Witmark, Remick, and that
of DeSylva, Brown, and Henderson. R.K.O. controlled the
firms of Leo Feist and Carl Fischer. Robbins became a subsidi-
ary of Metro-Goldwyn-Mayer. Paramount owned the Famous
Music Company and Twentieth-Century-Fox incorporated the
Red Star Publishing Company.[40]

This process of centralization gave a progressively smaller
number of executives more and more control over the choice
of material to be distributed. Owning or controlling affiliates in
almost every phase of the entertainment business, the men in
charge sought above all a standardized product which they
could sell through every medium to as many people in as many
places as possible. To be fully exploitable, music now had to
be suitable not only for dance halls, the stage, and phonograph
records (all of which could cater to minority tastes) but also
for radio and films, which reached the general, nationwide audi-

ence. Although collectively improvised jazz of Louis Armstrong's Hot Five or the blues sung by Bessie Smith sounded less strange than they had a few years earlier, they still had little market appeal for the general audience. Furthermore, the suggestive lyrics, which shocked traditionalists, met with the disapproval of the Radio Commission and the Hays office. The words of "It's Tight Like That" (VO 1216) by "George Tom" and "Tampa Red:" offer a good example.

> Now the girl I love is long and slim,
> When she gets it it's too bad, Jim.
> It's tight light that, beedle um bum,
> It's tight like that, beedle um bum.
> Hear me talkin' to you, it's tight like that.

Record companies continued to sell such material to the Negro audience,[41] but they knew that lyrics like these and the music associated with them could never be sold for use on radio or in films. Thus, centralization of the entertainment business helped to prevent the spread of collectively improvised jazz and certain blues.

In addition, the interlocking directorates fostered by centralization facilitated the suppression of jazz. Take for example, the power possessed by one company to implement its anti-jazz policy. The Radio Music Company was founded in 1929 primarily as a publishing affiliate of N.B.C. E. C. Mills, whom we encountered earlier as the head of the Music Publishers' Protective Association and of ASCAP, was the president of the Radio Music Company. He proclaimed that its employees intended to make "an active and intelligent use" of the N.B.C. facilities in order to improve American music, and he added: "The new firm will have its influence in putting jazz in the background of the American musical picture. We have had perhaps too much jazz, and there is no denying the influence of music on peoples' inclinations, it seems about time for someone to assume leadership in the movement away from jazz. I think we should go back to the melody and let it serve instead of noise to give us the inspiration we expect from music."[42] The following list of members of the board of directors of the Radio Music Company indicates the vast influence within the music business of the makers of this anti-jazz policy. The chairman of the board was the president of N.B.C., M. H. Aylesworth. Other board members were the executive vice-president of R.C.A., David Sarnoff; the president of the Radio Victor Corporation, E. E. Schumaker; the president of R.K.O., Hiram S. Brown; the president of Leo Feist, Inc., Leo Feist; the president of Westinghouse Electric and Manufacturing Company, H. P. Davis; the director of the Roxy Theater and a power in the music business, S. L. Rothafel; and the president of Carl Fischer, Walter J. Fischer. Other publishers and leading song-writers also co-operated. In 1921, when a leading figure in the business like Mills had tried to curtail jazz, he could count on only the help of several publishers and a few others in connected industries. By 1929, however, concentration of control of commercial entertainment had helped to pyramid his power so that he could expect the co-operation of many of the most prominent policy-makers in the music business.

In their attempts to control every production process and outlet, the large corporations in the entertainment business set up headquarters in New York or Hollywood and sought to divide the country into trade areas serviced by provincial cities.[43] New York was the center for the music industry. Here bands were booked for personal appearances, record dates, and radio jobs. Here talents were assayed, the largest salaries paid, and the biggest reputations made. For gifted jazz men in the late twenties earning $22.50 a week in Chicago, Kansas City, or Dallas, the glitter of Manhattan and the prospect of $100–$200 a week was hard to withstand.[44] "Most of the Chicago gang had gone to New York around 1928," wrote pianist Joe Sullivan, "and plenty more musicians were streaming into Manhattan to get their kicks and grab their share of the fantastically high salaries which were being paid at that time."[45]

Most of the jazz men who came to New York found their hopes of playing jazz for high salaries to be false. People who hired musicians had little use for jazz. Only a few clubs and ballrooms in New York or elsewhere employed collectively improvising jazz men. And the anti- or non-jazz policy of many producers of canned music made jazz musicians' jobs for record, radio, and film companies increasingly scarce as the entertainment business became progressively centralized.

In addition, the growing use of sound-reproducing devices directly affected the market for musicians in a manner that provided further hardship for jazz men. Whether or not mechanical sound devices destroyed more jobs than they ultimately created is a moot question. Yet, it is clear that their introduction resulted in at least temporary displacement for musicians of all types. Radio, to take one medium, sharply cut down the demand for live performances. A striking illustration of this obsolescence occurred in Boston in 1924. Three thousand seats had been sold for a Fritz Kreisler concert, but, when the news got out that the performance would also be broadcast, over half the ticket-holders returned their tickets and presumably listened to the concert over the radio.[46] After 1929 the Depression cut deeper into the opportunities of all musicians.

These circumstances forced many jazz men to abandon collectively improvised jazz for a living at least. The relatively few jobs calling for live performance were usually with refined jazz bands. And without an occasional job with one of the organizations that produced canned music it was difficult to make much money or a reputation that would lead to other jobs. Even before the centralization of the entertainment business, jazz men had recognized the importance of being heard on records and had sometimes paid record companies for the privilege of recording in the hope that the result would prove marketable. After centralization, however, the importance of canned performances to a musician's career became more obvious than ever before. Consequently, the temptation to yield to the demands of the entertainment industry grew. Many jazz men succumbed quickly to the temptation. Those who resisted it usually found that before long they had to submit if they wanted to continue to be musicians. Submission obliged jazz men to replace the most "offensive" characteristics of jazz with elements of traditional popular music. Too often the results were musical trash and jazz men gave in to them with varying degrees of willingness. Some performers, such as Benny Goodman and Louis Armstrong resigned themselves without complaint. In 1954, defending himself against charges that he had wasted his talents on bad popular songs, Armstrong said, "They put a piece of music up in front of you — you ain't supposed to tell the leader 'I don't want to play this.' And I was brought up that way." In discussing this quotation, Chadwick Hansen has pointed out that since Armstrong has almost always led his own band, he is not the leader here, and thus his statement is a metaphor for the entertainment business.[47] Other jazz men resigned themselves more reluctantly to Tin Pan Alley material. "I never knew one of them," wrote clarinetist Artie Shaw, "who didn't feel exactly the same as I did about what we were doing. Which could be put into the following words: "Sure it stinks, but it pays good dough so the hell with it."[48] Still other jazz men could not give in to the dictates of the industry because they lacked sufficient traditional training or would not comply because they disdained refined jazz. They generally retired from music, at least temporarily, sometimes for good.

In yielding to the demands of the market many jazz men surrendered outright to refined jazz. Others, men like Louis Armstrong, Duke Ellington, and Benny Goodman, found ways to mix their music with traditional popular music and yet retain the essential elements of jazz. The results of their efforts prepared the way for a new kind of jazz called "swing."

CHAPTER SIX

SHIFTS TOWARD TRADITIONAL STANDARDS

IN his article "Social Influences on Jazz Style: Chicago, 1920–30," Chadwick Hansen argues that the musical changes which led to swing resulted from pressure from both inside and outside the Negro community. He briefly discusses what he calls the external pressures — the centralization of the entertainment industry, the extension of the jazz audience among whites, and the standardization of material — but he maintains that the strongest pressure came from the wish of northern Negroes to improve their social position by conforming to "socially approved standards." Hansen maintains that one consequence of this desire was "the Negroes' own compulsion to reject a music identified in his mind with a degraded past, and to replace it with socially respectable popular music of the white middle-class majority."[1]

I have two comments about Hansen's argument. It ignores the role of white jazz men. Admittedly, the best jazz performers have generally been Negroes, and their influence in determining jazz style has surpassed that of white musicians. Nevertheless, in the thirties the styles of whites like Benny Goodman, the so-called King of Swing, and of others like Bunny Berigan, Artie Shaw, and members of the Casa Loma Orchestra were often distinctive and influential. In my judgment any explanation of the development of swing style should take their work into account. More important, I believe Hansen overstates the significance of social pressure within the Negro community. Among the immediate causes of the change of style, what he calls the external pressures seem to have been of more consequence. As was suggested in the preceding chapter, the lure of high salaries for jobs in commercial bands and the lack of jobs in real jazz bands pushed jazz men to satisfy the demands of the lowest common denominator of public taste. Jazz men who failed to comply found only occasional jobs. Presumably the desire for more or less steady work outweighed the desire to improve one's social position. Social position was important as Hansen maintains, but, it seems fair to assume that most musicians had to eat regularly before status could become their primary concern.

Whatever the relative importance of the immediate reasons for the change of style, behind them was pressure from the dominant traditional culture. This pressure made suppression or modification of "offensive" elements necessary before mechanical devices could diffuse jazz to the general audience.

II

The modifications affecting the music and the practitioners of jazz occurred gradually, almost imperceptibly, during the twenties and thirties, but a radical change in the content of jazz lyrics took place about 1928. Before this time jazz lyrics came largely from rags, stomps, blues, and the like. After 1928, when jazz words came largely under the control of the centralized entertainment industry, the drastic influence of Tin Pan Alley on the lyrics becomes quite clear.

Here, for example, are two Louis Armstrong vocals recorded before 1928:

Big Fat Ma and Skinny Pa
(Okeh 8370, recorded in 1926)

Voice talking:
Fall in line, grab your partner, and get back on time.
Big fat ma and skinny pa gonna do a dance you never saw.
Armstrong singing:
Big fat ma and skinny pa start dancin'.
Ah the latest steps with a lot of pep goin prancin'.
Aw fo' she cut out boy he did a million wings.
Everybody thought they could shake that thing,
When big fat ma and skinny pa did their dance.

Hey big fat ma and skinny pa start dancin'.
All the latest steps with a lot of pep goin' prancin'.
Now looka here when old ma and pa made an "O,"
And every shoulder shakin' started shaken some mo'.
Hey big fat ma and skinny pa, thats all, hi hi.

I'm Not Rough
(Okeh 8551, recorded in 1927)

Now I ain't rough and I don't bite,
But the woman that gets me got to treat me right,
Cause I'm crazy 'bout my lovin and I must have it
  all the time.
It takes a brown skin woman to satisfy my mind,
To satisfy my mind.

And here are two Louis Armstrong vocals recorded after 1928:

When You're Smiling
(Okeh 41298, recorded in 1929)

When you smiling, When you smiling,
The whole world smiles with you ba-ba-ba-bo.
Ah when you laughing babe, when you laughing,
The sun comes shining through,
But when you crying, you bring on the rain,

So stop your crying, be happy again,
And keep on smiling, keep on smiling,
And the whole world smiles with you.

When Your Lover Has Gone
(Okeh 41498, recorded in 1931)

When you alone, who cares for starlit skies,
When you alone, the magic moonlight dies,
At break of dawn there is no sun, sunrise,
When your lover has gone, when your lover has gone,
    when your lover has gone.
What lonely hours the evening shadows fall,
What lonely hours with memories lingering,
Like faded flowers, life can't mean anything bay-bay-bee,
Oh baby baby when your lover has gone.

These examples illustrate the relative primitiveness and spontaneity of jazz lyrics before 1928 and the comparative sophistication and sentimentality of later ones. In an attempt to measure some of these changes I analyzed the contents of random samples of leading Negro jazz singers before and after 1928. A full report on the procedure and results of the analysis is in Appendix B. Here I want only to outline the nature of the samples, to list some of the positive findings, and to discuss the results briefly.

The most influential jazz vocalist during the twenties and thirties, and one of the few to survive the transformation of jazz after the centralization of the music business, was Louis Armstrong. Random samples were taken of his early output, 1925–27, and compared with some of his post-centralization recordings of 1929–31. To check the results of this comparison, I collected and examined two more random samples: certain Bessie Smith records, 1923–25, which further represented pre–1928 lyrics; and some Billie Holiday disks, 1936–39, which typified later lyrics.

The following tables list only the positive findings of the analyses. In the left-hand column are the elements tested and to the right of them are the results of the tests. In the column headed "songs" are the percentages of songs which contain the elements; in the column under "words" are the percentages of words referring to the elements.

The findings show that the largest degrees of difference lie between the vocals of Bessie Smith and of Billie Holiday. This result is not surprising because the lapse of eleven years or more between the Smith and Holiday recording dates allowed ample time for the lyrics to change noticeably. Yet taken by itself, the Smith-Holiday comparison seems unreliable because to some extent the degree of the differences arises from the different personalities and vocal styles of the two singers. Thus the comparison between the two Armstrong samples is more valid. In most instances, however, the Smith-Holiday contrast bears out the findings of the Armstrong contrast.

The lyrics invite more thorough sampling and analysis than they receive here, but the foregoing statistics seem sufficient to indicate progressive saturation with traditional values. The tables alone, however, do not satisfactorily describe the saturation. They require exemplification and commentary to be understood adequately.

Among the elements of jazz lyrics to diminish after 1928 was humor. Early jazz lyrics were often humorous (e.g., Armstrong's "Big Fat Ma and Skinny Pa" [2]), and singers laughed in the middle of them and added their own amusing words or intonations which slanted the joke in the direction desired. Singers viewed sex humorously referring to the sexual relationship ironically or metaphorically. Thus, on "I'm Not Rough" Louis Armstrong speaks of sexual gratification in terms of mental satisfaction, "It takes a brown skin woman to satisfy my mind"; and on "Dropping Shucks" he responds to his lover's infidelity with the lines: "I told you sweet mama way last fall,/ You come and find another mule in your stall."

Sometimes early jazz vocalists regarded sex or love more seriously. Infidelity or mistreatment evoked lines like "Pretty

Elements Which Decreased

Elements	Bessie Smith 1923–1925		Louis Armstrong 1925–1927		Louis Armstrong 1929–1931		Billie Holiday 1936–1939	
	Songs	Words	Songs	Words	Songs	Words	Songs	Words
Cynical Outlook: Distrust of human nature, conduct motivated by self-interest	.67		.32		.11		.10	
Materialism (words referring to money)		.006		.009		.002		.0004
Economic problems	.35		.15		0		.03	
Action as solution to unhappiness	.38		.36		.16		.06	
Words referring to violence		.01		.007		.004		0
Death (implicit or explicit)	.35		0		.17		0	
Love viewed largely in terms of sex	.35		.32		.14		0	
Words referring to intercourse		.004		.02		.006		0
Infidelity or mistreatment	.76		.37		.38		.17	
Adjustment to unhappiness in love (excluding dreams)	.26		.18		.06		.16	
Love viewed humorously	.03		.29		.06		0	
Songs containing humor of any sort	.11		.50		.11		.06	
Songs with reference to music	.06		.21		.16		.13	
Songs with reference to dancing	0		.21		0		.06	
Basic twelve-bar blues	.41		.16		0		0	
Language associated primarily with the Negro		.06		.05		.02		0
Sex treated metaphorically	.12		.07		.05		0	

Elements Which Increased

1928

Elements	Bessie Smith 1923–1925		Louis Armstrong 1925–1927		Louis Armstrong 1929–1931		Billie Holiday 1936–1939	
	Songs	Words	Songs	Words	Songs	Words	Songs	Words
Hope, happiness or contentment (actual or possible)	.06		.21		.36		.50	
Wishing for, or dreaming of, ideal persons or circumstances	0		.07		.33		.27	
Dreams as a solution to unhappiness	0		.04		.28		.20	
Love as an ideal state	0		.11		.19		.46	
Love associated with magic	0		0		.03		.07	
Sentimental ballads of Tin Pan Alley variety	0		.10		.56		.80	
Romantic words (e.g., moon, paradise, heart) excluding terms of endearment		0		.01		.28		.10
Personification of nature	0		0		.25		.10	
Inflated or elevated language	0		.10		.25		.37	
Ornate imagery	.03		.04		.30		.43	
Use of related images	.03		0		.30		.33	
Religious imagery	0		0		.03		.07	
Intercourse treated with abstract periphrasis	.11		.14		.22		0	
Terms: love, loving		.003		.003		.03		.02
Terms: dream, reverie, memory		0		.0007		.009		.005

papa, tell me what's on your mind./You keep my poor heart achin,' I'm worried all the time" (Bessie Smith, "Bleeding Hearted Blues") or, "Now momma, momma, momma, why do you treat me so. . . . You treat me mean baby, just because I'm gully [gutter] low" (Louis Armstrong, "Gully Low Blues").

Economic problems also received serious treatment before 1928. Bessie Smith's lyrics in "Keeps on Rainin'" complain about bad weather shortening working hours:

> In the winter time, when it starts to snow,
> You know your pretty mama gotta have some dough.
> Keeps on rainin', look how it's rainin',
> Poppa he can't make no time.

Sometimes concern for money led to out-and-out materialism. On "S.O.L. Blues" Louis Armstrongs sings, "I'm witcha sweet mamma as long as you have barucks bucks bucks./When the bucks run out sweet mamma, I mean you are out of luck, out of luck mamma."

Responses to economic or other problems usually took the form of activity, sometimes violence — the expression of which early jazz lyrics by no means suppressed. In "That's When I'll Come Back to You" May Alix sings to Louis Armstrong, "You can knock me down, treat me rough, and even kick me,/Black both my eyes, but daddy please don't quit me." And vocalists like Bessie Smith often sang about violent death. "Goin' down to the river take a rope and rock,/Tie it round my neck and jump over the dock./That's why I'm sinful as can be" ("Sinful Blues"); or "The judge said, 'Listen Bessie, tell me why you kilt your man.'/I said 'Judge you ain't no woman and you cain't understand'" ("Sing Sing Prison Blues").

Many early jazz lyrics described man as cynical or immoral and singers' attitudes often communicated a distrust of sincerity and rectitude. The following bit of gossip reported by Bessie Smith in "Eavesdropper's Blues" illustrated the tendency to find badness in others: "They talked about my pa who was blind in

one eye./They said he was a sinner and was too mean to cry."
More often than not pre–1928 jazz lyrics stated explicitly or im-
plicitly that evil outweighed good in the world and that life
was a lonesome, unrewarding experience.

These songs took a variety of forms, but the conventional
blues was most common. Conventional blues consisted of a
series of twelve-bar, three-line units. The first line provided
a complication, question, or description; the second line repeated the first; and the third line resolved, answered, or commented upon the first two. Take the following stanza from
Bessie Smith's "Eavesdropper's Blues":

> They said I had a man I give my money to.
> They said I had a man I give my money to.
> And if I was broke, he would turn my eyes all blue.

Such units provided a flexible form for a narrative or description of indefinite length.

After 1928 these characteristics of early jazz lyrics tended to
give way to those of traditional popular music. Although occasionally expressions of self-pity, early jazz lyrics usually conveyed an unsentimental view of life, on the other hand Tin Pan
Alley lyrics, which now provided the basis for jazz vocals, were
generally mawkish.

Sigmund Spaeth and S. I. Hayakawa have pointed out that
the words of Tin Pan Alley songs have long ignored "the facts
of life."[3] One manifestation of this disregard of reality was un-
warranted optimism. After 1928 jazz lyrics increasingly asserted
the existence or implied the possibility of happiness. The words
of "When You're Smiling," for example, suggest that a smile
can solve the world's problems. The roseate view of male-female
relationships was equally unrealistic. Tin Pan Alley lyrics suggested that love effected a heavenly magic which removed
lovers from the context of ordinary experience. In "The Man I
Love" Billie Holiday imagines her first encounter with the man
of her dreams: "He'll look at me and smile, I'll understand,/

Then in a little while he'll take my hand,/And though it seems absurd, I know we both won't say a word." Such experiences occurred in idyllic environments:

> A sailboat in the moonlight and you,
> Wouldn't that be heaven, heaven just for two.
> A soft breeze on a June night and you,
> What a perfect settin' for lettin' dreams come true.
> (Billie Holiday, "A Sailboat in the Moonlight")

Ostensibly such songs ignored sex or sublimated it into love, but little imagination was required to read sexual implications into the genteel abstractions that filled Tin Pan Alley lyrics. In Louis Armstrong's record of "All of Me," for instance, the listener could construe lines like "You took the part that once was my heart,/So why not take all of me?" as an invitation to sexual intercourse.

Dreams and reverie played an important role in the jazz lyric after 1928. They replaced action as the characteristic response to dissatisfaction. Singers daydreamed about, or yearned for, ideal mates — "Some day he'll come along, the man I love,/And He'll be big and strong, the man I love" (Billie Holiday, "The Man I Love"); or about ideal places, "Night cover all, and though fortunes may forsake me,/Oh, sweet dreams will ever take me home" (Louis Armstrong, "Home"); or about ideal times, "Yesterdays, Yesterdays,/Days I knew as happy, sweet, sequestered days,/Olden days, golden days,/Days of mad romance and love" (Billie Holiday, "Yesterdays"). Sometimes lyrics implied confusion between the content of dreams and reality. In "Dream of Life" Billie Holiday sang about her lover's return: "Now that you've come back/My dream of life is here to stay." In general such lyrics represented dreams not merely as devices for temporary escape or relief, but also as sources of values which listeners might apply to actual circumstances.

After 1928 the weaknesses of jazz lyrics lay not only in what was said but also in how it was said. Frequently they stated banalities in tones of high seriousness and in language that was affectedly poetic. On a record like Louis Armstrong's "Home" thoughts were "ever wending," a heart was "forever yearning," and songs such as "Stardust" (Louis Armstrong) contained words such as "inspiration," "paradise," and "nightingale." Flat and sometimes ornate images crowded many of the songs. On "Without Your Love" Billie Holiday sang that in the absence of her lover she was like a "song without words," "a nest without birds," "a violin without strings," "a plane without wings," that "the sun will never shine at [her] door," and that she was "lost at sea." On the other hand, when her lover was present, she was "on the crest of the wave." Although such wildly-mixed figures of speech cluttered some lyrics, others contained several related but similarly hackneyed figures of speech. Thus the lyrics of Armstrong's version of "When Your Lover Has Gone" alluded to "starlit skies," "magic moonlight," "the break of dawn," and "sunrise." Occasionally, inanimate objects received personalities. For instance, the words of "Home" told how "trees whisper day is ending" and "stars begin to peep in one by one."

Before 1928 jazz lyrics reflected the life of the Negro sub-culture. Usually they were frank statements of fundamental human problems and feelings, uninhibited utterances of joy, humor, love, sensuality, anger, sorrow, pain. They found ex-pression in simple, salty language, concrete figures of speech, and strong rhythms. Such lyrics allowed jazz singers to impro-vise easily and to evoke deep feelings in some listeners. But after 1928 jazz lyrics exemplified the traditional inclination of Americans to divorce music from practical affairs. A shallow idealism replaced the realism of early lyrics. Tin Pan Alley words were full of superficial philosophizing and manifesta-tions of escapism. Significantly, despite the hardships accom-panying the Depression, post-1928 jazz lyrics generally ignored economic problems. At their worst the words of these songs con-stituted a collection of cliches which resemble parodies of bad, nineteenth-century, romantic poetry. Their elevated sentiments seem empty and sometimes ridiculous because the inflated diction, trite imagery, and sugary tone communicate little conviction or depth of emotion.

Formerly, the artistic effect of the vocalist depended heavily upon the contents of the lyrics, but after 1928 it was largely contingent upon how they were sung. Obliged to use vapid Tin Pan Alley material, a Louis Armstrong or a Fats Waller deliberately changed the meaning of songs by adding and subtracting words and syllables, by altering pitch, stress, and rhythm, and by making facial and bodily gestures. As Hazard Adams and Bruce Park have pointed out [4] harsh tones constituted disdainful commentary on absurd words or saccharine tunes. Mock seriousness over trivia conveyed satire. By emphasizing generalities or euphemisms which originally avoided sexual implications, jazz singers gave words a ribald effect, often with the help of a meaningful movement of an eye or hip. While the original words spoke of love, the performer sometimes transformed them into sexual allusions. At times, he communicated emotion by deliberately garbling the words, or he used his voice as a musical instrument in order to sing "through" the lyrics in "scat" (nonsense) syllables which left only the framework of the verse.

III

In the late twenties and afterward, traditional values radically affected the music, as well as the lyrics, of jazz.

Earlier jazz bands usually had from five to seven men who relied heavily, sometimes exclusively, on collective improvisation. After the mid-twenties, however, jazz bands increasingly took on some of the characteristics of refined jazz orchestras which used sixteen or more musicians organized into conventional string, wind, and percussion sections. Written scores of refined jazz orchestras ruled out almost all improvisation and banished or diluted "offensive" jazz elements. To play the numerous and difficult arrangements, refined jazz orchestras required conductors of high, traditional musical capabilities and proficient traditionally trained musicians who underwent long and arduous rehearsals.

By the late twenties there had emerged several big bands (similar to refined jazz orchestras, but without string sections) which could play both real and refined jazz. At first these were large Negro groups, led by men like Fletcher Henderson, Bennie Moten, and Duke Ellington. There were also white orchestras, such as those of Ben Pollack, Jean Goldkette, and, after 1927, even Paul Whiteman, all of which played refined arrangements yet had a few men who could play real jazz if the occasion arose.

There was a wide public demand for big bands and gradually new technical advances encouraged the music industry to exploit it. In 1927 Paul Whiteman explained: "With highly improved methods of capturing sound and with new scientific principles, it has grown more and more practicable to record large bodies of instruments without losing volume, without having a large quantity of tone dilute and diffuse itself. . . . The possibilities of the orchestra began to loom large and the original plan with a single player for each type of instrument began to expand."[5] Jazz bands of men like Ellington, Henderson, and Red Nichols grew larger as their ties with recording companies and booking agents increased. The Henderson group expanded from ten men in 1922 to fourteen in 1924. Nichols used five performers for recording purposes in 1926, but by 1930 he was using up to fifteen.[6] Discussing the enlargement of the Ellington band, Barry Ulanov wrote: "The change was made without any formal ceremony, and nobody, except Duke, perhaps, was especially aware of it. But change it was, the ineluctable growth from music for its own sake to music for big business, from booking one's own jobs to booking through Irving Mills [the agent, who was chiefly responsible for augmenting the band], from seven pieces to ten, eleven, twelve and fifteen, from wildcat recording for a dozen companies under as many pseudonyms to a contract with Victor, then with Brunswick."[7] By 1935 arrangers and booking agents found that the best instrumentation for a big band was five brass, four reed, and four rhythm instruments — a combination which produced enough volume to fill the largest theater or ballroom and which provided a pleasing balance of sounds. Bands seeking a wide reputation conformed increasingly to this instrumental pattern. As a local group, playing in and around Kansas City, Count Basie's early band consisted of nine men, but in 1935, when it began to make records for Decca and the Music Corporation of America became its booking agent, the band expanded to the standard five brass, four reed, and four rhythm instruments — the same instrumentation with which Benny Goodman was launching the "swing era."[8]

Extensive use of written arrangements also brought jazz closer to traditional music norms. Small groups of jazz men could improvise collectively without getting into one another's way, or could memorize short rehearsed passages in their heads. To learn a new song, explained Louis Armstrong of small band procedures, "all one man in the band had to do was to . . . hear a good number. He keeps it in his head until he reaches us. He hums it couple of times, and from then on we had a new number."[9] Large bands, however, could not learn a new song so easily; they needed written arrangements, which many jazz men believed smothered the spirit of jazz. In the early twenties Fletcher Henderson and his arranger, Don Redman, developed arrangements which allowed big bands to retain much of the jazz spirit. The Henderson-Redman formula called upon the reeds to play together as one voice and the brass as another, the two complementing each other in repeated figures called "riffs." These provided introductions and conclusions and furnished backgrounds for improvised solos. Of the numerous bands which adopted this formula or variations of it, the band of Benny Goodman had the widest appeal.

Much of the success of this group resulted from arrangements purchased from Fletcher Henderson. As Goodman explained:

> Up to that time [1934] the only kind of arrangements that the public had paid much attention to, so far as knowing who was responsible for them was concerned, were the elaborate ones such as Ferde Grofe's for Whiteman. But the art of making an arrangement a band can play with swing — and I am convinced it is an art — one that really helps a solo player to get off, and gives him the right background to work against — that's something that very few musicians can do.
>
> The whole idea is that the ensemble passages where the whole band is playing together or one section has the lead, have to be written in more or less the same style that a soloist would use if he were improvising. That is, what Fletcher [Henderson] really could do so wonderfully was to take a tune like "Sometimes I'm Happy" and really improvise on it himself, with the exception of certain parts of the various choruses which would be marked solo trumpet or solo tenor or solo clarinet. Even here the background for the rest of the band would be in the same consistent vein, so that the whole thing really hung together and sounded unified. Then, too, the arranger's choice of the different key changes is very important, and the order in which the solos are placed, so that the arrangement works up to a climax.[10]

Henderson infused jazz feeling not only into the up-tempo numbers but also into what were, to begin with, sentimental Tin Pan Alley tunes. John Hammond, a jazz critic and close friend of Goodman's, explained: "Benny let Fletcher make arrangements of current pop tunes with a beat and irreverence he had never dared to employ with his own band. I firmly believe it was this approach to ballads that gave the Goodman band the style that made it conquer the nation."[10] Goodman agreed.[11] After 1935 all but the most commercial bands tried to imitate the Henderson-Redman formula by using antiphonal riffs and by permitting occasional unwritten solos.

It was one thing to find good jazz arrangements, but it was quite another to make a band jell as a unit. To get thirteen or more men playing written scores precisely and yet with the spontaneity basic to the jazz feeling was difficult. Goodman wrote, "I wanted to create a tight small band quality. . . . A driving beat, a rhythmic brass section and a sax section that would be smooth but with lots of punch."[12] And of his augmented orchestra Count Basie declared: "I wanted my fifteen-piece band to work together just like those nine pieces [of his early group] did. I wanted fifteen men to think and play in the same way. I wanted those four trumpets and trombones to bite with real guts. BUT I wanted that bite to be just as tasty and subtle as if it were the three brass I used in Kansas City."[13] To get such an effect a big jazz band needed many long rehearsals which closely resembled those of traditional orchestras. In rehearsals jazz band leaders worked on *tempi*, balance, attack, and phrasing; they tried to draw the proper amount of "punch" from the reeds, the most effective "sting" from the brass, and a powerful, yet relaxed beat from the rhythm section.[14] In 1939 Goodman, who had played chamber music with Szigeti and the Budapest String Quartet, compared the problems of big-band jazz men and of academic musicians:

> I discovered that they go about things pretty much the same way. First they want to take the music apart and find out just what the composers put into it, as far as each note in the individual parts is concerned. Then, after that they try to express what the composer meant in their own way, or as they say, *interpret* [Goodman's italics] it. . . .
>
> These links between jazz music and concert hall music really exist (as more people are finding out all the time). . . . In other kinds of music, it's the idea of measuring yourself against what a great composer was thinking, of playing with a fine quality of tone and blending in with the other instruments, phrasing with them, and trying to hit just the right tempo on which the music sounds best. When everything blends, and all the players feel the same idea in back of what they're playing — well that's the same thing jazz musicians mean when they say that something swings.[15]

As the format and procedures of the big band approached academic standards, the music itself moved toward traditional norms.[16] As jazz historian Marshall Stearns has suggested, a comparison between those records made in 1917 by the five-man Original Dixieland Jazz Band and those by Benny Goodman's band of the mid-thirties reveals an astonishing transformation. To traditionalist ears the collective improvisation of the Dixieland Band sounds like confused, unrestrained polyphony and gives an impression of wildness and unrelenting pressure. The Goodman band seems far more dignified; its music sounds smoother, fuller, more flowing, and less confused [17] — in short more akin to traditional music.

This proximity to traditional norms helped to create wide interest in swing. From the early twenties a number of big Negro jazz bands had been playing music which was largely unheard by the general public. Most white jazz men admired a Negro band like Henderson's for its fire and bite, but by traditional standards its music seemed crude and awkward, its section work ragged, and its soloists out of tune.[18] Goodman was the first to apply traditional polish to the jazz of big Negro bands. Goodman bought and turned into nationwide hits arrangements that the Henderson band had used for years with only fair commercial success. In 1932 the Henderson band made a record called the "New King Porter Stomp" (Okeh 41565). Two and a half years later Goodman used the same arrangement on "King Porter Stomp" (Victor 25090). Today Henderson's version sounds better to most jazz enthusiasts, but in the thirties Goodman's record was far more acceptable to the general public.[19] Again, in 1937 Count Basie's big Negro band recorded "One O'Clock Jump" (Decca 1363), a large part of which was taken from a Don Redman arrangement. Six months later Goodman borrowed the number (Victor 25792). Basie's version sold well but not compared to the Goodman record, which, coupled with "Don't Be That Way," a similar selection, sold over a millian copies.[20]

Goodman spoke of "digging" the music out of Henderson arrangements. "Digging" out their music meant closely adhering to certain traditional norms when rehearsing a piece. Goodman declared,

> I am such a bug on accuracy in performance, about playing in tune, and with just the proper note values — because I think that a good musician should do that automatically when he sees something in an arrangement. For example, when we first rehearsed Edgar Sampson's 'Don't Be That Way,' some of the fellows were playing a triplet kind of uneven, with more time on one note than another, instead of making them all even. Well, we went over that and rehearsed it as carefully as we could, till everybody was playing it just the same way. That was one of the reasons that we got such a terrific rock on that arrangement, and why it turned out to be one of the biggest things we ever had.[21]

Other white bands, like those of Woody Herman, and Jimmy and Tommy Dorsey benefited from Goodman's success and developed and extended jazz (in so far as they played it) along the traditional lines he had worked out.

Despite alterations which brought the music closer to traditional values, certain essential jazz elements remained. Powerful riffs and strong rhythm sections helped retain the rhythmic character of jazz. And even though big bands offered few opportunities to improvise collectively, "ad-libbing" remained a common practice in solos allotted to the best performers. The retention of these characteristics allowed much of the jazz spirit to remain intact. As Benny Goodman contended in 1939:

> There is nothing essentially new in what is now called swing — it is just the same jazz that bands like the Original Dixieland Jazz Band and the New Orleans Rhythm Kings and Louis [Armstrong] and Jimmy Noone used to play. Of course it has been altered somewhat by the use of bigger bands with more instruments, playing arrangements instead of jamming [improvising] all the time; and almost every outstanding band realizes

the need for . . . a good rhythm section — which is the foundation of all swing. But the most important element is still improvisation, the liberty a soloist has to stand up and play a chorus
in the way he feels — sometimes good, sometimes bad, but still
as an expression of *himself* [Goodman's italics], rather than of
somebody else who wrote something for him.[22]

Louis Armstrong had said the same thing in 1936 when he gave
the would-be jazz man the following advice about improvisation, "I would tell him never to forget for one minute of his
life that the true spirit of swing music lies in free playing and
that he must always keep his own musical feeling free. He
must always try to originate and not just imitate. . . . A young
man who is willing to follow his score, and stop there, can
never be a swing man no matter how many swing songs he
plays. . . . And I say to young men, paste that on your music
rack."[23]

Although swing bands of the thirties moved real jazz nearer
to refined jazz, an all-important difference between the two
remained. Instead of embroidering traditional music with jazz
elements as Whiteman and his colleagues had done, swing
musicians modified jazz with traditional elements. The difference is not merely rhetorical. For whereas refined jazz
exponents imposed traditional elements which neutralized the
spirit of jazz, the swing musicians applied certain traditional
devices but tried to preserve the spontaneity and vitality of
the music. Writing of this difference Irving Kolodin argued
on behalf of swing: "Everything that was written down was
put in jazz terms, as part of a consistent pattern. . . . No attempt was made to have jazz sound like anything other than it
basically was: the only desire was to make it more orderly,
more integrated, more unified — the strongest possible concen-
trate of its best qualities."[24] When Kolodin made this statement
(1939), he reflected contemporary enthusiasm for swing. Today,
his words sound too strong. As jazz bands became larger they
lost something of the excitement and creativity of small groups.

Yet, the best of the swing bands of the thirties preserved enough of the jazz spirit to make the music they recorded esthetically rewarding.

IV

Traditional standards also affected the jazz men themselves. To succeed or survive they needed enough traditional musical training to play the complex written arrangements which big bands performed at dance engagements, theater appearances, recording dates, radio shows, and occasionally at film studios. The average dance band needed a library of forty or fifty arrangements, at the very least, to get through an evening without repeating too many.[25] Radio shows often meant playing through twenty pieces in an hour, including five or six new arrangements for each program.[26] Competition obliged band leaders to insist on first-rate, traditional musicianship from their men. Mrs. Fletcher Henderson wrote of her husband's band in the twenties: "It had the hardest book in the business, and many a musician just couldn't play those arrangements. Why, there were times when there was an empty chair on the bandstand. Jimmy Harrison couldn't make it. Fletcher turned him away and he went out and studied before Fletcher would take him back."[27]

Complex arrangements required big-band jazz men to read traditional notation precisely and easily. In 1936 Louis Armstrong urged the would-be jazz man "to read expertly and be just as able to play the score as any 'regular' musician."[28] Pressure to learn how to read came also from the musicians' union. Many locals required a musical literacy test for prospective members. Sometimes this requirement was not enforced, but occasionally it kept jazz men from jobs. In the early twenties inability to read prevented Eddie Condon from joining the union's Cedar Rapids, Iowa, local, and Bix Beiderbecke had similar difficulties in Davenport.[29]

Other traditional skills were important also. "What most folks don't realize," explained Benny Goodman, "is that a top-notch jazz band has just as high standards of technical performance as any top-ranking musical organization. Jazz musicians think just as much about things like attack, and intonation, and phrasing as legitimate players do, even if you don't hear much talk about it."[30] Particularly in need of these skills were soloists, whose improvisation demanded not only original ideas, but also first-rate technical ability to perform them clearly against the most fiery ensemble passages. Swing band soloists, sometimes short of ideas, usually could execute a broad range of difficult and striking effects.

Jazz men with traditional musical training, men like members of the Duke Ellington band, and individuals, such as Louis Armstrong, Fletcher Henderson, Red Nichols, Benny Goodman, Miff Mole, were best equipped to survive the shift away from collective improvisation. Many such men became band leaders. A few jazz men with little traditional training but with exceptional improvising ability found jobs in big bands and somehow managed to make their way through the scores. Trumpeter Joe Smith had his own way of reading his parts in the Henderson band. "He finally learned to read — but not according to Hoyle," recalled Henderson. "He used his own system by remembering if a note was so far from another note, then it had to be *that* [Henderson's italics] note it was supposed to be. Lines and spaces meant nothing to him and he did very well with this curious method."[31] Often jazz men in Smith's position learned to read correctly. In the thirties, Benny Goodman hired saxophonist Vido Musso, a good improviser but a stranger to notation. In order to keep his job, Musso slowly learned to read with the help of patient colleagues. Still other poor readers proved less adaptable. As early as 1923 all but one of the "ear men" of the Original Dixieland Jazz Band had given way to musically literate jazz men and had retired, temporarily at least, from music. A major reason for the failure of

Bix Beiderbecke in the late twenties was his difficulty with written arrangements.[32]

As big bands replaced small ones the non-musical as well as the musical behavior of the jazz man changed. The shift to large bands minimized or destroyed the sense of belonging and frequent opportunities for explorative personal expression that had existed in small bands. Instead of a large role in a small organization there was journeyman's work in a large group; and in place of improvisation regimented reading of section passages. Only lucky and highly talented jazz men were permitted improvised solos. The impersonal, businesslike organization of the big band, its trips (frequently up to four hundred miles) between one night stands, its meals often eaten quickly in roadside diners, the living and sleeping on buses, the numerous rehearsals and performances, the constant pressure to read many scores precisely, and the high-level teamwork — all these combined to fray nerves and reduce most jazz men to mere hired craftsmen.[33]

This harried existence isolated the jazz man from the life of most Americans. In 1941 Carlo Lastrucci, a sociologist and sometime jazz musician, studied the environment and social behavior of jazz men. Most of the musicians he investigated were whites between the ages of seventeen and thirty, since the competition and working conditions discouraged middle-aged men. Constant traveling and job changes usually destroyed the sense of belonging to a conventional community. Because jazz men worked at night and slept or rehearsed during the day, they had little opportunity or desire for non-musical interests or friends. Jazz men usually lived as lavishly as their incomes allowed and made no provisions for the future. There was a lower incidence of marriages and children than expected in their age, sex, and race group. When marriages did occur, domestic difficulties were frequent and the divorce rate high. Jazz men gambled, associated with "loose" women, and had a higher incidence of venereal disease than other Americans but seldom used marijuana. More often than not, they considered themselves, however vaguely, as creative artists rather than commercial entertainers, as they were thought to be by the general public. Perceptive jazz men felt unappreciated, and, they disdained the audience. All these characteristics bound them together in a common interest.[34]

Lastrucci's study indicates that jazz men of the thirties in many ways resembled their counterparts of the twenties, yet the high traditional musical standards, long hours, and hard work drove the later jazz men toward a certain respectability. Spontaneous behavior, "kicks," and horseplay both on and off the bandstand had characterized jazz men in small bands. In large bands, however, such behavior was less tolerable. Leaders preferred the consistently solid performers to the inconsistent star; the man who was brilliant one night and erratic the next five found few jobs in big bands.[35] There could be joking between big band performances, but, except for such premeditated, crowd-pleasing, tricks as the tousled-haired, eye-rolling drummer's pretense of being caught under the spell of his own wild solo, musicians had to look staid and to play in a dignified manner before the paying audience.

Moreover, most jazz men could not misbehave off the bandstand and still keep up high standards of musicianship or meet rigorous schedules of big bands. Mrs. Fletcher Henderson wrote of her husband's group: "They rehearsed 'most every night, and while there were drinkin' men in the band, I don't remember when any of them was ever drunk on the job. And, at that time, I don't think there was any of that reefer [marijuana] smokin'."[36] Speaking of drinking and marijuana, Goodman said, "That may go for fellows in a little ginmill or hole in the wall someplace, but it simply doesn't go for the musicians in the big bands, if for no other reason than they couldn't hit the stuff and still keep in shape to play seven hours a night, or do five shows a day in a theatre."[37] Most big bands had rules that kept musicians in line. Glen Gray explained that in the

Casa Loma Band, which he led, "Most stringent of the rules
. . . is that relating to drinking. None is allowed before or
during the job. . . . If a man should show up on a job with a
few drinks under his belt, the treasurer would automatically
debit him fifty dollars on the books. . . . Less severe but
equally certain fines are assessed the men for lateness on the
job or at rehearsals, [and] for unnecessary or unexplained
absences."[38]

Although most jazz men stopped playing professionally after
thirty, a few middle-aged jazz men acquired a wide public
following in the 1930's and projected a new image of the white
jazz man that helped make jazz acceptable. These jazz men,
notably Benny Goodman, Artie Shaw, Tommy and Jimmy
Dorsey, and Woody Herman, had begun their jazz careers as
adolescents in the 1920's and became successful band leaders
before 1940. Whatever their behavior as youngsters, by the
time they became bandleaders, age, responsibility, or the desire for security led them toward respectable conduct.

The duties of the bandleader often demanded particular
decorum. Among other things the leader concerned himself
with his band's room, board, transportation, debts, salaries,
discipline, morale, musical arrangements, rehearsals, and
standards of musicianship. Moreover, he was supposed to be
a good soloist, and he had to look and behave in a manner that
would appeal to the general public. By the early 1940's the
most successful leaders of swing bands earned over $150,000
annually,[39] and many of them had settled down (in so far as
their jobs permitted) with wives and children who served as
restraining influences. Age and responsibility brought out the
reserve both in the behavior and appearance of such men.
Benny Goodman and Tommy Dorsey looked like reputable
businessmen, and in 1946 a writer described Jimmy Dorsey as
a small man in a blue suit who looked "more like a bank teller
than a great hot saxophone" player.[40] These leaders were by no
means typical jazz men, but their fame often matched that of

leading movie stars, and the image of the jazz musician they provided did much to make jazz and its practitioners more and more respectable in the eyes of the general audience.

After 1928 changes which brought the lyrics, music, and performers of jazz closer to traditional norms helped to cut the ground out from under traditionalist opposition to the music. The lyrics, once earthly and frank, lost their offensiveness and most of their emotional power as well. The unfamiliar sounds that once made jazz seem barbaric had changed or disappeared. And the jazz man, whom many persons had once viewed as an irresponsible rebel out to undermine American society, was beginning to look more like the boy next door,[41] or, if famous, his father. Having undergone these changes, jazz was ready for wide acceptance. Gradually more and more Americans began to think of jazz men as artists rather than entertainers, and to consider jazz as art instead of popular music.

CHAPTER SEVEN

THE BEGINNINGS OF
GENERAL ACCEPTANCE

IN the twenties Americans generally regarded jazz as a low form of popular music, yet only a decade later more and more of them were beginning to think of it as art music. This surprisingly quick change of taste had resulted from the breakdown of traditional values, the esthetic needs jazz seemed to fulfil, its increased diffusion by new sound-reproducing devices, and the modifications which made it increasingly acceptable. But, aside from these developments, certain other events facilitated the transition of the image of jazz from popular music to art music.

Among these events was the rise of jazz criticism. One function of the art critic is to stand between artist and audience in order to assist in the clarification, interpretation, and formulation of emotional symbols. Criticism involves placing works in their historical context, defining their nature and their differences, and judging their faults and merits. In the performance of these tasks, the first jazz critics encountered several difficulties.

First, they faced a barrier of ignorance. Until well into the thirties a large majority of Americans could not distinguish between jazz and commercial jazz; only a handful of jazz men and enthusiasts knew about real jazz and its esthetic value. Attempting to overcome this ignorance, the jazz critic faced a problem in communication. Since the new music employed unfamiliar elements and techniques and evoked unconventional sensations and emotions, traditional musical terms and concepts often proved inadequate for jazz criticism. Words like polyrhythm and syncopation cannot define the rhythmic characteristics of jazz, and microtones do not adequately describe its blue notes. Nor did traditional standards provide fair criteria for judging the esthetic values of the new music. It required appraisal largely on its own terms as a separate form of music.

Because traditionalist critics and musicians of the twenties failed to recognize the need for separate standards their writings on jazz are dated. Men like Daniel Gregory Mason, Dr. Henry van Dyke, and Paul Rosenfeld, who judged it almost entirely in terms of traditional music, could only regard it with disgust or disdain. Supporters of symphonic jazz, such as Paul Whiteman, H. O. Osgood, Gilbert Seldes, and Edward Burlingame Hill, measured real jazz by looser traditional criteria and concluded that it needed refinement. Symphonic jazz advocates like Whiteman could provide a limited technical explanation and a qualified esthetic justification of jazz, but at first they were untouched by, or opposed to, the real spirit of the music.

Gradually, a school of jazz critics arose to correct the misconception of authorities like Mason and Whiteman. Charles Edward Smith was the first to point out in an American publication some of the differences between jazz and its various derivatives. In October, 1930, his article in *Symposium*, "Jazz: Some Little Known Aspects," began, "It may be said, almost without qualification, that jazz is universally misunderstood, that the men of jazz, those of the authentic minority, have remained obscure to the last." He went on to explain that both refined and symphonic jazz were dilutions of a "genuine originality of expression" and he traced the confusion over the various types of jazz to the first part of the twentieth century. After briefly outlining the history of the music, he concluded that real jazz was art and its practitioners artists.[1] In general, the jazz critics of the thirties and early forties were occupied with further exploration and elaboration of these points.

The best-known spokesman for real jazz was the French enthusiast, Hugues Panassié. In 1936 his *Le Jazz Hot* (Paris, 1934) was revised and published in the United States as *Hot Jazz*. Whereas Smith's article was informal and suggestive, Panassié's book was a serious and fully developed argument. "My single aim here," Panassié stated in his foreword, "is to give a precise idea of jazz in its definitive form, to put an end to the deplorable misunderstandings about jazz. . . . All I ask of the reader is that he free himself of all prejudices he has thus far acquired and that he pay attention to opinions which are not so much mine as a faithful expression of the opinions of the great jazz musicians."[2] Panassié explained at some length the nature and merits of real jazz, and showed how it differed from diluted jazz and academic music. Then he catalogued, and offered his judgments of, the leading performers, bands, arrangers, and styles; the so-called Chicago style, Louis Armstrong, and Duke Ellington had separate chapters of their own. A long appendix provided a discography of many of the best records.

Panassié deserves great credit as the first critic to try to set down systematically a real-jazz esthetic. In the light of recent jazz scholarship and criticism, however, his judgments often seem misleading and too impressionistic. Yet, whatever its shortcomings for present-day readers, *Hot Jazz* greatly advanced acceptance of the new music. Panassié's enthusiasm and strong opinions appealed to many readers who found his book a useful guide to an intriguing and little-understood subject. Throughout the thirties and forties *Hot Jazz* helped to justify jazz to Americans who were ignorant of, or diffident about, their native music.

Two other critics active in the thirties deserve particular mention: John Henry Hammond, Jr., and George Simon.[3] Hammond was a tireless writer, talent scout, and organizer of jazz performances and record dates. These activities together with his role in building the Benny Goodman and Count Basie bands made him one of the most influential figures in the growth and acceptance of jazz. After graduating from Harvard in 1935, George Simon became a critic for *Metronome*. In his reviews he focused his attention on big bands. He summed up the basic character of each organization and analyzed each instrumental section, both as a separate unit and as a part of the whole band. His reviews set a style of jazz criticism and rendered the inner workings of the big band more meaningful to the growing jazz audience.[4]

From its beginnings in the thirties, jazz criticism has been highly erratic. Too often the critic has stood between the artist and his audience in a negative rather than a positive way. Personal slurs, flippancy, and sensationalism frequently have obscured or twisted problems of evaluation. Unable to rely on the norms of academic music, the jazz critic had to begin without a tradition to guide and support his writings. The music developed so rapidly that only now have the language, values, and procedures of jazz and its criticism become relatively clear. As often as not, the early critic felt it necessary to be entertaining as well illuminating because only a small part of his audience was intelligently interested in the music. Undoubtedly some of the slurs and sensationalism of early jazz criticism stemmed from, or were condoned by, the idea that almost any sort of publicity helped at the box office.

At first jazz critics and historians had trouble finding publishers for their writings, but after the mid-thirties a number of publications, partly or wholly devoted to jazz, sprang up. The first two and most long-lived were the magazines of the professional dance musician. *Down Beat*, the earliest, began publication in 1934. Two years later *Metronome*, formerly devoted chiefly to traditional music, switched over to jazz and commercial jazz. Both magazines developed a steady circulation of about 50,000.[5] From the mid-thirties on, a series of shorter-lived but generally more serious periodicals emerged. Among those to appear by 1942 were the *Society Rag* of the Hot Record Society, *Tempo, Jazz Information, Music and Rhythm*, and *Jazz*.[6] In addition, several influential books on jazz had been published by 1940. In 1936 Louis Armstrong wrote *Swing That Music*, the first autobiography of a jazz musician. Three years later, with the help of Irving Kolodin, Benny Goodman told his story in *The Kingdom of Swing*. The first American edition of *Hot Discography* by Charles Delaunay — a Frenchman and the first man to attempt a thorough compilation of jazz records — was printed in 1938. It helped to bring some order to the chaos involved in collecting and appreciating jazz records. Also published in 1938, Winthrop Sargeant's *Jazz: Hot and Hybrid*, offered a valuable technical analysis of the nature of the music but gave a less knowledgeable commentary on the place of jazz in the world of art. Two analytical and historical volumes, *American Jazz Music* by Wilder Hobson and *Jazzmen*[7] edited by Frederic Ramsey, Jr., and Charles Edward Smith, were brought out in 1939. Both books stirred up interest and helped to correct misconceptions about jazz.

Many of the readers of these publications were record-collectors. By the early thirties they had grown in numbers and had got to know one another. In 1934 Charles Edward Smith's

"Collecting Hot" in *Esquire* [8] aroused much interest in jazz disks. As the number of collectors increased, records which had been available cheap became scarce. Jazz-record enthusiasts made house-to-house canvasses of promising neighborhoods and traveled miles to comb second-hand shops and Salvation Army bins. Disks that once sold at junk-shop prices of from one to five cents could bring forty or more dollars if they were rare. As jazz records became scarce, clearinghouses were established to distribute information and disks. Two such places opened in New York; the Hot Record Exchange ran record auctions, and the Commodore Music Shop became a meeting place for collectors. [9]

By the mid-thirties jazz enthusiasts had founded a number of hot clubs. Those in New York, New Haven, Chicago, Cleveland, Boston, and Los Angeles joined in 1935 in the United Hot Clubs of America under the leadership of Marshall Stearns and John Hammond. These organizations and a growing number of new jazz clubs helped to focus the activities of jazz enthusiasts by sponsoring concerts and record reissues.

Reissuance of jazz records required special arrangements with the large record companies. When a disk sold no more than 1,000 copies a year, record companies discontinued its unprofitable manufacture. Thus, numerous jazz records had been taken off the commercial market shortly after issue, but the master, or matrix, from which copies were made remained in the companies' files. By guaranteeing to dispose of 1,000 copies, Milton Gabler, the owner of the Commodore Music Shop and the organizer of the informal Commodore Record Club, persuaded record companies to reissue a few jazz sides. After fourteen such reissues had appeared, he joined with Marshall Stearns to distribute them through the United Hot Clubs of America. At the same time another group of enthusiasts organized themselves as the Hot Record Society and began to reissue jazz sides. The disks of both groups were quickly bought up as "collectors' items." [10] In view of the success of reissues, record companies closed their files to hot clubs and once again began to market some of the records themselves. By 1940 they had reissued sides by Louis Armstrong, Bessie Smith, Bix Beiderbecke, Fletcher Henderson, King Oliver, the Wolverines, the New Orleans Rhythm Kings, and others. In addition to these records and to the trickle of newly recorded jazz disks distributed by the large companies — Columbia, Victor, and Decca — small companies like Commodore and Blue Note began to supply records of current small jazz bands for enthusiasts of so-called pure jazz. (Pure jazz was characterized by much improvisation, more often than not, collective improvisation). From time to time such music reached a wide audience over the radio. As early as 1932 John Hammond played "pure" jazz records over WEVD, New York, and before long other jazz enthusiasts played records on radio stations in other cities.

The growing interest in "pure" jazz played by small bands was not nearly as large as the attention given to large swing organizations. Swing bands filled theaters and dance halls across the country. There were nationwide radio programs starring swing bands. In 1938 Benny Goodman played to approximately 2,000,000 people three times a week on N.B.C.'s "Camel Caravan."[11] Of the 50,000,000 records of all types sold in 1939, an estimated 17,000,000 were swing.[12] Swing or near-swing dominated the nation's juke boxes and the libraries of the growing number of "disk jockeys." The sounds of swing made their way into more and more films such as *Pennies from Heaven*, which presented Louis Armstrong, and *The Big Broadcast of 1937*, starring Benny Goodman.

Ultimately, however, the new interest in smaller "pure" groups was more significant than attention given big swing bands, which were largely to disappear after World War II. Jazz critics, jazz historians, and record-collectors, as well as reissues, and new records stimulated interest in "pure" jazz. Jazz men in their late thirties and older were recruited from big bands or retirement to play and record with so-called

"Dixieland" bands whose style descended from that of the Original Dixieland Band and from other small groups of the twenties and earlier. Slowly this music began to get official recognition. Old time, New Orleans pianist Jelly Roll Morton made a series of records for the Library of Congress in 1938. Four years later Eddie Condon presented the first in a series of concerts featuring Dixieland music at staid Town Hall, New York. The "Dixieland revival" was underway. On the heels of the introduction of swing, collectively improvised "Dixieland" jazz — which after 1918 had scandalized respectable musicians and moralists and had sounded wildly alien to the general public — was gaining acceptance as art among a growing number of Americans.

Along with this recognition came a certain amount of formalization. As early as 1936, Lyle and Eleanor Dowling had written in their translators' note to Panassié's *Hot Jazz*, "Jazz has now become, in its own right, a classic art exhibiting all the formal rigors and economy associated with classicism."[13] This statement seems to have been too strong, and yet many of the forms and procedures associated with the new music were becoming standardized. Most swing bands used the Henderson-Redman formula and employed the same five brass, four reed, and four rhythm instruments. There was talk of a "Chicago style" and of New Orleans and Dixieland formulas. Record companies advertised "jazz classics" and before long people would speak of "traditional jazz," to designate jazz associated with the years before 1940.

Partly as a reaction to this formalization a significant new kind of jazz emerged in the early forties. Creative young jazz-men, tired of what they regarded as the clichés and limitations of traditional jazz, made experiments which led to bebop, later called "bop." The rhythms of bop were diverse and complex, the melody full of unfamiliar phrasing and atonal sounds, and the harmony characterized by irregular intervals. Early bop bands were small groups whose instrumentation usually consisted of a trumpet and saxophone, a piano, drums and bass viol. The trumpet and saxophone carried most of the melody. They usually played arranged introductions and conclusions in unison, and took improvised solos in the middle. Many advocates of traditional jazz, to say nothing of supporters of traditional (pre-jazz) music, found modern (post-1940) jazz distasteful. For the first time since before World War I, when jazz was widely introduced to the general public, the new music was changing primarily in response to the esthetic demands of its practitioners rather than to the tastes of the audience.

II

It is difficult to exaggerate the European influence on the American acceptance of jazz. Foreign interest in the new music began as early as 1896, when Brahms wrote that he was attracted to ragtime and that, had he the inspiration, he would have liked to use it in his compositions.[14] Later Ravel and Rachmaninoff found jazz interesting, Debussy, Stravinsky, and Milhaud, among others, incorporated jazz elements into their work.[15] Other Europeans also found the new music to their taste. They received touring American jazz men as dignitaries. During a visit to London in the thirties Duke Ellington and his musicians received serious attention from the musical press and were invited to fashionable social events and greeted by crowds both in and out of concert halls.[16] When Louis Armstrong's band arrived for a concert in Copenhagen, 10,000 enthusiasts welcomed it at the railroad station.[17] The jazz following was particularly strong in France. Here appeared the first jazz magazine in the world as well as the forerunners of American hot clubs. The first book devoted to jazz, *Aux Frontières du Jazz* by the Belgian Robert Goffin, was published in Paris in 1932. Although enthusiastic and sensitive, Goffin's book was highly subjective and impressionistic and was never translated into English. The strong influence of Panassié in the field of criticism and the contribution of Delaunay (whose *Hot Discogra-*

phy became the standard reference book for recorded jazz) have already been noted.

Conditioned to importing virtually all their standards for art music from Europe, many Americans more readily accepted foreign rather than native judgments about jazz. During the twenties favorable and unfavorable European opinions on jazz tended to cancel out one another. By the late thirties and early forties, however, European approval easily outweighed European censure of jazz. Many affirmative European judgments were reprinted in America. For example, in 1939 critic Roger Pryor Dodge quoted an earlier statement of Milhaud: "One thing I want to emphasize very particularly and that is the beneficial influence upon all music of jazz. It has been enormous and in my opinion, an influence of good." [18] Two years later Louis Harap's article, "The Case for Hot Jazz," in *Musical Quarterly* quoted Ernest Ansermet's belief that the improvisations of an American jazz man had a "richness of invention, force of accent, and daring in novelty and the unexpected. Already they gave the ideas of a style, and their form was gripping, abrupt, harsh, with a brusque and pitiless ending like that of Bach's Second Brandenburg Concerto. I wish to set down the name of this artist of genius, as for myself I shall never forget it: Sidney Bechet." [19]

Such European interest helped to justify serious attention by Americans. In 1936 in an article explaining jazz to the readers of the *Delineator*, a diffident author vindicated his interest in jazz by declaring, "We read that Europe first appreciated swing: that 'swing clubs' are scattered from Oslo to Rome, that scholarly treatises by French music critics forecast a great future for this 'new' American music." [20] In 1937 an author in *Etude* took much the same attitude in a similar article, "Whatever we think of [jazz] it has certainly captured the world. . . . there is just no escaping it. Serious musicians here and abroad have started to dissect it with great solemnity." [21]

Also helpful in winning respectability and recognition for

jazz was the rise of jazz concerts. At first jazz enthusiasts and musicians sponsored these in theaters, hotels, and night clubs. In 1936, when the Chicago Rhythm Club presented Benny Goodman at the Congress Hotel, the event received publicity from several national magazines and helped to launch the "swing era" and the success of the Goodman band. Thereafter, numerous jazz concerts, held both in and out of doors, drew large crowds. In January of 1938 Goodman gave the first real-jazz concert ever presented at Carnegie Hall. To the surprise of no one, the audience was extremely enthusiastic. Olin Downes wrote: "When Mr. Goodman entered, he received a real Toscanini send-off from the excited throng. It took some minutes to establish quiet. There was quivering excitement in the air, an almost electrical effect, and much laughter. The audience broke out, before the music stopped, in crashing applause and special salvos as one or another of the heroes of the orchestra arose in his place to give his special and ornate contribution to the occasion. That was almost the sum of it. . . . The great audience was almost off its head with joy."[22]

This successful event cleared the way for others. The largest jazz concert in 1938 featured twenty-five bands in a Carnival of Swing at Randall's Island, New York. Twenty-three thousand people packed the stadium for this forerunner of the present-day jazz festival.[23] Other concerts took place in Madison Square Garden, and one was planned for Soldier Field, Chicago. In 1942 Fats Waller gave a recital at Carnegie Hall, and Eddie Condon began a series of programs at Town Hall. The next year Duke Ellington took his band into Carnegie Hall. Such performances were directed primarily to serious listeners. When couples tried to dance at the first Goodman concert sponsored by the Chicago Rhythm Club, they were booed off the floor, and at his first Carnegie Hall concert, dancers were prevented from dancing in the aisles. But larger concerts occurred under less decorous circumstances. When the Goodman and Count Basie bands in a joint concert attracted 6,000 people to

Madison Square Garden, there were accommodations for both auditors and dancers. "As is customary with jitterbug audiences," explained a *New York Times* reporter, "most of the crowd clustered around the bandstand to listen. There were plenty, however, mostly youngsters in their teens, who came for serious dancing. They treated the spectators to an exhibition of some of the most tireless and violent shagging ever seen outside of Harlem."[24] The first Randall's Island Carnival employed 60 policemen and 140 park attendants to keep the crowd in check.[25]

In spite of jitterbugging and other enthusiastic responses to jazz, the music had acquired enough prestige to be played at benefits to support respectable organizations. In 1938 the New York area had a number of jazz concerts for charity. Duke Ellington played at a benefit of the League of Composers at the Hotel St. Regis. Two Randall's Island carnivals of jazz took place respectively in behalf of the hospital fund of Local 802, American Federation of Musicians, and the National Bureau of Blind Artists, and a Jam Session at Madison Square Garden benefitted the Los Angeles Sanitorium.

III

The accretion of this sort of prestige made jazz more and more respectable. Symphonic jazz devotees of the twenties had spoken of their music as indigenous art music; real-jazz enthusiasts in the thirties made similar statements. Charles Edward Smith declared, "A Bix [Beiderbecke] chorus expresses America completely and beautifully."[26] The monthly publication of the United Hot Clubs asserted: "Swing music is one of the unique contributions to the world. The fact that like our poets, Walt Whitman and Edgar Allan Poe, it was first truly appreciated abroad adds to our obligation to study it and spread an understanding of it at home. Like the skyscrapers it remains typically American."[27] By the late thirties articles in the non-

musical press also began to take jazz seriously. Writing in
Harper's, Reed Dickerson concluded a piece on the new music
by saying, "It possesses all the elements found in any valid
work of art whether a poem by Keats or a canvas of Manet.
And in the deft hands of a Goodman, Armstrong, or Rollini it
becomes a pliable and rich pigment embracing all the virtues
of strength without overstatement, cadence without monotony,
and above all an intense feeling of aliveness and beauty."[28]
Gama Gilbert wrote in the *New York Times*: "Jazz . . . is now
become of age and . . . is on its way toward founding a tradition: characteristic elements are taking definite form, technical
modes of expression are crystallizing. In other words it is established as a legitimate artistic medium."[29]

The prestige of the jazz men themselves increased in the
wake of growing acceptance of their music. As famous bandleaders like Goodman, Jimmy and Tommy Dorsey, and Artie
Shaw became celebrities; young people recognized them everywhere, sought their autographs, and even tried to get into taxi
cabs with them. Fan clubs worshipped the latest jazz idols and
civic officials turned out to welcome them.[30]

Attention focused not merely on the leader but also on other
band members, called sidemen. Record-collectors played
through old records in search of hitherto little-appreciated
solos. Discographers called upon jazz men to remember who
performed with them on particular record dates. For the first
time, record companies marketed not only reissues but a few
new recordings with all the participants listed on the label.
In 1939 speaking about one of his recorded performances,
Goodman commented, "It struck me funny to see that this
record has just been reissued, after ten years, with the names
of players on the labels, whereas nobody gave a damn about
that when the record was made."[31]

Gradually, academic musicians as well as other members of
the music audience began to regard traditionally trained jazz

men with a measure of respect. In 1932 the New York Schools of
Music gave their annual award for an American composer to
Duke Ellington. Benny Goodman was invited to play and re-
cord with well-known academic musicians. Jazz pianist Teddy
Wilson played the harpsichord in a concert of the New York
Bach Circle. In New York drummer Gene Krupa gave lecture-
demonstrations on jazz at the American Museum of American
History and Metropolitan Museum of Art. Dr. Robert West,
director of the Radio Artists' Guild of America declared, "Benny
Goodman has brought to popular music a virtuosity which
many symphonic instrumentalists envy." [32] And speaking of the
way Duke Ellington wrote his material, critic Howard Taubman claimed, "Though it may shock the idolators of the masters,
it is fair to say that Ellington is a composer in the tradition of
Bach and Haydn." [33]

Yet for many people, the jazz man still carried with him unsavory associations. In most of the North and in the South, Negro musicians were far less acceptable than their white
colleagues. By the thirties colored jazz men could record with
whites, but attempts to take Negroes on tours with predomi-
nantly white bands led to difficulties. Negro performers were
excluded from restaurants and hotels and suffered a variety of
other indignities both on and off the bandstand. Whites in the
music business discriminated against Negro musicians. Booking agents and theater and club owners frequently restricted
Negro bands to playing in clubs in colored or marginal sections of town. With the exception of New York and Detroit,
Musicians' Union locals were segregated, cutting down job
opportunities of Negroes. It was extremely difficult for them to
find work at radio stations. Except for a handful of famous performers Negro jazz men were still awaiting acceptance as first-
class citizens, let alone recognition as artists.

White jazz men often felt a lack of recognition also. Their
biographical and other writings about the thirties often indicate a defensive attitude toward traditional values, most nota-

bly vis à vis the academic music tradition. Thus, as the members of the Goodman band nervously watched Carnegie Hall fill up before their first concert there, trumpeter Harry James said, "I feel like a waitress on a date with a college boy."[34] As respect for jazz men grew, their sense of inferiority began to disappear and they increasingly regarded themselves as artists rather than entertainers. But the recognition process was slow. As Nat Shapiro pointed out in 1957, some traditional jazz men still consider their music a skill or trade meaningful primarily in terms of making a living. For these performers, the conscious effort to communicate feeling, if it does exist at all, is almost inconsequential.[35]

IV

In the twenties there was a wide gap between the two sides in the argument over jazz. At one extreme were rebellious adolescents espousing the new music in its undiluted form. At the other were traditionalist adults who regarded jazz as the symbol or the substance of what was undermining American society. Between these two poles were those less articulate and harder to categorize who regarded jazz with varying degrees of enthusiasm and indifference. This polarity still obtained in the forties but antagonistic feelings about the new music had by now lost most of their vehemence. Moreover, the strength had shifted from the anti- to the pro-jazz side and the distance between the two poles had greatly narrowed.

In the 1930's and early 1940's young men were still the most enthusiastic white supporters of jazz. The most avid group of advocates was, as before, the rising crop of young jazz men. Many were still psychological adolescents rebelling against the values of their parents, but the violence of their rebellion was milder for several reasons — notably the growing general breakdown of traditional values which had by now removed some of the targets of earlier revolts, and the formal and rigorous professional requirements of jazz men which encouraged propriety. Almost nowhere in the 1930's does there appear the self-conscious iconoclasm or bitterness of the sort jazz men of the 1920's directed at traditionalists.

Young non-playing enthusiasts were still almost as absorbed in the music as the jazz men themselves. The number of these enthusiasts had grown rapidly. In 1934 Charles Edward Smith discovered record-collectors in almost every college and preparatory school in the country.[36] On weekends and school vacations students crowded into small clubs, like Nick's in New York. Many of them studied jazz with far more interest than they did more conventional subjects. By the late 1930's enthusiasm for jazz had become a fad.[37] As critic Wilder Hobson wrote, "There was one year when you could see it coming from week to week with those big loads of prep school and college assurance multiplying [sic] and those healthy handsome young girls who were so squirmingly eager to hear 'Wingy' Manone or 'Stuff' Smith or go skiing or sit up and see the sunrise or whatever People Were Doing."[38]

Other adolescents were ardent, though often undiscriminating, supporters of swing bands. Eagerly crowding around the bandstand or jitterbugging on the dance floor, these youngsters filled the nation's ballrooms. They formed lines in front of theater box offices hours before their favorite bands were scheduled to play. Once inside, their shouts sometimes drowned out the music, and at other times they had to be stopped from climbing onto the bandstand or dancing in the aisles.[39]

Again, as in the twenties, what we have loosely called intellectuals formed a small but influential part of the jazz following. Some became jazz critics and helped to explain the place and function of the new music to the growing audience. Other articulate men, who had made their mark in fields such as literature, also lent their talent and interest. As Benny Goodman explained: "We were popular not only among the swing-crazy kids, but among the intelligentsia too. The literary set took us up. Clifton Fadiman . . . did two scripts for our 'Caravan'

radio show. He was succeeded by Robert Paul Smith, the novelist. Robert Benchley appeared with us on the program and he
introduced the band to a group of writers for the *New Yorker*,
including S. J. Perleman and E. B. White. They used to show
up in the Madhattan [*sic*] Room of the Hotel Pennsylvania in
New York every Saturday night."[40] Besides such notables jazz
interested other intelligent people who, as Barry Ulanov noted,
took pride in being broad-minded and who liked to be abreast
of the latest musical developments.[41]

Some of the types of people who had opposed jazz in the
twenties tended to support to tolerate it a decade later. Occasionally the very same men who had earlier condemned it
changed their minds. In 1924 Virgil Thompson had dismissed
jazz saying that its "rhythm shakes but it won't flow. There is
no climax. It never gets anywhere emotionally. . . . It is exactly analagous to the hoochee-coochee."[42] Twelve years later
he called Louis Armstrong "a master of musical art. . . . His
style of improvisation would seem to have combined the highest reaches of instrumental virtuosity with the most tensely disciplined melodic structure and the most spontaneous emotional
expression."[43] In 1925 Fritz Kreisler had rejected "jazz" as non-
art and called it a caricature of music, but in 1936 he defended
it as the true expression of restless mankind and argued that
nobody should condemn it. "There is good music and bad music," he pointed out, and suggested that jazz like academic
music could be good or bad.[44] Walter Damrosch, Artur Rodzin-
ski, and Jerome Kern,[45] each of whom had earlier denounced
"jazz," were among those to sign a plaque given to Duke
Ellington before his Carnegie Hall concert. Other notable sig-
natories were academic composers Deems Taylor, Roy Harris,
Aaron Copland; conductors Albert Coates, Leopold Stokowski,
Eugene Ormandy; singers Laurence Tibbett, Margery Law-
rence, John Charles Thomas; and the impresario of the
Metropolitan Opera, Edward Johnson.[46]

Academic music critics, too, were more open-minded about

jazz than they had been in the twenties. There were still some who disliked or ignored it, but others like Howard Taubman and Irving Kolodin [47] gave it serious attention or outright support. Tolerance characterized the treatment of jazz in the academic music press and a number of articles explained the various types of the new music and its elements.

Moreover, jazz was beginning to engage the curiosity of the relatively conservative concert-goer who had ignored or scoffed at it in the twenties. In 1938 the final instalment of a concert-lecture series at New York's Town Hall presented Benny Goodman playing jazz between explanatory comments by the president of the Julliard School of Music, John Erskine. A reporter for the *New York Times* wrote:

> The audience might have assembled to hear a program of Bach, Beethoven and Brahms. For subscribers of a series that had presented serious lecture-recitals on lieder, the symphony, the string quartet and other sober manifestations of the musical art, the response to what was perhaps their first face-to-face experience in swing must have been altogether encouraging to friends of swing. Although no one even attempted to 'truck' down the aisles . . . the applause and cheers that followed Mr. Goodman's music left no doubt that the classics had not spoiled the audience forever for the delights of hot jazz or swing. Although occupants of the orchestra seats maintained a concert-going reserve, those in the balcony were not ashamed to sway their shoulders and paid no heed to restless feet.[48]

By the late thirties social and civic leaders who, as guardians of public morality, were earlier opposed to "jazz," had generally dropped their complaints. Their protests and fearful predictions had virtually disappeared from the press. Some social and civic leaders patronized the acceptance of swing by sponsoring jazz concerts given as charity benefits. Among the patrons of one swing session at Randall's Island were Mrs. James Roosevelt (who in the twenties had been one of a group of Episcopal churchwomen to organize against "improper" dancing), the New York Commissioner of Welfare, William Hodson, and Controller Joseph D. McGoldrick.[49] In 1937, when the New York City Board of Education planned a program to introduce high school students to the fundamentals of jazz and academic music, it secured the support of the mayor of New York City and the governor of the state.

This program was symptomatic of the changing views of educators toward the new music. The plan was to invite jazz men Benny Goodman, Duke Ellington, Tommy Dorsey, and Red Nichols, along with commercial jazz performers and academic musicians to visit different schools for a series of lectures. This proposal did not mean that educators in general had come to like jazz but rather that they were beginning to tolerate it. George B. Gartlan, the board's director of music, defended the program by arguing that it would bring children "within the fold" and give guidance to their natural inclinations. "We cannot stop a chld from doing what he wants to do."[50] Implicit in his statement was the new tendency to regard children as organic individuals who were expected to behave according to the needs of children rather than according to traditional concepts of them as miniature adults. In 1939 Lilla Bell Pitts, the vice-president of the Music Educators' National Conference, told the Eastern Music Educators' Convention that times had changed; the youth of the country were no longer controlled exclusively by the old standards. "The home, the church, the school and the conservatory," she continued, "are no longer unrivalled in developing the musical taste of youth." Miss Pitts did not like the child's preference for swing, but she urged the teacher to learn about it and its various derivatives in order to reach children at the level of their own tastes. She concluded that jazz should not be scorned and agreed with Alec Templeton that "if Johann Sebastian Bach were alive today he and Benny Goodman would be the best of friends."[51]

Others connected with education were more outspoken, if sometimes less knowledgeable, in their support of jazz. In 1937 Carleton Sprague Smith, head of the music division of the

New York Public Library and later president of the American Musicological Association, called "swing," by which he meant popular music, "appropriate musical expression" deserving serious consideration.[52] Professor J. F. Brown of the University of Kansas declared, "The difference between Beethoven's *Fifth Symphony* and Benny Goodman's *Opus 1/2* is one of degree and not of kind."[53]

Gradually, a few forward-looking teachers brought jazz or refined jazz into the classroom. It was taught in the New York High Schools of Music and Art, the Rye (New York) High School, New York University, the New School for Social Research, and the New England Conservatory of Music.[54]

We have little precise knowledge of how the inarticulate mass of Americans felt about jazz in the 1930's. Yet it seems clear that most of these people were now far more sympathetic to jazz than their forebears in the 1920's had been. Newspaper and magazine pictures of audiences at swing concerts in the thirties show a wide range of types: whites and Negroes — more often than not apparently under thirty-five years of age — displaying a wide variety of dress and a broad range of enthusiasms. The *New York Times* reported that the audience at the first Carnival at Randall's Island drew almost every sort of person "young and old, rich and poor." "They were all races, all colors, all walks of life."[55]

Furthermore, the kind of newspapers and magazines that in the twenties had ignored or condemned jazz now treated it with approval or tolerance. In the thirties the *New York Times Magazine Section, Saturday Evening Post, Life, Parents' Magazine, Reader's Digest, Delineator, Harper's, Scribner's, Time, Newsweek*,[56] and other publications printed articles explaining the history of jazz, its verbal language, and the differences between the real thing and its dilutions.

Side by side with various degrees of enthusiasm and forbearance, opposition to jazz continued in the thirties. By now, however, the opponents were far fewer and their voices heard less and less. They were usually the conservative members of society, whose status or sensibility still depended heavily on traditional values. An occasional outcry arose from a keeper of public morality. The Most Reverend Francis Beekman, Archbishop of Dubuque, Iowa, told the National Council of Catholic Women in 1942, "We permit, if not freely endorse by our criminal indifference, 'jam sessions,' 'jitterbugs,' and cannibalistic rhythmic orgies to occupy a place in our social scheme of things, wooing our youth along the primrose path to hell!"[57] Professor H. D. Gideonese of Columbia told four hundred Barnard undergraduates that "swing is musical Hitlerism. There is a mass sense of letting one's self go."[58] And there were still Americans, such as William Allen White, to whose musical taste jazz "squawked and shrieked and roared and bellowed in syncopated savagery."[59]

"You know I'm no friend of jazz," conductor Bruno Walter told an interviewer in 1939. "This thing called swing hits the lower strings of mankind and sets them in vibration. I must confess that I do find the rhythmic variety of jazz very interesting, but it is drowned by wildness of sound; my ears become unhappy."[60] Alfred L. Dennis, a prominent businessman and president of the Bach Society of New Jersey, spoke out indignantly against jazz and demanded and end to jazzing of classics over the air.[61] Donald Grant, president of the Dancing Teacher's Business Association, told the annual convention of his organization that young people found in swing "neurotic and erotic expressions of physical activity."[62]

Opposition to jazz remained (and still exists), but acclaim from almost every quarter easily drowned out the protests which decreased annually. By the early forties public complaints about jazz had virtually disappeared.

CONCLUSION

AT the beginning of this study I set up a working hypothesis about the reception of esthetic novelty, a theory which seems to account for the acceptance of jazz between the two world wars. The hypothesis was useful as a guide, but at the end of the project I had to alter some of its points. In general, however, it remained intact. I present the revised version here as a theory which seems to illuminate the acceptance of jazz, and which may, after some modification, apply to the reception of other esthetic innovations in modern Western civilization:

A new art form or style, touching upon the basic assumptions of a culture-system, usually provokes controversy. Traditionalists, that is, those who hold strongly to conventional values (esthetic and non-esthetic), tend to disregard or oppose the innovation. On the other hand, modernists, who find that the innovation satisfies esthetic and other needs, react against traditionalist opposition by drawing together in an area of understanding or brotherhood and often ignore or flout important traditional values. Before long, a group of moderates arises and tries to bridge the gap between the sensibilities of the two camps.

With the passage of time the controversy cools and the moderate viewpoint gains while both the traditionalist and modernist sides lose strength. Traditionalist opposition weakens as new circumstances alter or undermine traditional values and as people increasingly recognize the value of the innovation or become accustomed to its previously unconventional aspects. On the other hand, the modernist cause suffers when the demands of the general audience force the innovation to undergo modifications which bring it closer to traditional norms. The more basic the innovation, the more slowly opposition to it dissolves and the more numerous the successive modifications. Promoted chiefly by moderates with close ties to the traditional culture, early modifications (refined and symphonic jazz, for example) tend to dilute the innovation in ways which diminish its esthetic value. Later modifications (like swing) are usually the work of moderates who are less tied to traditional values and who restore many of the techniques first associated with the innovation and much of its former esthetic value. Before the final modification occurs critical values pertaining to the innovation emerge and gain currency. At the same time customs, organizations, and institutions arise to promote the development and appreciation of the innovation.

By this time the moderate viewpoint begins to lose adherents as the audience increasingly recognizes the weaknesses of the early modifications and begins to question the value of some of the later ones. Eventually, the innovation begins to be widely adopted in its original state (popularity of reissues of early jazz records is a case in point), or in a state similar to the original (for instance, the music of the Dixieland revival). But by now many of its characteristics have become so formalized and static that they no longer satisfy many modernists who feel compelled to create further innovations (e.g., bop). At this point the earlier innovation has become the basis or rallying point for the resistance to further innovation. Then the pattern of social response to esthetic novelty may begin anew — often before the earlier innovation has become a fully accepted part of the dominant complex of values.

II

It is too early to make a definitive judgment, but the events of the acceptance of modern jazz seem in many ways analogous to those of the acceptance of traditional jazz. There was the same opposition by people dependent on the status quo. Bop musicians and their advocates formed an unofficial brotherhood against this opposition and often ignored or disdained the standards of both traditional academic and traditional jazz musicians. Time again brought a compromise. Bop has been gradually modified. Early modifications leaned strongly toward traditional jazz. Woody Herman, Duke Ellington, and Stan Kenton were swing musicians who in the 1940's used some of the rhythmic, melodic, and harmonic elements of bop. Later modifications, the work of modernists such as Miles Davis, Lennie Tristano, and George Shearing (called "cool" jazz men) more closely resembled original bop. As the recent reissues of Parker and Gillespie records indicate, there has been a rebirth of interest in the founders of bop. And in the late fifties, the music of a hard-bop musician such as Sonny Rollins sounded very similar to the work of these originators. Critics and historians have emerged to define and evaluate the new music and to defend it against the complaints of traditional jazz advocates. Modern jazz clubs have sprung up. The distinguishing characteristics of the music, once wild-sounding, have become familiar and appealing to many ears. Opposition to jazz has declined and growing evidence shows that bop, the original style of modern jazz, is becoming conventional and acceptable. In the meantime, saxophonist Ornette Coleman and others, dissatisfied with the conventions of bop, have introduced a new style of jazz which sounds as alien to modern jazz men as bop first sounded to traditional jazz men and almost as strange as traditional jazz sounded initially to followers of traditional (pre-jazz) music. Possibly the pattern of acceptance is beginning once again. The bop cycle of the acceptance pattern was less convulsive than that of traditional jazz because with traditional jazz the audience had to accustom itself to an entirely new form of music, whereas bop was only a new style of jazz.

III

The controversy over the place of jazz in American life and in the world of art goes on. Influential people in the music audience (for example, many music teachers in our colleges and universities) still oppose jazz or fail to consider it seriously. For such people the acceptance of new kinds of music is exceedingly difficult. In 1932 French pianist Stepane Mougin wrote in regard to the controversy over traditional jazz:

> We are creatures of habit, we inherit conventions which cannot be infringed upon without serious disturbance. It takes tolerance and willingness to accept these new art forms. One must forget all that one's previous artistic education has taught one. The mind must be like fresh wax, ready to receive these new impressions. Otherwise, your entire being, everything you are accustomed to and have learned to like, will be shaken and even wounded — nevertheless, there is no reason why you should renounce classical music; it is simply necessary that you take along with classical music an entirely different set of emotions, those belonging to jazz.[1]

This statement illuminates the predicament of the traditionalist confronted by esthetic innovation. I think, however, that Mougin oversimplifies the difficulties: The traditionalist cannot make his mind "like fresh wax" by forgetting his earlier esthetic feelings. With great difficulty he may partially and temporarily suppress them, but he cannot forget them; he cannot "simply . . . take along with classical music, a new set of emotions, those belonging to jazz." New sets of emotions follow only after significant personality and cultural changes. Thus, in the 1920's traditionalists could not accept jazz because their culture had molded sensibilities unable to appreciate the new music. Acceptance required new sets of feelings which were part of a new culture. Only as relative norms replaced ideal standards, as people who matured after World War I became as numerous as those who grew up before it, did jazz find large numbers of adherents.

Many of the determinants of taste seem beyond the direct control of the audience, yet perhaps Mougin is right when he implies there is some freedom of choice in acceptance of art. In any event, an effort to keep an open mind seems essential. Certainly, no new form or style of art should be rejected merely because it is unconventional. We need to examine it carefully and as sympathetically as possible, to expose ourselves to it at least until its shock or strangeness wears off, before we can judge it fairly. If we limit our taste to the art of one time, we lose much; the lover of Beethoven's music who hates jazz is as unfortunate as the traditional jazz enthusiast who abhors bop, or the Webern devotee who dislikes Palestrina. Old and new art should not be in competition with one another. Both have a place in our sensibilities and the acceptance of one need not involve renunciation of the other. Although sometimes we cannot appreciate art of the past, more often we fail to fathom that of the present. The works of the past conform comfortably to our patterns of taste, but current art often seems strange. It confuses or disturbs us, and naturally we tend to doubt its merit or to dislike it. In doing so, both artists and audiences ignore that one of art's most important functions is to convey emotional symbols for contemporary experience. Bop saxophonist Charlie Parker said: "Music is your own experience, your thoughts, your wisdom. If you don't live it, it won't come out of your horn. They teach you there's a boundary line to music. But, man, there's no boundary line to art."[2] Today, approximately 150 years after the first attempts to create an indigenous music in the United States, more and more Americans are learning of both this truth and its implications. Both are difficult to grasp because artists and audiences of each generation have to apply them in new ways.

APPENDIX A

DEFINITIONS

THE FOLLOWING are not intended to be all-inclusive descriptions, but rather working definitions of what I consider to be the leading characteristics of the kinds of music referred to in this book. Since the book is a study of the reception of jazz by the whole music audience, I have based the definitions upon groups of sounds recognized by the public as well as upon definitions made by musicians, critics, and musicologists.

First some brief classifications:

Folk music is anonymous and of varying esthetic value. It is orally transmitted from generation to generation and is adapted to the current needs of a primitive or agrarian society. The singing and playing of Huddie "Leadbelly" Ledbetter, for example, is folk music.

Popular music is of minor esthetic value. Usually it is of known or assigned authorship, written down, copyrighted, published, and sold — e.g., "Always" or "Nearer My God to Thee."

Art music has high esthetic content and embraces two kinds of music. The first is *academic music*, which until the first part of the twentieth century was virtually the only sort of music played and studied in our concert halls and accredited music schools. A Bach mass, a Beethoven symphony, and Bartók quartet are examples. A second type of art music is *jazz* (*q.v.*) such as that found on most Louis Armstrong and Charlie Parker records.

The following definitions sometimes cut across the above classifications and in other instances make them more specific.

Traditional music consists of popular, art, and to a lesser extent, folk music of Western civilization in the eighteenth and first three quarters of the nineteenth centuries. When written down, the rhythm of traditional music is divided into regular measures separated by bar lines. Each measure contains two or three (or multiples of them) metric units. The time values within measures are designated by whole, half, quarter, eighth, sixteenth, and thirty-second notes. A time signature indicates the number and nature of beats, or metrical units, in the measure. For example, three-four (3/4) time means that there are three beats to a measure and a quarter note receives one beat. The common time signatures in traditional music are two-four (2/4), four-four (4/4), three-four (3/4) and six-eight (6/8).

Melody in traditional music is based on the twenty-four diatonic scales built upon the twelve half-tones of the octave, or chromatic scale. The seven tones of the diatonic scale tend to behave in an identifiable manner called tonality, which defines traditional melodic characteristics and helps to determine harmonic practices. Traditional melodies tend to center on the first step (called the tonic) of the diatonic scale. The fifth step, or degree, is next in the power of attraction, followed by the fourth and then the seventh degree. Modulation to different but related keys is often temporary, and a return to the original key is usually implied and carried out.

In its simplest form, harmony in traditional music involves the superimposition of intervals of a third over the root (the note which the chord is built on). Tonality helps to determine harmony. The chords most important to traditional music are the tonic, built on the first degree of the diatonic scale, and often designated as I; the dominant (V), constructed on the fifth degree; and the subdominant (IV), based on the fourth degree.

The ends of phrases or points of repose in music are called cadences. They help to confirm the tonality and to regulate and define the feeling and flow of the music. Traditionally the most important harmonic cadence is the shift from the dominant to the tonic chord (V–I), known as the authentic cadence. Others listed in the order of their importance in traditional music are the plagal cadence, subdominant to tonic (IV–I); half cadence, tonic to dominant (I–V); and deceptive cadence, tonic to submedient (V–VI).

The tone color, or characteristic sound, of traditional music comes from a recognizable way of playing certain instruments and of balancing their sounds in certain conventional groups. Traditional orchestras consist of section, or choirs, of strings, woodwinds, brasses, and percussion. Traditional marching bands have woodwinds, brasses, and percussion, but no strings. All but the smallest instrumental groups require a leader who conducts rehearsals and performances. He balances the sounds of the various instruments and gives a unified and consistent interpretation to the music. With the exception of traditional folk music, almost all traditional music is written down by the composer or arranger.

Examples of traditional folk music are early Burl Ives performances of "The Blue Tail Fly" or "Cowboy's Lament." "Ballads" like "Sweet Adeline," waltzes like "Three O'Clock in the Morning," and marches like "El Capitan" can be classified as traditional popular music. Examples of traditional academic music are Haydn's symphonies and Beethoven's quartets.

Modern academic music emerged partly as a revolt against traditional academic music. The seeds of the revolt took root in the works of Franck, Tchaikovsky, Wagner, Mahler, Fauré, and Sibelius. Most music historians also include Ravel and Debussy as transitional figures. It remained for twentieth-century composers like Schoenberg, Stravinsky, Bartók, Berg, and Webern to complete the break with traditional academic music. Romanticism, the dominant mood of traditional academic music in the nineteenth century, no longer expressed the feelings of these men. They found little room for expansion within the confines of traditional tonality and harmony, and even the impressionism of Ravel and Debussy appeared vague, precious, and capable of only limited development.

Modern academic music differs from traditional music in several ways. Among other things, modern academic composers expanded and supplemented traditional rhythmic usage; not limiting themselves to traditional duple or triple time, they sometimes used such signatures as 5/4, 7/8 and even 3½/4. Occasionally they wrote rhythm outside of bar lines, and called for frequent changes of time in a single piece. Moreover, they began to use polyrhythm, which Winthrop Sargeant describes as the "simultaneous use of two or more independent rhythms of different phrase lengths but of identical metric units."[1] Traditional music contains polyphonic effects known as "two against three" or "three against four," but in every instance the first beat of each rhythm coincides at the beginning of each measure. In modern academic compositions the first beats of independent rhythms do not coincide at the beginning of each measure except accidentally.

Modern composers also turned away from traditional melodic practices. They variously abandoned the conventional scales and notions of tonality, sometimes disregarding diatonic limitations and even attempting to employ the twelve half-tones of the chromatic scale more or less equally. This last practice came to be known as "atonality" or more precisely "non-tonality" or "pan-tonality." Other modern academic composers retained the diatonic scale but introduced non-traditional harmonic ideas, a method called "pan-diatonicism." Still other modern academic composers resorted to the whole-tone or pentatonic scale and even introduced micro-tones — third, quarter, and sixth tones — into their compositions.

Most nineteenth-century traditional music is homophonic. In other words, it consists of a single melody usually supported by harmony. Modern academic music often contains counterpoint and polyphony, devices which involve two or more melodies played at the same time. Consequently, modern academic works are more easily heard (or at least more easily explained) horizontally rather than vertically, the way we listen to traditional music. Harmony in modern academic music sometimes consists merely of coinciding sounds of simultaneously played melodies. Some modern composers wrote homophonic music but broke with harmonic tradition by superimposing seconds, fourths, fifths, and occasionally sevenths above the root.

The tone color of modern academic music also differs from that of traditional music. Unconventional rhythmic, melodic, and harmonic practices are chiefly responsible for this difference. Also significant is the treatment of unconventional subjects, neurotic, brutal, and mechanical themes. The presentation of such subjects called for new instrumental and vocal usages which further contributed to a non-traditional tone color.

Jazz is a difficult term to define. Since 1917 when it first came into public use, the word has denoted several different types of music, dress, behavior, and miscellaneous subjects.[2] In present-day music terminology jazz is a form of art music usually at least partially improvised and possessing a distinctive rhythmic feeling, tonality, and tone color. For present purposes I have divided jazz into traditional (pre-1940) and modern (post-1940) types. This essay deals almost entirely with the acceptance of traditional jazz. In order to simplify matters the term jazz will refer to traditional jazz unless otherwise specified.

In jazz, more than in traditional music or in modern academic music, rhythm is the main organizing element. The leading rhythmic characteristic of jazz is an effect which we shall call the swinging sensation. This sensation is indefinable in words; it must be felt to be known. But two of the devices used to produce it are relatively clear. The first is syncopation, a device which upsets the basic rhythmic pulse of a piece by anticipating or retarding the ordinary accent(s) of the measure. The second device is polyrhythm, the simultaneous use of two or more independent rhythms, which like syncopation, results in displacement of accent(s) in the basic rhythm of the music.

Although in some ways traditional jazz melody resembles that of traditional music, non-traditional practices and elements give jazz melody its characteristic qualities. Much jazz is based on the so-called blues scale. Like the diatonic, the blues scale consists of two similar tetrachords. It differs from the diatonic, however, in that the third tone of each tetrachord, in other words the third and seventh degrees of the scale, are variable in pitch. In some renditions of blues the second degree of the scale is variable also.

Notes of the blues scale tend to behave in certain characteristic ways which create a blue tonality. Winthrop Sargeant has shown that the notes most frequently used by traditional jazz men are the first, second, blue third, and the sixth of the octave below. The first degree acts as the tonic, the center of the melodic movement and the final note in cadences. The second, blue third, and sixth below have an affinity for the tonic both in cadences and throughout jazz melody. Easily the most common cadences are through the blue third or the sixth below to the tonic. Often in cadences the second degree acts as a passing-note between the blue third and the tonic. Unlike the blue third the major third has no affinity for the tonic, and moves readily upward to the sixth, or fourth, the least employed tone of the blue scale. As these remarks suggest, the lower tetrachord of the blues scale gets more use than the upper. When the upper tetrachord is used, the behavior of its

notes corresponds to that of the lower; for example, its movements
center around the fifth in the same way that the movements of the
lower tetrachord center around the tonic. The following illustration, borrowed from Winthrop Sargeant,[3] indicates the parallel
tendencies of notes in two tetrachords. He arranged the notes of
the blues scale in terms of their importance and characteristic behavior rather than in the usual tonic to tonic extension.

Jazz, unlike traditional music, is not architectonic, or construc-
tional. Because it relies so heavily on improvisation, jazz requires a
relatively simple harmonic basis. Jazz men repeat or imply the
same harmonic pattern several times during the course of a piece
and this pattern permits them to ad lib without losing their relationships to the notes of other musicians. The following is a harmonic pattern often used by jazz men:[4]

In this illustration the conventional symbols I, V, and IV designate
the tonic, dominant, and subdominant harmonies respectively; the
figure 7 marks the seventh chord) formed like the dominant seventh, with two minor thirds standing above a major third), and
the diamond indicates a blue note.

This harmonic pattern resembles that used in traditional (pre-
jazz) popular music such as hymns and barbershop songs. There
are, however, important differences. The pseudo-dominant seventh
chord, built on the tonic (I[7]) and on the subdominant (IV[7]), is
rarely found in traditional music. Frequently employed in jazz,
this chord often has a blue note foreign to the diatonic scale.
Many harmonic cadences in jazz are unconventional also. The
next-to-last chord must frequently conform harmonically to the
major or blue third, the second, or the sixth of the octave below.
Therefore, the most generally employed cadences are hybrid forms
of the authentic and plagal harmonies.

The tone color of jazz differs markedly from the characteristic sounds of traditional music. Various rhythmic, melodic, and harmonic "irregularities" are partly responsible for this difference. In addition, the music of the first jazz bands was seldom homophonic. On the other hand, their improvisations could not be considered polyphonic in the traditional sense of two or more melodies fitted tightly together according to a strict set of rules.

As a rule trumpets, trombones, clarinets, and later saxophones carried the melodic burden. Performers departed from the traditional range of these instruments by playing sounds which resembled human or animal laughs, moans, growls, and other cries unheard in traditional music. Further, jazz performers abandoned string instruments traditionally used chiefly for melodic purposes or else assigned to a rhythm section which might contain the following instruments: piano, guitar or banjo, bass or tuba, and drums.

Modern jazz emerged after 1940, partly as a reaction to traditional jazz. I shall briefly discuss only its earliest form, bop, which falls within the chronological limits of this study. The chief characteristic of bop, as of traditional jazz, is the swinging quality produced by means of syncopation and polyrhythm. Yet, the rhythms which create the swinging quality in modern jazz are far more diverse and complex than those in traditional jazz. Whereas the half and quarter note had usually been the basis of rhythm in traditional jazz, the eighth note became the fundamental rhythmic unit in bop. Bop players often broke up time even further. On a record of "Night in Tunisia," for example, Charlie Parker, generally conceded to be the most influential figure in the bop movement, plays a series of sixty sixteenth notes vehemently accented on various "off" beats.

Dissatisfied with traditional jazz tunes, bop musicians radically paraphrased them or composed new ones with abrupt accents and irregular phrasing that did not conform to traditional bar lines. Bop performers occasionally used the harmonic sequences of old songs, but they superimposed different melodies upon them and altered the harmonics to suit their purposes. They continued to use the blues scale but they extended tonal usage in the direction of atonality. Such novel practices produced not only new melodies but also new harmonies full of chromatic notes and unconventional intervals.

APPENDIX B

CONTENT ANALYSIS
OF LYRICS

IN chapter vi, I summarized the nature of the samples and the results of a content analysis of jazz lyrics. The purpose of this appendix is to give further details of the procedures and findings of the analysis. Throughout much of it I had the guidance of an expert in this kind of research, Sanford M. Dornbusch, who saved me from several mistakes. Whatever errors appear in the following paragraphs were doubtless made while I was no longer guided by him.

I chose the samples in the following way. Using Charles Delaunay's *New Hot Discography*, edited by Walter Schaap and George Avakian (New York, 1948), I determined how many vocals the various singers had recorded in the years under examination. I assigned a number to each title. Employing a random numbers table I chose twenty sides and used for my sample as many of the twenty as I could locate and transcribe.[1]

Bessie Smith recorded 78 sides in 1923–25. Of the first twenty to appear on the random numbers table, I obtained the seventeen listed here with their original matrix numbers: "Gulf Coast Blues"

Co (for Columbia) A3844, "Keeps On Rainin'" CoA3898, "Tain't Nobody's Business If I Do" CoA3898, "Baby Won't You Please Come Home" Co3888, "Bleeding Hearted Blues" CoA3936, "Midnight Blues" CoA3936, "Jail House Blues" CoA4001, "I'm Goin' Back to My Used To Be" Co13007D, "Any Woman's Blues" Co-13001D, "Mistreatin' Daddy" Co14000D, "Eaves Dropper's Blues" Co14010D, "The Bye Bye Blues" Co14042D, "Follow the Deal on Down" Co14052D, "Sinful Blues" Co14052D, "Sing Sing Prison Blues" Co14051D, "Soft Pedal Blues" Co14075D, "He's Gone Blues" Co14083D.

Of the forty-five sides made by groups led by trumpeter and vocalist Louis Armstrong 1925–27, twenty-one have vocals. I selected twenty by the same random sampling method used above. Sixteen were available. "Heebie Jeebies" Ok (for Okeh) 8300, "Don't Forget To Mess Around" Ok8343, "I'm Gonna Gitcha" Ok8343, "Droppin Shucks" Ok8357, "Big Fat Pa and Skinny Ma" "Ok8379, "Big Butter and Egg Man from Way Out West" Ok4323, "You Made Me Love You" Ok8447, "S.O.L. Blues" Ok8496, "Gully Low Blues" Ok8474, "Put 'Em Down Blues" Ok8503, "That's When I'll Come Back to You" Ok8519, "The Last Time" Co35838, "I'm Not Rough" Ok8551, "Gut Bucket Blues" Ok8261. "Skit-Da-De-Dat" Ok8436 and "Keyhole Blues" Ok8496 had only "scat" vocals. Therefore, these records were averaged in with the other statistics only in reference to the item listed as "songs containing 'scat' singing."

Of sixty-two disks Armstrong made between 1929–31, forty-four had lyrics. Again, I chose twenty as samples, of which eighteen were available: "Ain't Misbehavin'" Ok8774, "Sweet Savanah Sue" Vo (for Vocalion) 3136, "Some of These Days" Ok41,298, "When Your're Smiling" Ok41298, "Rockin' Chair" Co2668D, "I'm in the Market for You" Ok41422, "Confessin'" Ok41448, "If I Could Be with You" Ok41448, "Just a Gigolo" Ok41486, "Shine" Ok41486, "Walkin' My Baby Back Home" Ok41497, "I Surrender Dear" Vo3202, "You Rascal You" Ok41504, "When Your Lover Has Gone" Ok41498, "Stardust" (first version) Ok41530, "Home" Ok41552, "All of Me" Ok41552, "Chinatown My Chinatown" Ok41534, "St. Louis Blues" Ok41350, I used the same system to select twenty samples of the fifty-eight records Billie Holiday made in 1936–39. Of the twenty chosen, fifteen were obtainable: "Did I Remember" Vo3276, "I've Got My Love To Keep Me Warm" Vo3431, "Me, Myself and I" Vo3593, "Without Your

Love" Vo3593, "A Sailboat in the Moonlight" Vo3605, "Born To Love" Vo3605, "Trav'lin' all Alone" Vo3748, "Now They Call It Swing" Vo3605, "On the Sentimental Side" Vo3947, "If I Were You" Vo4151, "Dream of Life" Vo4631, "Yesterdays" CMS (for Commodore) 527, "I've Got a Right To Sing the Blues" CMS527, "Some Other Spring" Vo5021, "The Man I Love" Vo5377.

Analyzing the contents of the samples was harder than selecting them. Meaning in jazz vocals often differs greatly from the denotation of the words that appear on the sheet music. The singer may alter the sense of words and of entire songs by adding or subtracting syllables or words and by changing emphasis, pitch, or rhythm. As a result, more than one meaning can often be justified.

In an effort to be objective I asked another person familiar with jazz lyrics to help judge their content. First, we set up a series of hypotheses regarding the changes in lyrics before and after 1928.[2] Then, using the samples, we independently tested the validity of the hypotheses and as far as possible represented the findings statistically. Later we averaged our results together and translated them into percentages. The hypotheses are at the extreme left; the raw data are at the top of each box — mine on the left, my associate's on the right; and the percentages are in the bottom half of the box. Since each sample did not contain the same number of songs and each song had a different number of words, the percentages, rather than the raw data, should be used for comparison purposes.

These statistics show the growing influence of traditional values. In some instances the trend toward traditional norms seems to waver, in others it is not fully clear, and in a few cases the hypotheses seem to be false. Yet the number of negative findings is small and doubtless some of them result from the different personalities and vocal styles of the singers.

Traditional Elements Expected To Increase
1928

Elements	Bessie Smith 1923–1925		Louis Armstrong 1925–1927		Louis Armstrong 1927–1930		Billie Holiday 1936–1939	
	Songs	Words	Songs	Words	Songs	Words	Songs	Words
Hope, happiness or contentment (actual or possible)	1 / 1 .06		3 / 3 .21		7 / 6 .36		9 / 6 .50	
Wishing for, or dreaming of, ideal persons or circumstances	0		1 / 1 .07		5 / 7 .33		4 / 4 .27	
Dreams as a solution to unhappiness	0		1 / 0 .04		5 / 5 .28		3 / 3 .20	
Love as ideal state	0		1 / 2 .11		3 / 4 .19		7 / 7 .46	
Love as a spiritual experience which goes beyond sex	2 / 1 .09		3 / 1 .14		8 / 5 .36		12/ 8 .67	
Love associated with magic	0		0		1 / 0 .03		1 / 1 .07	
Sentimental ballads of Tin Pan Alley variety	0		2 / 1 .10		13/ 7 .56		12/13 .80	
Romantic words excluding terms of endearment		0		14/23 .01		92/111 .28		94/112 .10
Personification of nature	0		0		5 / 4 .25		2 / 1 .10	
Inflated or elevated language	0		2 / 1 .10		6 / 3 .25		7 / 4 .37	
Ornate imagery	1 / 1 .03		1 / 0 .04		6 / 5 .30		7 / 6 .43	
Use of related images	1 / 1 .03		0		6 / 5 .30		6 / 4 .33	
Religious imagery	0		0		1 / 1 .03		2 / 0 .07	
Sexual intercourse treated with abstract periphrasis	2 / 2 .11		3 / 1 .14		4 / 4 .22		0	
Terms: love, loving		9 /10 .003		5 / 4 .003		21/23 .03		40/45 .02
Terms: dream, reverie, memory		0		1 / 1 .0007		7 / 8 .009		10/10 .005
Words of more than two syllables		56/49 .02		13/12 .004		54/53 .07		64/60 .03

Elements of Early Jazz Lyrics Expected To Decrease

1928

Elements	Bessie Smith 1923–1925		Louis Armstrong 1925–1927		Louis Armstrong 1927–1930		Billie Holiday 1936–1939	
	Songs 17	Words 2,698	Songs 14 + 2 Scat	Words 1,331	Songs 18	Words 716	Songs 15	Words 2,035
Cynical Outlook: distrust of human nature, conduct motivated by self-interest	11/12 .67		5 / 4 .32		2 / 2 .11		1 / 2 .10	
Materialism (words referring to money)		17/19 .006		13/13 .009		1 / 2 .002		1 / 1 .0004
Economic problems	7 / 5 .35		2 / 2 .15		0		1 / 0 .03	
Action as solution to unhappiness	7 / 6 .38		6 / 4 .36		3 / 2 .16		1 / 1 .06	
Words referring to violence		34/32 .01		10/10 .007		3 / 3 .004		0
Death (implicit or explicit)	6 / 6 .35		0		3 / 3 .17		0	
Love viewed largely in terms of sex	6 / 6 .35		4 / 5 .32		3 / 2 .14		0	
Words referring to sexual intercourse		11/ 1 .004		30/21 .02		4 / 5 .006		0
Infidelity or mistreatment	13/13 .76		6 / 5 .37		6 / 5 .38		2 / 3 .17	
Adjustment to unhappiness in love (excluding dreams)	5 / 4 .26		4 / 1 .18		1 / 1 .06		2 / 2 .16	
Love viewed humorously	1 / 0 .03		4 / 4 .29		1 / 1 .06		0	
Songs contain-ining humor of any sort	3 / 2 .11		6 / 8 .50		2 / 2 .11		1 / 1 .06	

(continued)

Elements of Early Jazz Lyrics Expected To Decrease (continued)

1928

Elements	Bessie Smith 1923–1925		Louis Armstrong 1925–1927		Louis Armstrong 1937–1930		Billie Holiday 1936–1939	
	Songs 17	Words 2,698	Songs 14 + 2 Scat	Words 1,331	Songs 18	Words 716	Songs 15	Words 2,035
Songs with reference to music	1 / 1 .06		3 / 3 .21		3 / 3 .16		2 / 2 .13	
Songs with reference to dancing	0		3 / 3 .21		0		1 / 1 .06	
Basic twelve-bar blues	7 / 7 .41		3 / 3 .16		0		0	
Language associated primarily with Negro		155/137 .06		73/76 .05		13/15 .02		0
Songs containing scat (nonsense) syllables	1 / 0 .03		4 / 4 .25		9 / 8 .47		1 / 1 .07	
Sex treated metaphorically	2 / 2 .12		1 / 1 .07		1 / 1 .05		0	
Songs dealing with love or sex	15/15 .88		10/ 9 .68		13/14 .75		14/13 .90	

NOTES

INTRODUCTION

1. David D. Boyden, *An Introduction to Music* (New York, 1956), p. 382.
2. Nicholas Slonimsky, *Music since 1900* (New York, 1949), p. 131.
3. Morroe Berger, "Jazz: Resistance to the Diffusion of a Culture-Pattern," *Journal of Negro History*, XXII (January, 1947), 461–94.

CHAPTER ONE. BACKGROUND

1. Gilbert Chase, *America's Music*, (New York, 1955), p. 150.
2. Isaac Goldberg, *Tin Pan Alley* (New York, 1930), p. 218.
3. Joe Laurie, Jr., *Vaudeville* (New York, 1953), p. 66.
4. J. Walker McSpadden, *Light Opera and Musical Comedy* (New York, 1936), p. 274.
5. Oscar Thompson (ed.), *International Cyclopedia of Music and Musicians* (New York, 1946), p. 1772; see also John Philip Sousa, *Marching Along* (Boston, 1928), *passim.*
6. Chase, *America's Music*, pp. 270, 272, 277.
7. Marshall W. Stearns, *The Story of Jazz* (New York, 1956), pp. 141–44.
8. Nat Shapiro and Nat Hentoff (eds.), *Hear Me Talkin' to Ya* (New York, 1955), p. 53.
9. Stearns, *Story of Jazz*, pp. 3–14, 72–75.
10. Louis Armstrong, *Swing That Music* (New York, 1936), p. 74.

11. Stearns, *Story of Jazz*, pp. 154–55.

12. H. O. Brunn, *The Story of the Original Dixieland Jazz Band* (Baton Rouge, La., 1960), p. 70; Barry Ulanov, *A History of Jazz in America* (New York, 1952), p. 142.

13. See pp. 72–78, 119–20 for further discussion of refined jazz.

14. Abel Green and Joe Laurie, Jr., *Show Biz from Vaude to Video* (New York, 1951), p. 317.

15. See Stearns, *Story of Jazz*, p. 56.

16. See John H. Mueller, *The American Symphony Orchestra* (Bloomington, Ind., 1951), pp. 14–18.

17. *Seventh Census of the United States* (Washington, D.C., 1850) p. xxxiii.

18. Chase, *America's Music*, p. 634.

19. Walter Damrosch, *My Musical Life* (New York, 1923), p. 334.

20. See Mueller, *American Symphony Orchestra*, pp. 30, 292–93.

21. Theodore Thomas, *Theodore Thomas: A Musical Autobiography*, ed. George Upton (Chicago, 1905), I, 234–35. Mueller, *American Symphony Orchestra*, p. 292.

22. Thomas, *Autobiography*, Vol. I, epigraph.

23. John T. Howard, *Our American Music* (New York, 1931), p. 185.

24. For discussion of this subject see James H. Stone, "Mid-Nineteenth Century American Beliefs in the Social Value of Music," *Musical Quarterly*, XLIII (January, 1957), 38–49; also Charles Seeger, "Music and Class Structure in the United States," *American Quarterly*, IX (Fall, 1957), 285.

25. David Ewen, *Music Comes to America* (New York, 1942), pp. 76–77; Olga Samaroff-Stokowski, *An American Musician's Story* (New York, 1939), *passim*.

26. Arthur Mees, *Choirs and Choral Music* (New York, 1911), pp. 106–211; U.S. Bureau of Education, "The Study of Music in Public Schools," *Circular of Information*, I, (1886), 76–77.

27. Damrosch, *My Musical Life*, pp. 186–87; Ewen, *Music Comes to America*, pp. 81–83; Mueller, *American Symphony Orchestra*, p. 36.

28. See Roland Gelatt, *The Fabulous Phonograph* (New York, 1953), pp. 137–57, 307–8.

29. Ewen, *Music Comes to America*, pp. 155, 161, 181.

30. *Ibid.*, pp. 99, 176.

31. Deems Taylor, "Music," in *Civilization in the United States*, ed. Harold Stearns (New York, 1922), pp. 204–5; D. G. Mason, *The Dilemma of American Music* (New York, 1928), p. 91.

32. Ewen, *Music Comes to America*, pp. 4–5.

33. Chase, *America's Music*, pp. 327, 333.

34. Ewen, *Music Comes to America*, pp. 4–8.

35. Taylor, "Music," p. 206; Ewen, *Music Comes to America*, pp. 14–15, 83, 206–7.

36. Ewen, *Music Comes to America*, pp. 96–97.

37. Edward Mims, *Sidney Lanier* (Boston, 1905), p. 16; Chase, *America's Music*, pp. 342–69.

38. Damrosch, *My Musical Life*, pp. 323–24.

39. *Fourteenth Annual Census*, (Washington, D.C., 1920) IV, 42.

40. Howard, *Our American Music*, pp. 255–57; Chase, *America's Music*, p. 377.

41. Thompson, *Cyclopedia*, pp. 51–52, 1139–43; Ewen, *Music Comes to America*, p. 133; Chase, *America's Music*, p. 635.

42. This average was extrapolated from a chart in Mason's *Dilemma of American Music*, pp. 63–64; the five orchestras were the New York Philharmonic, and the New York, Philadelphia, Chicago, and Boston Symphony Orchestras.

43. Mason, *Dilemma of American Music*, p. 5.

44. Taylor, "Music," pp. 207–11.

45. Chase, *America's Music*, pp. 324, 385–86.

46. *Ibid.*, pp. 332–33, 634.

47. *Ibid.*, p. 391.

48. *Ibid.*, p. 390.

49. *Ibid.*, pp. 391–95; see also Edward N. Waters, "The Wa-Wan Press: An Adventure in Musical Idealism" in *A Birthday Greeting to Carl Engel*, ed. Gustav Reese (New York, 1943), pp. 217–18.

50. Waters, "The Wa-Wan Press," p. 222.

51. *Ibid.*, p. 223.

52. Rupert Hughes, "A Eulogy of Ragtime," *Musical Record*, CDXLVII (1899), 157.

53. Rudi Blesh and Harriet Janis, *They All Played Ragtime* (New York, 1950), p. 271.

54. *Ibid.*, p. 135; see also Goldberg, *Tin Pan Alley*, p. 234.

55. Blesh and Janis, *Ragtime*, p. 135.

56. Frederick Lewis Allen, "When America Learned To Dance," *Scribner's Magazine*, CII (September, 1937), 15, 17.

57. Hiram K. Moderwell, "Two Views of Ragtime. I, A Modest Proposal," *Seven Arts*, II (July, 1917), 368.

58. *Ibid.*, p. 370.

59. Hiram K. Moderwell, "Ragtime," *New Republic*, IV (October 16, 1915), 286.

60. Moderwell, "Two Views," p. 375.

61. D. G. Mason, "Concerning Ragtime," *New Music and Church Review*, XVII (March, 1918), 116.

62. D. G. Mason, "Folk Song and American Music," *Musical Quarterly*, IV (July, 1918), 324.

63. *Ibid.*, p. 337.

CHAPTER TWO. TRADITIONALIST OPPOSITION

1. J. Hartley Manners, *The National Anthem*, (New York, 1922), p. xiii.

2. *Metronome*, XXXVIII (August, 1922), 27–28.

3. See Howard Mumford Jones, *Guide to American Literature and Its Backgrounds since 1890* (Cambridge, Mass., 1959), p. 111.

4. I have slightly modified the definitions of these two groups which Morroe Berger gives in "Jazz: Resistance to the Diffusion of a Culture-Pattern," *Journal of Negro History*, XXXII (January, 1947) 461–62.

5. Gilbert Chase, *America's Music* (New York, 1956), p. 365.

6. Jones, *Guide to American Literature*, p. 113.

7. Anne Shaw Faulkner (Mrs. Marx Obendorfer), "Does Jazz Put the Sin into Syncopation," *Ladies' Home Journal*, XXXVIII (August, 1921), 34.

8. Sigmund Spaeth, "Jazz Is Not Music," *Forum*, LXXX (August, 1928), 270.

9. John R. McMahon, "Back to Pre-War Morals," *Ladies' Home Journal*, XXXVIII (November, 1921), 13.

10. Paul Whiteman and Mary Margaret McBride, *Jazz* (New York, 1926), pp. 5–6.

11. *New York Times*, November 14, 1924, p. 16.

12. "Where Is Jazz Leading America?" (second installment), *Etude*, XLII (September, 1924), 595.

13. *New York Times*, April 17, 1928, p. 26.

14. *Ibid.*, October 7, 1928, Section V, p. 19.

15. Whieman and McBride, *Jazz*, pp. 137–38; see also *New York Times*, February 12, 1922, p. 1.

16. H. O. Osgood, *So This Is Jazz* (Boston, 1926), pp. 5–6.

17. *New York Times*, April 14, 1926, p. 15.

18. Oscar Handlin, *Race and Nationality in American Life* (Anchor Edition, New York, 1957), pp. 119–22.

19. John R. McMahon, "Unspeakable Jazz Must Go!" *Ladies' Home Journal*, XXXVIII (December, 1921), 34.

20. Frederick Lewis Allen, *Only Yesterday* (New York, 1931), pp. 90, 92.

21. John R. McMahon, "Our Jazz-Spotted Middle West," *Ladies Home Journal*, XXXIX (February, 1927), 38. No reliable figures on illegitimate births exist for the years before 1917. Since then the rate of such births has risen steadily. From 1917 to 1922, the year Miss Barrow made this statement, the national rate rose from 20.2 to 25.2 per 1,000 births. *Vital Statistics of the United States* (Washington, D.C., 1937), Part I, p. 7.

22. *New York Times*, January 30, 1922, p. 16.

23. H. O. Brunn, *The Original Dixieland Jazz Band* (Baton Rouge, La., 1960), p. 173.

24. John R. McMahon, "Unspeakable Jazz Must Go!" p. 34.

25. *New York Times,* June 19, 1920, p. 24.

26. Anne Shaw Faulkner, "Does Jazz Put the Sin into Syncopation?" p. 34.

27. "Where Is Jazz Leading America," (first instalment), *Etude,* XLII (August, 1924), 520.

28. "What's the Matter With Jazz?" *Etude,* XLII (January, 1924), 6.

29. *Literary Digest,* LXV (January 12, 1920), 40.

30. Milton Mezzrow and Bernard Wolfe, *Really the Blues* (New York, 1946), p. 61.

31. *New York Times,* March 3, 1922, p. 15.

32. *Ibid.,* May 7, 1926, p. 10.

33. Allen, *Only Yesterday,* p. 92.

34. Sherwood Boblitz, "Where Movie Playing Needs Reform," *Musician,* XXV (June, 1920), 8.

35. Elise F. White, "Music Versus Materialism," *Musical Quarterly,* VII (January, 1922), 42.

36. "Is Jazz the Pilot of Disaster?" *Etude,* XLIII (January, 1925), 6.

37. *Metronome,* XXXIX (February, 1923), 59.

38. *New York Times,* February 4, 1926, p. 4.

39. "Too Much Jazz Basis for New Role of Laurette Taylor." This newspaper clipping, dated January 29, 1922, is wihout a masthead; it is in the Theater Collection of the Harvard College Library, where it is filed with a series of reviews of *The National Anthem.*

40. Handlin, *Race and Nationality in American Life,* pp. 125–28.

41. Faulkner, "Does Jazz Put the Sin into Syncopation?" p. 16; see also Amy Keith Carroll, "Jazz Is Savage, Says Oumiroff," *Musical Leader,* XLV (March, 1923), 259.

42. Nat Shapiro and Nat Hentoff (eds.), *Hear Me Talkin' to Ya* (New York, 1955), p. 332.

43. Whiteman and McBride, *Jazz,* pp. 139–40.

44. See *New York Times,* January 30, 1922, p. 16; and January 27, 1925, p. 12.

45. McMahon, "Back to Pre-War Morals," p. 13.

46. Walter Damrosch, *My Musical Life* (New York, 1923), p. 268.

47. Elise F. White, "Music Versus Materialism," pp. 42–43.

48. *New York Times,* October 8, 1924, p. 20.

49. "Where Is Jazz Leading America?" (first instalment), p. 518.

50. *New York Times,* April 17, 1928, p. 26.

51. Edwin Franko Goldman, "A Growing Demand for Wind Instrument Players," *Musician,* XXVII (December, 1922), 8.

52. *Literary Digest,* LXV (June, 1920), 40.

53. Frank Patterson, "'Jazz' — The National Anthem(?)," *Musical Courier,* LXXXIV (May 11, 1922), 6.

54. *New York Times,* May 3, 1925, Section VIII, p. 6.

55. "Where Is Jazz Leading America?" (first installment), p. 520.

56. See for examples *New York Times,* October 7, 1928, Section V, p. 19; and October 11, 1922, p. 15.

57. Whiteman and McBride, *Jazz,* pp. 137–38; McMahon, "Unspeakable Jazz Must Go!" p. 34.

58. Brunn, *Original Dixieland Jazz Band,* p. 173.

59. *New York Times,* September 21, 1919, Section VII, p. 6.

60. J. W. Studebaker, "The Age of Jazz," *Journal of Education,* CIX (January, 1929), 68.

61. *New York Times,* September 26, 1926, p. 26.

62. *Ibid.,* January 11, 1925, p. 34.

63. *Ibid.,* November 24, 1928, p. 16; and June 14, 1926, p. 1.

64. *Ibid.,* August 31, 1919, p. 4; Faulkner, "Does Jazz Put the Sin into Syncopation?" p. 16; McMahon, "Unspeakable Jazz Must Go!" pp. 34, 116.

65. Faulkner, "Does Jazz Put the Sin into Syncopation?" p. 34; P. G., "Representatives of 2,000,000 Women Meet To Annihilate 'Jazz,'" *Musical Courier,* LXXXVI (May 21, 1923), 5, 29.

66. McMahon, "Our Jazz-Spotted Middle West," p. 38.

67. *New York Times,* October 14, 1922, p. 16.

68. *Ibid.,* July 12, 1925, Section II, p. 2.

69. Allen, *Only Yesterday,* p. 92.

70. *New York Times,* February 12, 1922, p. 1.

71. Brunn, *Original Dixieland Jazz Band,* p. 175. *New York Times,* October 4, 1922, p. 16; and July 12, 1925, Section II, p. 2; Allen, *Only Yesterday,* p. 92.

72. Brunn, *Original Dixieland Jazz Band,* p. 175; Helen B. Lowry, "Putting the Music into Jazz," *New York Times,* February 19, 1922, Section III, p. 8; Ella Gardner, *Public Dance Halls,* Publication of U.S. Children's Bureau, No. 189 (Washington, D.C., 1929), pp. 3–35.

73. *New York Times,* January 11, 1926, p. 1; McMahon, "Our Jazz-Spotted Middle West," p. 181; Faulkner, "Does Jazz Put the Sin into Syncopation?" p. 16.

74. Berger, "Jazz: Resistance to the Diffusion of a Culture-Pattern," p. 463.

75. *Literary Digest,* LXXX (July 5, 1924), 31.

76. *New York Times,* November 14, 1924, p. 17.

77. *Ibid.,* December 6, 1927, p. 29.

78. *Ibid.,* December 7, 1927, p. 28.

CHAPTER THREE. ACCEPTANCE OF JAZZ IN THE TWENTIES.

1. Oscar Handlin in lectures given in 1957 for History 163, Harvard University. Handlin's insights strongly influenced the first part of this chapter.

2. *Ibid.*

3. Milton Mezzrow and Bernard Wolfe, *Really the Blues* (New York, 1946), p. 92.

4. Edward B. Marks, *They All Sang: From Tony Pastor to Rudy Vallee*, as told to A. J. Liebling (New York, 1934), p. 212.

5. Langston Hughes, *The Big Sea* (New York, 1945), pp. 250, 254.

6. Abel Green and Joe Laurie, Jr., *Show Biz: From Vaude to Video* (New York, 1951), pp. 79, 178, 213, 315.

7. *Ibid.*, pp. 48, 142, 245, 251.

8. Mark Sullivan, *The Twenties*, Vol. IV of *Our Times* (New York, 1935), pp. 382 n. 7A, 424; for *Collier's* advertisements see Vol. LXXVI, October 25, 1924, p. 51, and June 28, 1924, p. 35.

9. This summary of the psychology of adolescence derives from two articles by psychiatrists, Aaron H. Esman, "Jazz — A Study in Cultural Conflict," *American Imago*, VIII (1951), 225; Norman M. Margolis, "A Theory on the Psychology of Jazz," *American Imago*, XI (1954), 276, 277; Kenneth Keniston of Harvard told me that 90 per cent of psychiatrists working with adolescents would accept this theory.

10. Preston W. Slosson, *The Great Crusade and After*, 1914–1928 (New York, 1931; Vol. XII of A. M. Schlesinger and Dixon R. Fox [eds.], *A History of American Life*), p. 142.

11. For traditional ways of bringing up young persons see, for examples, Gustave Pollak (ed.), *Our Success in Child Training* (New York, 1902); Henry Barnard, *American Pedogogy*, (Hartford, 1876); Daniel Putnam, *A Manual of Pedagogics* (Boston, 1895). For examples of later books using psychological and sociological approaches associated with organic child rearing see Benjamin G. Gruenberg, *Outline of Child Study* (New York, 1922); Herbert Martin, *Formative Factors in Character* (New York, 1925); William S. and Lena K. Sadler, *Piloting Modern Youth* (New York, 1925).

12. U.S. Bureau of Education *Bulletins* 1927, No. 33, p. 10; and 1926, No. 40, pp. 1–3; Slosson, *The Great Crusade and After*, pp. 29, 320.

13. "These Wild Young People, by One of Them (John F. Carter, Jr.)" *Atlantic Monthly*, CXXVI (1920), 302–3.

14. Esman, "Jazz — A Study in Cultural Conflict," p. 225.

15. Margolis, "A Theory on the Psychology of Jazz," pp. 278–80.

16. The books are: Benny Goodman and Irving Kolodin, *The Kingdom of Swing* (New York, 1939); Eddie Condon and Thomas Sugrue, *We Called It Music* (New York, 1947); Hoagy Carmichael, *The Stardust Road* (New York, 1946); Milton Mezzrow and Bernard Wolfe, *Really the Blues*, (New York, 1946).

17. Carmichael, *Stardust Road*, pp. 7–8.

18. Mezzrow and Wolfe, *Really the Blues*, pp. 103–4.

19. *Ibid.*, pp. 125, 127.

20. Goodman and Kolodin, *Kingdom of Swing*, p. 101.

21. Condon and Sugrue, *We Called It Music*, p. 62.

22. E. J. Nichols, "Bix Beiderbecke" in Frederic Ramsey, Jr. and Charles Edward Smith (eds.), *Jazzmen* (New York, 1939), pp. 151–52, and insert at pp. 128–29.

23. Carmichael, *Stardust Road*, p. 17.

24. Condon and Sugrue, *We Called It Music*, p. 107.

25. Carmichael, *Stardust Road*, pp. 6–7.

26. *Ibid.*, p. 53.

27. Nat Shapiro and Nat Hentoff (eds.), *Hear Me Talkin' to Ya* (New York, 1955), p. 279.

28. Mezzrow and Wolfe, *Really the Blues*, p. 110.

29. Goodman and Kolodin, *Kingdom of Swing*, p. 101.

30. Mezzrow and Wolfe, *Really the Blues*, p. 61.

31. Condon and Sugrue, *We Called It Music*, p. 110.

32. This idea was suggested by William B. Cameron, "Sociological Notes on the Jam Session," *Social Forces*, XXXIII (1954), 181. While this and other comments of Cameron's are helpful, many of them go too far and are inapplicable to the majority of jazz men of any generation thus far. If anything, his remarks are more meaningful in terms of jazz men of the twenties and forties than of their less rebellious counterparts of the thirties (see chapter vi) of the fifties, whom Cameron has in mind.

33. Barry Ulanov, *History of Jazz in America* (New York, 1952), pp. 130–31.

34. Mezzrow and Wolfe, *Really the Blues*, p. 182.

35. See Cameron, "Sociological Notes on the Jam Session," p. 181.

36. Carmichael, *Stardust Road*, p. 53.

37. Mezzrow and Wolfe, *Really the Blues*, pp. 72–73.

38. Goodman and Kolodin, *Kingdom of Swing*, p. 97.

39. Mezzrow and Wolfe, *Really the Blues*, pp. 120–24; Condon confirms Mezzrow's description of life at Hudson Lake in his own account of a visit there, Condon and Sugrue, *We Called It Music*, pp. 138–39.

40. H. Brook Webb, "The Slang of Jazz," *American Speech*, XII (1937), 179–84, contains a glossary of jazz slang; for another glossary and some questionable material on the subject see Mezzrow and Wolfe, *Really the Blues*, pp. 216–28, 354–60.

41. Okeh recording 8300.

42. Carmichael, *Stardust Road*, p. 40.

43. *Ibid.*, p. 105.

44. Mezzrow and Wolfe, *Really the Blues*, pp. 222–23.

45. Carmichael, *Stardust Road*, p. 143.

46. Louis Armstrong, *Swing That Music* (New York, 1936), p. 78.

47. Mezzrow and Wolfe, *Really the Blues*, p. 142.

48. Carmichael, *Stardust Road*, p. 140.

49. *Ibid.*, pp. 116–17.

50. Cameron, "Sociological Notes on the Jam Session," pp. 179, 180.

51. Mezzrow and Wolfe, *Really the Blues*, p. 79.

52. *Ibid.*, p. 80; Nichols, "Bix Beiderbecke," pp. 145–46; Condon and Sugrue, *We Called It Music*, pp. 102, 115.

53. *Ibid.*, p. 102.

54. Shapiro and Hentoff, *Hear Me Talkin' to Ya*, p. 161.

55. *Ibid.*, p. 153.

56. Mezzrow and Wolfe, *Really the Blues*, p. 83.

57. Ulanov, *History of Jazz*, p. 139.

58. Carmichael, *Stardust Road*, p. 72.

59. Shapiro and Hentoff, *Hear Me Talkin' to Ya*, p. 151.

60. For examples, see Nichols, "Bix Beiderbecke," pp. 145, 158; Shapiro and Hentoff, *Hear Me Talkin' to Ya*, p. 163.

61. George Hoefer, "Bix Beiderbecke," in Nat Shapiro and Nat Hentoff (eds.), *Jazz Makers* (New York, 1957), p. 90.

62. For these and similar stories see Nichols, "Bix Beiderbecke," p. 144.

63. Armstrong, *Swing That Music*, p. 76.

64. See Stephen Smith, "Hot Collecting," in Ramsey and Smith, *Jazzmen*, pp. 288–89.

65. André Hodeir, *Jazz: Its Evolution and Essence*, trans. David Noaks (New York, 1956), p. 12.

66. Carmichael, *Stardust Road*, p. 143.

67. Malcolm Cowley, *Exiles' Return* (Compass Books edition, New York, 1956), p. 279.

68. Edward Lueders, *Carl Van Vechten and the Twenties* (Albuquerque, N.M., 1955), pp. 44–45, 85–90.

69. Hughes, *The Big Sea*, pp. 251–52.

70. Shapiro and Hentoff, *Hear Me Talkin' to Ya*, p. 245.

71. Hughes, *The Big Sea*, p. 249; and in conversation with me April 10, 1956.

72. Armstrong, *Swing That Music*, pp. 88–90.

73. Marshall W. Stearns, *The Story of Jazz* (New York, 1956), pp. 183–84.

74. Condon and Sugrue, *We Called It Music*, pp. 204–9.

75. *Ibid.*, p. 73.

CHAPTER FOUR. THE BREAKTHROUGH OF COMMERCIAL AND SYMPHONIC JAZZ

1. Commercial jazz, especially refined jazz was ordinarily played in these halls. Occasionally, however, the patrons heard a real jazz band. For examples: Fetcher Henderson's band alternated with Vincent Lopez's commercial group at the Roseland Ballroom, and the Wolverines performed at the Cinderella Ballroom in 1924.

2. Maria W. Lambin and Leroy S. Bowman, "Evidence of Social Relations as Seen in Types of New York City Dance Halls," *Social Forces*, III (January, 1925), 286–90.

3. *Ibid.*, pp. 288–90.

4. For examples of complaints which symphonic jazz advocates made about traditional manners and morals see Paul Whiteman and Mary Margaret McBride, *Jazz* (New York, 1926), pp. 154–55, 256–58; H. O. Osgood, *So This Is Jazz* (Boston, 1926), pp. 246–47; Gilbert Seldes, *The Seven Lively Arts* (New York, 1924), p. 98.

5. Whiteman and McBride, *Jazz*, pp. 34–35.

6. Alfred Frankenstein, *Syncopating Saxophones* (Chicago, 1925), p. 40.

7. Samuel Chotzinoff, "Jazz: A Brief History," *Vanity Fair*, XX (June, 1923), 104.

8. Sigmund Spaeth, "Jazz Is Not Music," *Forum*, LXXX (August, 1928), 271.

9. Osgood, *So This Is Jazz*, pp. 7–8.

10. Whiteman and McBride, *Jazz*, p. 155.

11. Seldes, *Seven Lively Arts*, p. 97.

12. Helen B. Lowry, "Putting the Music into Jazz," *New York Times*, February 19, 1922, Section III, p. 8.

13. *New York Times*, September 13, 1926, p. 21.

14. Frank Patterson, "Jazz — The National Anthem (?)" (second instalment), *Musical Courier*, LXXXIV (May 11, 1922), 6.

15. Spaeth, "Jazz Is Not Music," p. 269.

16. *Literary Digest*, LXXIX (November 4, 1922), 31.

17. Merle Armitage (ed.), *George Gershwin* (New York, 1938), p. 25.

18. Whiteman and McBride, *Jazz*, p. 94.

19. *Ibid.*, pp. 19–20, 95–96, 99.

20. Armitage, *George Gershwin*, p. 25.

21. Whiteman and McBride, *Jazz*, p. 105; see also *Musical America*, XXXIX (February 23, 1924), 32.

22. Osgood, *So This Is Jazz*, p. 158; Chadwick Hansen, "Social Influences on Jazz Style: Chicago, 1920–30," *American Quarterly*, XLII (Winter, 1960), 500.

23. Walter Damrosch, *My Musical Life* (New York, 1923), p. 268.

24. Osgood, *So This Is Jazz*, p. 204; Olin Downes, "A Piano Concerto in the Vernacular To Have Its Day with Damrosch," *New York Times*, November 29, 1925, Section VIII, p. 6.

25. *Etude*, XLII (August, 1924), 515.

26. *New York Times*, August 11, 1924, p. 12.

27. Edwin J. Stringham, "Jazz — an Educational Problem," *Musical Quarterly*, XII (April, 1926), 190–91.

28. The Osgood book was published in Boston, the Whiteman in New York.

29. Aaron Copland, *Our New Music* (New York, 1941), p. 88.

30. Osgood, *So This Is Jazz*, p. 26.

31. Whiteman and McBride, *Jazz*, p. 210.

32. *Literary Digest*, XCII (March 26, 1927), 26–27.

33. *Ibid.*, pp. 26–27; see also Isaac Goldberg, "Copland and His Jazz," *American Mercury*, XII (September, 1927), 63–65.

34. George Gershwin, "Relation of Jazz to American Music," in Henry Cowell (ed.), *American Composers on American Music* (Palo Alto, 1933), pp. 186–87.

35. For examples see Whiteman and McBride, *Jazz*, pp. 3–20; Chotzinoff, "Jazz: A Brief History," p. 69; Lowry, "Putting the Music into Jazz," p. 8.

36. Osgood, *So This Is Jazz*, pp. 249–50.

37. *Literary Digest*, LXXXVIII (March 13, 1926), 24–25.

38. Mark Sullivan, *The Twenties*, Vol. IV of *Our Times* (New York, 1935), p. 480; George Gershwin, "The Composer in the Machine Age," in Oliver Sayler (ed.), *Revolt in the Arts* (New York, 1930), p. 266.

39. Whiteman and McBride, *Jazz*, pp. 130–32.

40. For examples see *ibid.*, pp. 9–10, 20, 137–42; Osgood, *So This is Jazz*, pp. 246–49; Chotzinoff, "Jazz: A Brief History," p. 59.

41. See the following articles in this connection: "A Defense of Jazz," *New York Times*, September 18, 1926, p. 14; "Newman Resumes Attack on Jazz," *New York Times*, December 26, 1926, p. 30; Ernest Newman, "Summing Up Music's Case against Jazz," *New York Times*, March 6, 1927, Section IV, pp. 3, 22; Paul Whiteman, "In Defense of Jazz and Its Makers," *New York Times*, March 13, 1927, Section IV, pp. 4, 22.

42. See Osgood, *So This Is Jazz*, p. 249; *Musical Courier*, LXXXVII (July 5, 1923), 21.

43. See Whiteman and McBride, *Jazz*, pp. 26, 88–91, 125–29, 187–88; W. J. Henderson, "Ragtime, Jazz, and High Art," *Scribner's*, LXXVII (February, 1925), 200–203.

44. Carl Van Vechten, "George Gershwin: An American Composer Who Is Writing Notable Music in the Jazz Idiom," *Vanity Fair*, XXIV (March, 1925), 40.

45. Olin Downes, "Concerning 'Modern American Music' — Recent Delusions and Experiments," *New York Times*, November 23, 1924, Section VIII, p. 6.

46. Henderson, "Ragtime, Jazz, and High Art," pp. 200–203; *Musical Leader*, XLVII (April, 1924), 400; *Musical Courier*, LXXXVIII (March 27, 1924), 36.

47. Whiteman and McBride, *Jazz*, pp. 263, 287–88; *Musical America* XLIII (November 14, 1925), 31; *New York Times*, April 15, 1928, Section V, p. 3; Percy Grainger, "What Effect Is Jazz Likely To Have on the Music of the Future?" *Etude*, XLII (September, 1924), 593.

48. *New York Times*, June 28, 1926, p. 17; Osgood, *So This Is Jazz*, p. 23; Whiteman and McBride, *Jazz*, pp. 61–62; 121, 158.

49. Statement of Paul Specht in "Where Is Jazz Leading America?"

(second instalment), *Etude,* XLII (September, 1924), 596; Whiteman and McBride, *Jazz,* pp. 145–50.

50. H. L. Mencken, *Prejudices: Fifth Series* (New York, 1926), p. 293
51. *Current Opinion,* LXXVII (December, 1924), 746.
52. Whiteman and McBride, *Jazz,* pp. 76, 142–43.

CHAPTER FIVE. THE IMPACT OF MECHANIZATION

1. Arthur Whiting, "The Mechanical Player," *Yale Review,* VIII (July, 1919), 830.
2. Roland Gelatt, *The Fabulous Phonograph* (Philadelphia, 1954), pp. 83–171, 189, 212–13, 308; U.S. Bureau of Census, *Biennial Census of Manufacturers,* 1923, p. 1012; Edward B. Marks and Abbott J. Liebling, *They All Sang* (New York, 1934), pp. 104–5; Julius Weinberger, "Economic Aspects of Recreation," *Harvard Business Review,* XV (Summer, 1937), 452.
3. David Ewen, *Music Comes to America* (New York, 1942), pp. 200, 202; Weinberger, "Economic Aspects of Recreation," p. 452; Gelatt, *Fabulous Phonograph,* p. 213; *Biennial Census of Manufacturers,* p. 1012; Abel Green and Joe Laurie, Jr., *Show Biz: From Vaude to Video* (New York, 1951), p. 234; Francis Chase, *Sound and Fury* (New York, 1942), pp. 265–67.
4. Green and Laurie, *Show Biz,* p. 231; Barry Ulanov, *A History of Jazz in America* (New York, 1952), p. 114; Gelatt, *Fabulous Phonograph,* p. 216; Ewen *Music Comes to America,* p. 208.
5. Foster R. Dulles, *America Learns To Play: A History of Popular Recreation, 1607–1940* (New York, 1940), p. 327.
6. Ewen, *Music Comes to America,* p. 210.
7. *Etude,* IV (January, 1924), 5.
8. Charles Merz, *The Great American Bandwagon* (New York, 1928), pp. 47–48. Other evidence may be found in G. A. Lundberg, "The Content of Radio Programs," *Social Forces,* VII (1928), 59. Checking New York City radio stations during February, 1927, Lundberg found only 22 per cent of their time given to what he called "dance music" and 48 per cent given to "other music." The apparent inconsistency between these and Merz's figures seems to result from geographical differences in taste and, more important, from the vague terminology of both reports. Merz speaks of all music with a jazz sound, whereas Lundberg apparently refers to music listed in newspaper program-schedules as dance music. Probably much of the "other music" Lundberg speaks of sounded like jazz even though newspapers did not list it as "dance music."
9. Merz, *Great American Bandwagon,* pp. 48–49.
10. Llewellyn White, *The American Radio* (Chicago, 1947), p. 16.
11. Dulles, *America Learns To Play,* pp. 287–97, 301–2; Jesse P. Steiner, "Recreation and Leisure Time Activities," in *Recent Social Trends,* II (New York, 1933), 940–41; David Ewen, *Panorama of*

American Popular Music (Englewood Cliffs, N. J., 1957), pp. 280–82; Green and Laurie, *Show Biz*, pp. 247, 251, 270.

12. See Isaac Goldberg, *Tin Pan Alley* (New York, 1930), pp. 308–9.

13. Marks, and Liebling, *They All Sang*, pp. 207–8.

14. Merz, *Great American Bandwagon*, pp. 46–50.

15. George Avakian, "The History of Columbia Is the Saga of Jazz," *Down Beat*, XXIII (December 12, 1956), 14.

16. H. O. Brunn, *The Original Dixieland Jazz Band* (Baton Rouge, La., 1960), p. 70.

17. William Russell and Stephen W. Smith, "New Orleans Music" in Frederic Ramsey, Jr., and Charles Edward Smith (eds.), *Jazzmen* (New York, 1939), p. 22.

18. Nat Shapiro and Nat Hentoff (eds.), *Hear Me Talkin' To Ya* (New York, 1955), pp. 119–20.

19. *New York Times*, July 6, 1924, Section VIII, p. 14.

20. *Ibid.*, February 3, 1927, p. 3.

21. *Ibid.*, April 6, 1927, p. 30.

22. *Ibid.*, June 10, 1927, p. 23.

23. Carl Dreher, "In Defense of Broadcasting," *Radio Broadcast*, VIII (December, 1925), 192.

24. Ruth Brindze, *Not To Be Broadcast* (New York, 1937), p. 143; Chase, *Sound and Fury*, pp. 233, 236.

25. Robert West, *The Rape of Radio* (New York, 1941), p. 460.

26. *Ibid.*, p. 461.

27. White, *American Radio*, p. 70.

28. Chase, *Sound and Fury*, pp. 226–27; West, *Rape of Radio*, p. 462.

29. Green and Laurie, *Show Biz*, p. 292.

30. Chase, *Sound and Fury*, pp. 227–67.

31. *New York Times*, May 31, 1929, p. 26.

32. *Ibid.*, November 3, 1938, p. 25.

33. *Ibid.*, March 14, 1927, p. 19; and March 15, 1927, p. 28.

34. Kingsley Welles, "The Listeners' Point of View: Is the Popularity of Jazz Music Waning?" *Radio Broadcast*, VIII (December, 1925), 177–78.

35. *Ibid.*, p. 178.

36. Maurice Bardèche and Robert Brasillach, *The History of Motion Pictures*, trans. Iris Barry (New York, 1938), pp. 205–9; Green and Laurie, *Show Biz*, pp. 253–55; Dulles, *America Learns To Play*, pp. 299–300.

37. George Hoefer, "Bessie Smith," in Nat Shapiro and Nat Hentoff (eds.), *Jazz Makers* (New York, 1957), p. 137.

38. George Avakian, liner notes of Vol. II of "The Louis Armstrong Story," Columbia Record CL 852.

39. White, *American Radio*, p. 35.

40. Gelatt, *Fabulous Phonograph*, pp. 247, 251, 273; Green and Laurie, *Show Biz*, pp. 247, 266; Goldberg, *Tin Pan Alley*, pp. 312–14.

41. For discussion of this subject see Samuel Charters, *The Country Blues* (New York, 1959), *passim*.

42. *Musical Courier*, XCIX (December 14, 1929), 49.

43. See Paul S. Carpenter, *Music: An Art and a Business* (Norman, Okla., 1950), pp. 3–5.

44. Otis Ferguson, "The Five Pennies," in Ramsey and Smith, *Jazzmen*, p. 240.

45. Shapiro and Hentoff, *Hear Me Talkin' to Ya*, p. 269.

46. Green and Laurie, *Show Biz*, p. 243.

47. Chadwick Hansen, "Social Influences on Jazz Style: Chicago, 1920–30," *American Quarterly*, XII (Winter, 1960), 505.

48. Artie Shaw, *The Trouble with Cinderella*, (New York, 1952), p. 259.

CHAPTER SIX. SHIFTS TOWARD TRADITIONAL STANDARDS

1. Chadwick Hansen, "Social Influences on Jazz Style: Chicago, 1920–30," *American Quarterly*, XII (Winter, 1960), 493–507.

2. All illustrations are from records in the content analysis. Their matrix numbers can be found in Appendix B.

3. Sigmund Spaeth, *The Facts of Life in Popular Song* (New York, 1934), *passim*; S. I. Hayakawa, "Popular Songs vs. the Facts of Life," *Etc.: General Review of Semantics*, XII (Winter, 1955), 83–95.

4. Throughout this paragraph I drew heavily on Hazard Adams and Bruce Park, "The State of the Jazz Lyric," *Chicago Review*, X (Autumn–Winter, 1956), 5–20. Also helpful were Sidney Finkelstein, *Jazz: A People's Music* (New York, 1948), pp. 38–40, 143; George Avakian, "Louis Armstrong" in Nat Shapiro and Nat Hentoff (eds.), *Jazz Makers* (New York, 1957), p. 149.

5. Paul Whiteman and Mary Margaret McBride, *Jazz* (New York, 1926), pp. 226–27.

6. Rudi Blesh, *Shining Trumpets* (New York, 1946), pp. 234, 276–77; Charles Delaunay in George Avakian and Walter Schapp (eds.), *New Hot Discography* (New York, 1948), pp. 180–84; For further discussion of enlargement of jazz bands see Leroy Ostransky, *The Anatomy of Jazz* (Seattle, 1960), pp. 202–6.

7. Barry Ulanov, *Duke Ellington* (New York, 1946), pp. 69–70.

8. Benny Goodman and Irving Kolodin, *The Kingdom of Swing* (New York, 1939), pp. 138–39; John Hammond, "Twenty Years of Count Basie," in Eddie Condon and Richard Gehman (eds.), *Eddie Condon's Treasury of Jazz* (New York, 1955), pp. 253–54; Marshall W. Stearns, *The Story of Jazz* (New York, 1956), p. 199.

9. Nat Shapiro and Nat Hentoff (eds.), *Hear Me Talkin' to Ya* (New York, 1955), p. 204.

10. Goodman and Kolodin, *Kingdom of Swing*, pp. 156–57, 161–62.

11. Nat Shapiro, "Benny Goodman," in Shapiro and Hentoff, *Jazz Makers*, p. 182; Benny Goodman, "That Old Gang of Mine" in Condon and Gehman, *Eddie Condon's Treasury of Jazz*, p. 263.

12. *Ibid.*, p. 261.

13. Shapiro and Hentoff, *Hear Me Talkin' to Ya*, p. 304.

14. See Goodman and Kolodin, *Kingdom of Swing*, pp. 140, 157–58; Artie Shaw, *The Trouble with Cinderella* (New York, 1952), pp. 314–24.

15. Goodman and Kolodin, *Kingdom of Swing*, pp. 242–44.

16. Ideally, a discussion of musical changes should follow lines similar to those employed in examining the lyrics: a series of "before and after" scores and records might be chosen by a random sampling system and their musical elements analyzed. Such a study was out of the question for the present project. A strong background both in jazz and traditional music as well as a good ear would be necessary. I am a musicologist only by avocation, and the problems involved should be left to more capable hands. Nevertheless, I have pointed out certain obvious things. For a more technical discussion of some of the musical changes see Ostransky, *Anatomy of Jazz*, pp. 185–222, 243–52.

17. Stearns, *Story of Jazz*, p. 198.

18. *Ibid.*, p. 202; Stearns declared that white jazz men found Henderson's music rough and clumsy. His statement seems to apply best to those adhering closest to traditional norms who found Henderson's music crude, along with other "raw" types of jazz. For example, in the twenties Goodman felt that Beiderbecke, Condon, Mezzrow, Dave Tough, Bud Freeman, and Frank Teschmacher "were terrifically talented buys, but most of them didn't read, and we [the members of Ben Pollack's big band] thought their playing was rough — we didn't pay them much mind." (Goodman and Kolodin, *Kingdom of Swing*, p. 74.) Beiderbecke, Condon, and Mezzrow, who played collective improvisation close to the New Orleans style probably did not find Henderson's band clumsy and rough. Perhaps it seemed refined or too smooth to some of them.

19. Stearns, *Story of Jazz*, p. 209.

20. *Ibid.*, p. 213.

21. Goodman and Kolodin, *Kingdom of Swing*, p. 241.

22. *Ibid.*, pp. 237–38.

23. Louis Armstrong, *Swing That Music* (New York, 1936), p. 124.

24. Goodman and Kolodin, *Kingdom of Swing*, p. 172.

25. Shaw, *Trouble with Cinderella*, p. 301.

26. Edward J. Nichols, "Bix Beiderbecke" in Frederic Ramsey, Jr., and Charles Edward Smith (eds.), *Jazzmen* (New York, 1939), p. 158.

27. Shapiro and Hentoff, *Hear Me Talkin' to Ya*, p. 219.

28. Armstrong, *Swing That Music*, p. 121.

29. Eddie Condon and Thomas Sugrue, *We Called It Music* (New

York, 1947), p. 70; Hoagy Carmichael, *The Stardust Road* (New York, 1946), p. 136.

30. Goodman and Kolodin, *Kingdom of Swing*, p. 166.

31. Shapiro and Hentoff, *Hear Me Talkin' to Ya*, p. 210.

32. Goodman, "That Old Gang of Mine," p. 271; Otis Ferguson, "The Five Pennies" in Ramsey and Smith, *Jazzmen*, p. 227; Stearns, *Story of Jazz*, p. 190; Blesh, *Shining Trumpets*, p. 213; H. O. Brunn, *The Original Dixieland Jazz Band* (Baton Rouge, La., 1960), pp. 256–57.

33. See for examples Shaw, *Trouble with Cinderella*, pp. 311–13, 318, 323, 327–28.

34. Carlo Lastrucci, "The Professional Dance Musician," *Journal of Musicology*, III (Winter, 1941), 168–72; see also Louis Bergman, "Small Time Musicians," *New York Times*, September 10, 1939, Section VII, pp. 12, 16.

35. Goodman and Kolodin, *Kingdom of Swing*, p. 238; and Ostransky, *Anatomy of Jazz*, pp. 229–31.

36. Shapiro and Hentoff, *Hear Me Talkin' to Ya*, p. 219.

37. Goodman and Kolodin, *Kingdom of Swing*, p. 239.

38. Doron K. Antrim (ed.), *Paul Whiteman . . . [et al.] Give Their Secrets of Dance Band Success* (New York, 1936), pp. 23–24.

39. Frank Norris, "Benny Goodman and the Big Band Period," in Ralph de Toledano (ed.), *Frontiers of Jazz* (New York, 1947), p. 159; Richard English, "The Battling Brothers Dorsey," in Condon and Gehman, *Eddie Condon's Treasury of Jazz*, p. 293; Dave Dexter, Jr., *Jazz Cavalcade: The Inside Story of Jazz* (New York, 1946), p. 110.

40. English, "Battling Brothers Dorsey," p. 290. For evidence of conservatism and concern with security among more typical jazz men of the thirties see Ostransky, *Anatomy of Jazz*, pp. 229–31.

41. See Wilder Hobson, *American Jazz Music* (New York, 1939), p. 150.

CHAPTER SEVEN. THE BEGINNINGS OF GENERAL ACCEPTANCE

1. Charles Edward Smith, "Jazz: Some Little Known Aspects," *Symposium*, I (October, 1930), 502–17.

2. Hugues Panassié, *Hot Jazz*, trans. Lyle and Eleanor Dowling (New York, 1936), p. xvi.

3. For thumbnail sketches of a number of critics of the thirties see "Who's Who in the Critics Row," *Down Beat*, VII (November 15, 1940), 2, 5; second instalment (December 1, 1940), 6.

4. Barry Ulanov, *History of Jazz in America* (New York, 1952), pp. 201–2; Nat Shapiro, "Count Basie," in Nat Shapiro and Nat Hentoff (eds.), *Jazz Makers* (New York, 1947), p. 235.

5. Dave Dexter, *Jazz Cavalcade: The Inside Story of Jazz* (New York, 1946), pp. 114–16.

6. For full list of both foreign and American publications on jazz to 1954 see Alan P. Merriam and Robert J. Benford, *Bibliography of Jazz* (Philadelphia, 1954), a publication of the American Folklore Society, Bibliographical Series, IV, 121–25.

7. All of these books were published in New York.

8. Charles Edward Smith, "Collecting Hot," *Esquire*, I (February, 1934), 79.

9. Stephen W. Smith, "Hot Collecting," in Frederic Ramsey, Jr., and Charles Edward Smith (eds.), *Jazzmen* (New York, 1939), pp. 289, 296–97; Eddie Condon and Thomas Sugrue, *We Called It Music* (New York, 1947), p. 236.

10. Smith, "Hot Collecting," p. 296; Condon and Sugrue, *We Called It Music*, pp. 236–39.

11. Frank Norris, "Benny Goodman and the Swing Period" in Ralph de Toledano (ed.), *The Frontiers of Jazz* (New York, 1947), p. 149; see also Dexter, *Jazz Cavalcade*, p. 166.

12. Irving Kolodin, "Number One Swing Man" in Ralph Gleason (ed.), *Jam Session* (New York, 1958), p. 81.

13. Panassié, *Hot Jazz*, p. vii.

14. *Boston Evening Transcript*, March 22, 1930, Part IV, p. 4.

15. See Robert Rogers, "Jazz Influence on French Music," *Musical Quarterly*, XXI (January, 1935), 53–68.

16. Barry Ulanov, *Duke Ellington* (New York, 1946), pp. 131–51, 209–17.

17. Louis Armstrong, *Swing That Music* (New York, 1936), p. 112.

18. Roger Pryor Dodge, "Consider the Critics," in Ramsey and Smith *Jazzmen*, p. 310.

19. Louis Harap, "The Case for Hot Jazz," *Musical Quarterly*, XXVII (January, 1941), 53n.

20. Holmes Harvey, "It's Swing!" *Delineator*, CXXIX (November, 1936), 10.

21. William R. Tilford, "Swing, Swing, Swing," *Etude*, LV (December, 1937), 777.

22. *New York Times*, January 17, 1938, p. 11.

23. *Ibid.*, May 30, 1938, p. 13.

24. *Ibid.*, June 13, 1938, p. 15.

25. *Ibid.*, May 30, 1938, p. 13.

26. Charles Edward Smith, "Heat Wave," *Stage*, XII (September, 1935), 46.

27. Armstrong, *Swing That Music*, pp. 108–9.

28. Reed Dickerson, "Hot Music: Rediscovering Jazz," *Harper's*, CLXXII (April, 1936), 574.

29. Gama Gilbert, "Swing: What Is It?" *New York Times*, September 5, 1937, Section X, p. 5.

30. Benny Goodman and Irving Kolodin, *The Kingdom of Swing* (New

York, 1939), p. 235; Bennie Goodman, "That Old Gang of Mine," in Eddie Condon and Richard Gehman (eds.), *Eddie Condon's Treasury of Jazz* (New York, 1956), p. 272; Artie Shaw, *The Trouble with Cinderella* (New York, 1952), pp. 340–54; *New York Times*, July 12, 1942, p. 27.

31. Goodman and Kolodin, *Kingdom of Swing*, p. 104; see also p. 100.

32. Robert West, *The Rape of Radio* (New York, 1941), p. 153.

33. Howard Taubman, "Swing and Mozart Too," *New York Times*, December 29, 1940, Section VII, p. 15.

34. Benny Goodman, "That Old Gang of Mine," p. 273.

35. Nat Shapiro, "Count Basie," in Shapiro and Hentoff, *Jazz Makers*, p. 232.

36. Smith, "Collecting Hot," p. 96.

37. See Barry Ulanov, *A History of Jazz* (New York, 1952), pp. 165–66.

38. Wilder Hobson, "Fifty Second Street" in Ramsey and Smith, *Jazzmen*, p. 251.

39. See Goodman, "That Old Gang of Mine," p. 272; Goodman and Kolodin, pp. 217–19; *New York Times*, May 30, 1938, p. 13; Shaw, *Trouble with Cinderella*, pp. 341–42.

40. Goodman, "That Old Gang of Mine," p. 272.

41. Ulanov, *History of Jazz*, p. 205; see also *New York Times*, May 30, 1938, p. 13.

42. Virgil Thompson, "Jazz," *American Mercury*, II (August, 1924), 467.

43. Virgil Thompson, "Swing-Music," *Modern Music*, XIII (May–June, 1936), 16–17.

44. *New York Times*, October 9, 1936, p. 30.

45. *Ibid.*, April 17, 1928, p. 26; Ulanov, *Duke Ellington*, p. 176.

46. *Ibid.*, p. 253.

47. See Howard Taubman, "Duke Invades Carnegie Hall," *New York Times Magazine*, January 17, 1943, Section VII, pp. 10, 30; and Taubman, "Swing and Mozart Too," p. 7; Irving Kolodin, "What About Swing?" *Parent's Magazine*, XIV (August 1939), 180–81; and Goodman and Kolodin, *Kingdom of Swing*, passim.

48. *New York Times*, December 15, 1938, p. 8.

49. Frederick Lewis Allen, *Only Yesterday* (New York, 1931), p. 92; *New York Times*, August 25, 1938, p. 13.

50. *Ibid.*, May 19, 1937, p. 25.

51. Lilla Belle Pitts, "Music and Modern Youth," *Music Educators' Journal*, XXVI (October, 1939), 18–19, 67–68.

52. *New York Times*, May 5, 1937, p. 28.

53. *Science News Letter*, XXXVIII (December 14, 1940), 377.

54. *New York Times*, July 18, 1937, Section X, p. 5; and July 15,

1937, p. 16; *Metronome*, LVIII (August, 1942), 7, and LVIII (October, 1942), 7; Dexter, *Inside Jazz*, p. 210; Charles Edward Smith, with Frederic Ramsey, Jr., Charles Payne Rogers, and William Russell, *The Jazz Record Book* (New York, 1944), p. 51.

55. Pictures in *Life*, V (August 8, 1938), 57 and *New York Times*, May 30, 1938, p. 13; quotes are from this *Times* article and editorial, May 31, 1938, p. 18.

56. For listings of articles on jazz in these and other magazines with wide circulation see Merriam and Benford, *Bibliography of Jazz, passim*.

57. *New York Times*, October 26, 1942, Section IX, p. 20.

58. *Ibid.*, November 2, 1938, p. 25.

59. David Ewen, *Panorama of American Popular Music* (Englewood, Cliffs, N. J., 1957), p. 159.

60. *New York Times*, March 26, 1939, Section X, p. 12.

61. *Ibid.*, October 30, 1938, Section IV, p. 2.

62. *Ibid.*, July 27, 1938, p. 19.

CONCLUSION

1. Hugues Panassié, *Hot Jazz*, trans. Lyle and Eleanor Dowling (New York, 1936), p. 278.

2. Nat Shapiro and Nat Hentoff (eds.), *Hear Me Talkin' to Ya* (New York, 1955), p. 405 .

APPENDIX A. DEFINITIONS

1. Winthrop Sargeant, *Jazz: Hot and Hybrid* (New York, 1939), pp. 230–31; Leroy Ostransky, *The Anatomy of Jazz* (Seattle, Wash., 1960), pp. 94–98, 166–69.

2. The origin of the term *jazz* and its premusical meaning are not clear. In the course of this study I encountered a number of comments on the first use of the word in our language. There are several theories and explanations, some of which are plausible, but no one of which is entirely convincing. See the five articles entitled, "The Word Jazz" by Fradley Garner and Alan P. Merriam in *Jazz Review* from Vol. III, March–April to August 1960.

3. For the illustration and comments on jazz tonality see Sargeant, *Jazz: Hot and Hybrid*, pp. 161–72; see also Ostransky, *Anatomy of Jazz*, pp. 118–21.

4. Borrowed from Sargeant, *Jazz: Hot and Hybrid*, p. 195.

APPENDIX B. CONTENT ANALYSIS OF LYRICS

1. Mayo Duca of North Quincy, Massachusetts, Richard Schmidt of Milton, Massachusetts, Marshall W. Stearns, executive director of the Institute of Jazz Studies, New York; and Donald C. Gallup, curator of the

James Weldon Johnson Memorial Collection of Negro Arts and Literature at Yale University kindly allowed me to use records from their collections.

2. A discussion with Lee S. Halprin and S. I. Hayakawa's article "Popular Songs vs. the Facts of Life," *Etc.: A General Review of Semantics,* XII (Winter, 1955), 83–95, were helpful in formulating these hypotheses.

BIBLIOGRAPHY

BOOKS CONSULTED

ALLEN, FREDERICK LEWIS. *Only Yesterday.* New York, 1931.

ALLEN, WALTER C., and BRIAN A. L. RUST, *King Joe Oliver.* Belleville, N.J., 1955.

ANTRIM, DORON K. *Paul Whiteman et al. Give Their Secrets of Dance Band Success.* New York, 1936.

ARMITAGE, MERLE (ed.). *George Gershwin.* New York, 1938.

ARMSTRONG, LOUIS. *Satchmo.* New York, 1954.

————. *Swing That Music.* New York, 1936.

ASBURY, HERBERT. *The French Quarter.* New York, 1936.

BARDÈCHE, MAURICE and ROBERT BRASILLACH. *The History of Motion Pictures,* trans. IRIS BARRY. New York, 1938.

BARNARD, HENRY. *American Pedagogy.* Hartford, Conn., 1876.

BAUER, MARION. *Twentieth Century Music.* New York, 1933.

BECHET, SIDNEY. *Treat It Gentle.* New York, 1960.

BLESH, RUDI. *Shining Trumpets.* New York, 1946.

BLESH, RUDI, and HARRIET JANIS. *They All Played Ragtime.* New York, 1950.

BOYDEN, DAVID D. *An Introduction to Music.* New York, 1956.

BRINDZE, RUTH. *Not To Be Broadcast.* New York, 1937.

BROONZY, WILLIAM. *Big Bill Blues,* as told to YANNICK BRUYNOGHE. London, 1955.

BRUNN, H. O. *The Original Dixieland Jazz Band.* Baton Rouge, La., 1960.

BURLIN, NATALIE CURTIS. *Negro Folk Songs.* 4 vols. New York, 1918–19.

CARMICHAEL, HOAGY. *The Stardust Road.* New York, 1946.

CARPENTER, PAUL S. *Music: An Art and a Business.* Norman, Okla., 1950.

CARSON, WILLIAM E. *The Marriage Revolt: A Study of Marriage and Divorce.* New York, 1915.

CHARTERS, SAMUEL B. *Jazz: New Orleans, 1885–1957.* Belleville, N.J., 1958.

——. *The Country Blues.* New York, 1959.

CHASE, FRANCIS. *Sound and Fury.* New York, 1942.

CHASE, GILBERT. *America's Music.* New York, 1955.

CLARKE, ERIC. *Music in Everday Life.* New York, 1935.

CHÁVEZ, CARLOS *Toward a New Music,* trans. HERBERT WEINSTOCK. New York, 1937.

CONDON, EDDIE, and RICHARD GEHMAN (eds.). *Eddie Condon's Treasury of Jazz.* New York, 1956.

CONDON, EDDIE. *We Called It Music,* narration by THOMAS SUGRUE. New York, 1947.

CONFREY, "ZEZ." *Modern Course in Novelty Piano Playing.* New York, 1923.

COPLAND, AARON. *Our New Music.* New York, 1941.

——. *What To Listen for in Music.* New York, 1957.

COWELL, HENRY (ed.). *American Composers on American Music.* Palo Alto, 1933.

COWLEY, MALCOLM. *Exiles Return.* New York, 1956.

CROSBY, BING, and PETE MARTIN. *Call Me Lucky.* New York, 1953.

CUNEY-HARE, MAUD. *Negro Musicians and Their Music.* Washington, D.C., 1926.

DAMROSCH, WALTER. *My Musical Life.* New York, 1923.

DE TOLEDANO, RALPH (ed.). *Frontiers of Jazz.* New York, 1947.

DELAUNAY, CHARLES. *Hot Discography.* Paris, 1936; American editions in 1938, 1940.

——. *New Hot Discography,* WALTER E. SCHAAP and GEORGE AVAKIAN, eds. New York, 1948.

DEXTER, DAVE, JR. *Jazz Cavalcade: The Inside Story of Jazz.* New York, 1946.

DULLES, FOSTER R. *America Learns To Play: A History of Popular Recreation. 1607–1940.* New York, 1940.

EDWARDS, GEORGE THORNTON. *Music and Musicians of Maine.* Portland, 1928.

ELSON, LOUIS C. *The History of American Music.* New York, 1904.

ENGEL, CARL. *Discords Mingled.* New York, 1931.

ERNST, MORRIS L., and PARE LORENTZ. *Censored.* New York, 1930.

EWEN, DAVID. *Men of Popular Song.* Chicago, 1944.

——. *Music Comes to America.* New York, 1942.

——. *Panorama of American Popular Music.* Englewood Cliffs, N.J., 1957.

——. *The Story of George Gershwin.* New York, 1943.

FEATHER, LEONARD. *The Encyclopedia of Jazz.* New York, 1955.

FINKELSTEIN, SIDNEY. *Jazz: A People's Music.* New York, 1948.

FRANKENSTEIN, ALFRED V. *Syncopating Saxophones.* Chicago, 1925.

GARNER, ELLA. *Public Dance Halls.* U.S. Children's Bureau, No. 189, Washington, D.C., 1929.

GELATT, ROLAND. *The Fabulous Phonograph.* Philadelphia, 1954.
GIEDION, SIEGFRIED. *Space, Time, and Architecture.* Cambridge, Mass., 1953.
GILBERT, DOUGLAS. *American Vaudeville.* New York, 1940.
―――. *Lost Chords: The Diverting Story of America's Popular Songs.* New York, 1942.
GLEASON, RALPH (ed.). *Jam Session.* New York, 1958.
GOFFIN, ROBERT. *Jazz: From the Congo to the Metropolitan.* New York, 1946.
―――. *Horn of Plenty: The Story of Louis Armstrong.* New York, 1947.
GOLDBERG, ISAAC. *George Gershwin: A Study in American Music.* New York, 1931.
―――. *Tin Pan Alley.* New York, 1930.
GOLDSMITH, A. N., and A. E. LESCARBOURA. *This Thing Called Broadcasting.* New York, 1930.
GOODMAN, BENNY, and IRVING KOLODIN. *The Kingdom of Swing.* New York, 1939.
GREEN, ABEL, and JOE LAURIE, JR. *Show Biz: From Vaude to Video.* New York, 1951.
GROSSMAN, WILLIAM L., and JACK W. FARRELL. *The Heart of Jazz.* New York, 1956.
GRUENBERG, BENJAMIN G. *Outline of Child Study.* New York, 1922.
HANDLIN, OSCAR. *Race and Nationality in American Life.* New York, 1957.
HANDY, W. C. (ed.). *A Treasury of the Blues.* New York, 1949.
―――. *Father of the Blues.* New York, 1941.
HANSEN, CHADWICK C. "The Ages of Jazz: A Study of Jazz in its Cultural Context." Unpublished doctoral dissertation, University of Minnesota, 1956.
HERSKOVITZ, MELVILLE J. *The Myth of the Negro Past.* New York, 1941.
HERZOG, GEORGE. *Research on Primitive and Folk Music in the U.S.: A Survey.* American Council of Learned Societies, Bulletin No. 24. Washington, D.C., 1936.
HODEIR, ANDRE. *Jazz: Its Evolution and Essence,* trans. DAVID NOAKES. New York, 1956.
HOLIDAY, BILLIE, and WILLIAM DUFTY. *Lady Sings The Blues.* New York, 1956.
HOWARD, JOHN T. *Our American Music.* New York, 1931.
―――. *Our Contemporary Composers.* New York, 1941.
HUGHES, LANGSTON. *The Big Sea.* New York, 1945.
JOHNSON, JAMES WELDON. *The Book of American Negro Spirituals.* New York, 1925.
―――. *Black Manhattan.* New York, 1930.
JOHNSON, ROSAMOND. *Rolling Along in Song.* New York, 1936.
JONES, HOWARD MUMFORD. *Guide to American Literature and Its Backgrounds, Since 1890.* Cambridge, Mass., 1953.
―――. *The Theory of American Literature.* Ithaca, N.Y., 1948.
KAUFMAN, HELEN K. *From Jehovah to Jazz.* New York, 1937.
KENNEDY, R. EMMET. *Mellows.* New York, 1925.
―――. *More Mellows.* New York, 1931.

KREHBIEL, H. E. *Afro-American Folk Songs.* New York, 1914.
LAHEE, HENRY C. *Annals of Music in America.* Boston, 1922.
LAMBERT, CONSTANT (ed.). *Music Ho!* London, 1934.
LARKIN, OLIVER W. *Art and Life in America.* New York, 1949.
LAURIE, JOE, JR. *Vaudeville.* New York, 1953.
LEWIS, AL. *From Rhymes to Riches.* New York, 1935.
LINDSAY, BEN, and WAINWRIGHT EVANS. *The Revolt of Modern Youth.* New York, 1925.
LOCKE, ALAIN L. *The Negro and His Music.* Washington, D.C., 1936.
LOMAX, ALAN. *Mister Jelly Roll.* New York, 1950.
LOMAX, JOHN A., and ALAN LOMAX. *American Ballads and Folk Songs.* New York, 1934.
————. *Folksong U.S.A.* New York, 1947.
LUEDERS, EDWARD G. *Carl Van Vechten and the Twenties.* Albuquerque, 1955.
LUTHER, FRANK. *Americans and Their Songs.* New York, 1924.
McSPADDEN, J. WALKER. *Light Opera and Musical Comedy.* New York, 1936.
MANNERS, J. HARTLEY. *The National Anthem.* New York, 1922.
MARTIN, HERBERT. *Formative Factors in Character.* New York, 1925.
MARKS, EDWARD B. *They All Sang: From Tony Pastor to Rudy Vallee,* as told to ABBOTT J. LIEBLING. New York, 1934.
MASON, DANIEL GREGORY. *Artistic Ideals.* New York, 1927.
————. *The Dilemma of American Music.* New York, 1928.
————. *Tune In, America.* New York, 1931.
MEES, ARTHUR. *Choirs and Choral Music.* New York, 1911.
MENCKEN, HENRY L. *Prejudices, Fifth Series.* New York, 1926.
MERRIAM, ALAN P., with ROBERT J. BENFORD. *Bibliography of Jazz.* Philadelphia, 1954.
MERZ, CHARLES. *The Great American Bandwagon.* New York, 1928.
METFESSEL, MILTON. *Phonophotography in Folk Music.* Chapel Hill, N.C., 1928.
MEZZROW, MILTON, and BERNARD WOLFE. *Really the Blues.* New York, 1946.
MOLEY, RAYMOND. *The Hays Office.* New York, 1945.
MORGUN, ALUN, and RAYMOND HORRICKS. *Modern Jazz: A Survey of Developments since 1939.* London, 1956.
MUELLER, JOHN H. *The American Symphony Orchestra.* Bloomington, Ind., 1951.
NEWTON, FRANCIS. *The Jazz Scene.* London, 1959.
ODUM, HOWARD W. *Rainbow 'Round My Shoulder.* Indianapolis, 1938.
ODUM, HOWARD W., and GUY B. JOHNSON. *Negro Workaday Songs.* Chapel Hill, N.C., 1926.
OSGOOD, HENRY. *So This Is Jazz.* Boston, 1926.
OSTRANSKY, LEROY. *The Anatomy of Jazz.* Seattle, 1960.
PANASSIÉ, HUGUES. *Hot Jazz,* rans. LYLE and ELEANOR DOWLING. New York, 1936.
————. *The Real Jazz.* New York, 1942.
PARRY, ALBERT. *Garrets and Pretenders.* New York, 1933.

PERRY, BLISS (ed.). *The Life and Letters of Henry Lee Higginson.* 2 vols. Boston, 1921.

POLLOCK, GUSTAV (ed.). *Our Success in Child Training.* New York, 1902.

PUTNAM, DANIEL. *A Manual of Pedagogics.* Boston, 1895.

RAMSEY, FREDERIC, JR., and CHARLES EDWARD SMITH (eds.). *Jazzmen.* New York, 1939.

REESE, GUSTAVE (ed.). *A Birthday Greeting to Carl Engel.* New York, 1943.

RITTER, FRÉDÉRIC L. *Music in America.* New York, 1883.

ROSENFELD, PAUL. *An Hour with American Music.* Philadelphia, 1929.

ROURKE, CONSTANCE. *The Roots of American Culture.* New York, 1942.

————. *Troupers of the Gold Coast.* New York, 1928.

SADLER, WILLIAM S., and LENA K. SADLER. *Piloting Modern Youth.* New York, 1925.

SANTAYANA, GEORGE. *The Genteel Tradition at Bay.* New York, 1931.

SAYLER, OLIVER (ed.). *Revolt in the Arts.* New York, 1930.

SCARBOROUGH, DOROTHY. *On the Trail of Negro Folk Songs.* Cambridge, Mass., 1925.

SELDES, GILBERT. *The Seven Lively Arts.* New York, 1924.

SIEPMAN, CHARLES A. *Radio, Television and Society.* New York, 1950.

SHAPIRO, NAT, and NAT HENTOFF (eds.). *Hear Me Talkin' to Ya.* New York, 1955.

————. *The Jazz Makers.* New York, 1958.

SHAW, ARTIE. *The Trouble with Cinderella.* New York, 1952.

SLONIMSKY, NICHOLAS. *Music Since 1900.* New York, 1937.

SLOSSOM, PRESTON W. *The Great Crusade and After, 1914–1928.* Vol. XII of *A History of American Life,* ARTHUR M. SCHLESINGER and DIXON R. Fox, eds. New York, 1931.

SMITH, CHARLES EDWARD, with FREDERIC RAMSEY, JR., CHARLES PAYNE ROGERS, and WILLIAM RUSSELL. *The Jazz Record Book.* New York, 1944.

SMITH, HUGH L., JR. "The Literary Manifestation of a Liberal Romanticism in American Jazz." Unpublished doctoral dissertation, University of New Mexico, 1955.

SONNECK, OSCAR G. *Suum Cuique, Essays in Music.* New York, 1916.

SOUSA, JOHN PHILIP. *Marching Along.* Boston, 1928.

SPAETH, SIGMUND. *A History of Popular Music in America.* New York, 1948.

————. *The Facts of Life in Popular Song.* New York, 1934.

————. *Read 'Em and Weep.* New York, 1927.

STEARNS, HAROLD E. (ed.). *Civilization in the United States.* New York, 1922.

STEARNS, MARSHALL W. *The Story of Jazz.* New York, 1956.

STEINER, JESSE FREDERICK. *Americans at Play.* New York, 1933.

STRAVINSKY, IGOR. *An Autobiography.* New York, 1936.

SULLIVAN, MARK. *The Twenties.* Vol. 4 of *Our Times: The United States.* New York, 1935.

THOMPSON, OSCAR (ed.). *The International Cyclopedia of Music and Musicians.* 6th ed., rev. by NICHOLAS SLONIMSKY. New York, 1952.

ULANOV, BARRY. *Duke Ellington.* New York, 1946.
————. *A History of Jazz in America.* New York, 1952.
UPTON, GEORGE (ed). *Theodore Thomas: A Musical Autobiography.* 2 vols. Chicago, 1905.
U.S. BUREAU OF CENSUS. *Biennial Census of Manufactures.* 1923.
WARE, CAROLINE. *Greenwich Village, 1920–1930.* Boston, 1935.
WEST, ROBERT. *The Rape of Radio.* New York, 1941.
WHITE, LLEWELLYN. *The American Radio.* Chicago, 1947.
WHITEMAN, PAUL, and MARY MARGARET MCBRIDE, *Jazz.* New York, 1926.
WILLIAMS, MARTIN T. (ed). *The Art of Jazz: Essays on the Nature and Development of Jazz.* New York, 1959.
WILSON, JOHN S. *The Collector's Jazz: Traditional and Swing.* New York, 1958.
————. *The Collector's Jazz: Modern.* New York, 1959.
WITMARK, ISADORE, and ISAAC GOLDBERG. *From Ragtime to Swingtime: The Story of the House of Witmark.* New York, 1939.
WITTKE, CARL. *Tambo and Bones.* Durham, N.C., 1930.
WORK, JOHN W. *American Negro Songs.* New York, 1940.

ARTICLES CONSULTED

ADAMS, HAZARD, and BRUCE PARK. "The State of the Jazz Lyric," *Chicago Review,* X (Autumn–Winter, 1956), 5–20.
ADORNO, T. W. "On Popular Music," *Studies in Philosophy and Social Science,* IX (1941), 17–48.
ALDRICH, RICHARD. "Drawing a Line for Jazz," *New York Times* (December 10, 1922), Sec. VIII, p. 4.
ALLEN, FREDERICK LEWIS. "When America Learned To Dance," *Scribner's* CII (September, 1937), 11–17, 92.
ANDERSON, W. R. "Jazz and Real Music," *Musical Times,* LXXXIII (October, 1932), 926–27.
ANTHEIL, GEORGE, "Jazz Is Music," *Forum,* LXXX (July, 1928), 64–67.
ANTRIM, DORON K. "Tin Pan Avenue," *Scribner's,* XCIV (February, 1936), 74–76.
AVAKIAN, GEORGE. "The History of Columbia Is the Saga of Jazz," *Down Beat,* XXXIII (December 12, 1956), 14.
BECKER, HOWARD S. "The Professional Dance Musician and His Audience," *American Journal of Sociology,* LVI (1951), 136–44.
BELL, CLIVE. " 'Plus de Jazz,' " *New Republic,* XXVIII (September 21, 1921), 92–96.
BERGER, MORROE. "Jazz: Resistance to the Diffusion of a Culture-Pattern," *Journal of Negro History,* XXXII (October, 1947), 461–94.
BERGMAN, LOUIS. "Small Time Musicians," *New York Times* (September 10, 1939), Sec. VII, pp. 12, 16.
BETTONVILLE, ALBERT. "Chicago Jazz, au Temps des Gangsters . . .," *Hot Club Magazine,* VI (June, 1946), 6–7, 9.
BOBLITZ, SHERWOOD K. "Where Movie Playing Needs Reform," *Musician,* XXV (June, 1920), 8, 29.
BOLGEN, KAARE A. "An Analysis of the Jazz Idiom," *Music Teachers' Review,* XI (September–October, 1941), 3–9.

BOYER, RICHARD O. "Bop," *New Yorker*, XXIV (July 3, 1948), 28–32, 34–37.

BUCHANAN, CHARLES. "Two Views of Ragtime," *Seven Arts*, II (July, 1917), 376–82.

BURK, JOHN N. "Ragtime and Its Possibilities," *Harvard Musical Review*, II (January, 1914), 11–13.

CAMERON, WILLIAM BRUCE. "Sociological Notes on the Jam Session," *Social Forces*, XXXIII (December, 1954), 177–82.

CARROLL, AMY KIETH. " 'Jazz Is Savage' Says Oumeroff," *Musical Leader*, XLV (March 15, 1923), 259.

CARTER, JOHN C. "These Wild Young People, by One of Them," *Atlantic Monthly*, CXXVI (April, 1920), 301–4.

CHASE, STUART. "Play" in CHARLES A. BEARD (ed.), *Whither Mankind: A Panorama of Modern Civilization* (New York, 1928), pp. 332–53.

CHOTZINOFF, SAMUEL. "Jazz: A Brief History," *Vanity Fair*, XX (June, 1923), 69.

CLARK, ROBERT. "Music Education vs. Radio and Dance-Hall Rhythm," *Music Educator's Journal*, XXIII (May, 1937), 33–34.

COVARRUBIAS, MIGUEL. "Impossible Interview; Fritz Kreisler vs. Louis Armstrong," *Vanity Fair*, XLV (February, 1936), 33.

CRANE, MAURICE. "Bebop," *Word Study*, XXX (October, 1954), 6.

DARRELL, R. D. "All Quiet on the Western Jazz Front," *Disques*, III (September, 1932), 290–94.

DICKERSON, REED. "Hot Music: Rediscovering Jazz," *Harper's*, CLXXII (April, 1936), 567–74.

DREHER, CARL. "In Defense of Broadcasting," *Radio Broadcast*, VIII (December, 1925), 191–93.

DOWNES, OLIN. "A Piano Concerto in the Vernacular To Have Its Day with Damrosch," *New York Times* (November 29, 1925), Sec. VIII, p. 6.

————. "American Popular Music in Europe," *New York Times* (August 1, 1926), Sec. VIII, p. 5.

————. "An American Composer," *Musical Quarterly*, IV (January, 1918), 23–26.

————. "Concerning 'Modern American Music' — Recent Delusions and Experiment," *New York Times* (November 23, 1924), Sec. VIII, p. 6.

EISENBERG, JACOB. "Clarence Adler Gives His Recipe for Success," *Musician*, XXIX (November, 1924), 29.

EMGE, CHARLES. "Venuti Part of 'Golden Era' of Jazz," *Down Beat*, XVII (December 1, 1950), 3.

ENGEL, CARL. "Jazz: A Musical Discussion," *Atlantic Monthly*, CXXX (August, 1922), 182–89.

————. "Jazz, In the Proper Light," *Journal of Proceedings of the Fifteenth Annual Meeting of the Music Supervisors' National Conference* (March 20–24, 1922), pp. 137–44.

————. "Views and Reviews," *Musical Quarterly*, XII (April, 1926), 306.

ESMAN, AARON H. "Jazz — A Study in Cultural Conflict," *American Imago*, III (Fall, 1954), 3–10.

FARNSWORTH, KEN. "Specht's 'Jass' Played a Big Part in Progress of Swing," *Down Beat*, VII (September 1, 1940), 7.

FAULKNER, ANNE SHAW. "Does Jazz Put the Sin in Syncopation?" *Ladies' Home Journal*, XXXVIII (August, 1921), 16, 34.

FERGUSON, OTIS. "A Mild Ribbing," *New Republic*, LXXXVI (March 11, 1939), 140.

——. "The Piano in the Band," *New Republic*, XCIII (November 24, 1937), 68–70.

——. "The Spirit of Jazz," *New Republic*, LXXXIX (December 30, 1936), 269–71.

FINCK, HENRY T. "Jazz — Lowbrow and Highbrow," *Etude*, XLII (August, 1924), 527–28.

FRANK, WALDO. "Jazz and Folk Art," *New Republic*, XLIX (December 1, 1926), 42–43.

FRENCH, WARREN G. "Behind the Popular Front," *Etc.: A Review of General Semantics*, XII (Winter, 1955–56), 127–32.

GALLAGHER, BUELL G. "The Negro's Participation in American Culture," in ALAIN LOCKE (ed), *When People Meet* (New York, 1942), pp. 548–51.

GILBERT, GAMA. "Swing: What Is It?" *New York Times* (September 5, 1937), Sec. X, p. 5.

GILLESPIE, JAMES F. with WESLEY STOUT. "Hot Music," *Saturday Evening Post*, CCIV (March 19, 1932), 10–11, 83, 86, 88.

GLEASON, RALPH J. "A Short Analysis of Hot Jazz Record Collecting," *Hobbies*, XLVI (May, 1941), 35–36.

GOFFIN, ROBERT. "Bix at Lake Forest," *Esquire*, XXI (March, 1944), 59, 144–45.

GOLDBERG, ISAAC. "Aaron Copland and His Jazz," *American Mercury*, XII (September, 1927), 63–65.

GOLDMAN, EDWIN FRANKO. "A Growing Demand for Wind Instrument Players," *Musician*, XXXVII (December, 1922), 8, 23.

GOMBOSI, OTTO. "The Pedigree of the Blues," in THEODORE M. FINNEY (ed.), *Volume of Proceedings of the Music Teachers' National Association, Fortieth Series* (Pittsburg, 1946), pp. 382–89.

GORDON, GRAY. "Experiment in Dance Music," *New York Times* (May 2, 1939), p. 22.

GORDON, JEAN. "Mental Snobs Who Never Succeed," *Musician*, XXXIX (January, 1924), 9.

GRAINGER, PERCY. "The Impress of Personality on Unwritten Music," *Musical Quarterly*, I (July, 1915), 416–35.

GUILLIAMS, A. E. "Detrimental Effects of Jazz on Our Younger Generation," *Metronome*, XXXIX (February, 1923), 59.

HAGGIN, B. H. "The Pedant Looks at Jazz," *Nation*, CXXI (December 9, 1924), 685–88.

HANSEN, CHADWICK C. "Social Influences on Jazz Style: Chicago, 1920–30," *American Quarterly*, XII (Winter, 1960), 493–507.

HARAP, LOUIS. "The Case for Hot Jazz," *Musical Quarterly*, XXVII (January, 1949), 47–61.

HAYAKAWA, S. I. "Popular Songs vs. The Facts of Life," *Etc.: A General Review of Semantics*, XII (Winter, 1955), 83–95.

HENDERSON, W. J. "Ragtime, Jazz, and High Art," *Scribner's*, LXXVII (February, 1925), 200–203.

HIATT, WALTER S. "Billions Just for Fun," *Collier's*, LXXIV (October 25, 1924), 19, 31.

HILL, EDWARD BURLINGAME. "Copland's Jazz Concerto in Boston," *Modern Music*, IV (May–June, 1927), 35–37.

HINCHCLIFFE, R. E. S. "Defends Jazzmen against 'Moronic Ravings' of Foes," *Down Beat*, VII (September 15, 1941), 7.

HODES, ART. "Bessie Smith," *Jazz Record*, LVIII (September, 1947), 8–9.

HOEFER, GEORGE. "Chicago Jazz Landmark Being Razed," *Down Beat*, XVII (January 27, 1950), 2.

————. "Committee To Perpetuate Memory of Beiderbecke," *Down Beat*, XVII (April 21, 1950), 7.

————. "Discographies Fill Vital Role in Collectors' Work," *Down Beat*, XVII (October 20, 1950), 11.

————. " 'Man, I Invented Jazz In ————' Claimed by More Folks!" *Down Beat*, XVI (July 1, 1949), 11.

HOUGHTON, JOHN ALAN. "Darius Milhaud: A Missionary of the 'Six,' " *Musical America*, XXXVII (January 13, 1923), 3, 42.

HUBBARD, W. L. "A Hopeful View of the Ragtime Roll," *Musician*, XXV (August, 1920), 6.

HUGHES, RUPERT. "A Eulogy of Ragtime," *Musical Record* (Boston) No. 447 (April, 1899), 157–59.

————. "Music for the Man of Today" in JAMES F. COOKE (ed.), *Great Men and Famous Musicians in the Art of Music* (Philadelphia, 1925), pp. 138–40.

————. "Will Ragtime Turn to Symphonic Poems?" *Etude*, XXXVIII (May, 1920), 305.

JOHNSON, GUY B. "Double Meaning in Popular Negro Blues," *Journal of Abnormal and Social Psychology*, XXII (April–June, 1927), 12–20.

JONES, S. TURNER. "Appreciation through Jazz," *Educational Music Magazine*, XX (January–February, 1941), 53, 55.

JUDSON, ARTHUR L. "Works of American Composers Reveal Relation of Ragtime to Art-Song," *Musical America*, XV (December 2, 1911), 29.

KEEPNEWS, ORRIN. "Definition of Jazz," *Record Changer*, VII (December, 1948), 9.

KOLODIN, IRVING. "Number One Swing Man," *Harper's*, CLXXIX (September, 1939), 431–40.

————. "What about Swing," *Parents' Magazine*, XLV (August, 1939), 18–19.

KOLISCH, MITZI. "Jazz in High Places," *Independent*, CXVI (April 10, 1926), 424.

KOOL, JAAP. "The Triumph of the Jungle," *Littell's Living Age*, CCCXXIV (February, 1924), 338–43.

KRAMER, A. WALTER. "I Do Not Think Jazz 'Belongs,' " *Singing*, I (September, 1926), 13–14.

L. "Jazz Analyzed," *Commonweal*, XXX (April 28, 1939), 22–23.

LACHENBRUCH, JEROME. "Jazz and the Motion Pictures," *Metronome*, XXXVIII (April, 1922), 94.

LAND, DICK. "Top Song Hits of 30 Years Are Recalled," *Down Beat*, VII (June 15, 1940), 22.

LASTRUCCI, CARLO L. "The Professional Dance Musician," *Journal of Musicology*, III (Winter, 1941), 168–72.

LAUBENSTEIN, PAUL FRITZ. "Jazz — Debit and Credit," *Musical Quarterly*, XV (October, 1929), 606–24.

LEVIN, MICHAEL. "Thirty Years of Dancing in U.S.," *Down Beat*, XVII (May 19, 1950), 1, 20.

LOCKE, BOB. "Waxman Tells of Early Day Jazz Era," *Down Beat*, IX (May 15, 1942), 9.

LOCKE, TED. "Says Most Jazz Critics Are Not Qualified," *Down Beat*, VIII (February 15, 1941), 8, 16.

LOPEZ, VINCENT. "Vincent Lopez Comments on His Unique Experiment," *Musical Observer*, XIII (May, 1924), 30.

LOWRY, HELEN B. "Putting the Music into Jazz," *New York Times* (February 19, 1922), Sec. II, p. 8.

LUNCEFORD, JIMMY. "Is Airtime Essential? Not on My Life — Lunceford," *Metronome*, LVIII (October, 1942), 9, 26.

LUNDBERG, G. A. "The Content of Radio Programs," *Social Forces*, VII (September, 1928), 59.

McCONATHY, OSBORNE. "The Great Gap," *Musician*, XXVII (September, 1922), 1, 26.

McCULLOCH, LYLE. "Intolerance and Jazz," *Melody*, VIII (September, 1924), 3.

McMAHON, JOHN R. "Our Jazz-Spotted Middle West," *Ladies' Home Journal*, XXXIX (February, 1922), 38, 181.

———. "The Jazz Path of Degradation," *Ladies' Home Journal*, XXXIX (January, 1922), 26, 71.

———. "Unspeakable Jazz Must Go!" *Ladies' Home Journal*, XXXIII (December, 1921), 34, 115–16.

MAGUIRE, HELENA. "The Revolt against Formalism," *Musician*, XXVII (September, 1922), 26.

MASON, DANIEL GREGORY. "Concerning Ragtime," *New Music Review and Church Music Review*, XVII (March, 1918), 112–16.

———. "Jazz for the Illiterate," *American Mercury*, LVII (December, 1943), 761.

———. "Stravinsky as a Symptom," *American Mercury*, IV (April, 1925), 465–68.

———. "The Jazz Invasion," in SAMUEL DANIEL SCHMALHAUSEN, *Behold America* (New York, 1931), pp. 499–513.

MARGOLIS, NORMAN H. "A Theory on the Psychology of Jazz," *American Imago*, XI (Fall, 1954), 263–91.

MATHEWS, HAYDN M. "Jazz — Its Origin, Effect, Future," *Flutist*, V (February, 1924), 32–34.

MAY, EARL CHAPIN. "The Reign of Reeds and Rhythm," *Saturday Evening Post*, CXCVII (January 10, 1925), 52, 54, 56.

MILHAUD, DARIUS. "The Jazz Band and Negro Music," *Littell's Living Age*, CCCXXII (October 18, 1924), 169–73.

MODERWELL, HIRAM K. "Hitching Jazz to a Star," *Musical America*, XLIX (March 10, 1929), 13, 55.

————. "Ragtime," *New Republic*, IV (October 16, 1915), 284–86.

————. "Two Views of Ragtime. I. A Modest Proposal," *Seven Arts*, II (July, 1917), 368–76.

MOONEY, HUGHSON F. "Songs, Singers, and Society, 1890–1954," *American Quarterly*, VI (Fall, 1954), 221–32.

NEVIN, GORDON BALCH. "Jazz — Whither Bound?" *Etude*, XLVII (September, 1929), 655, 699.

NEWELL, GEORGE. "George Gershwin and Jazz," *Outlook*, CXLVIII (February 29, 1928), 342–43, 351.

NILES, ABBE. "A Note on Gershwin," *Nation*, CXXVIII (February 13, 1929), 193–94.

————. "Lady Jazz in the Vestibule," *New Republic*, XLV (December 23, 1925), 138–39.

————. "Sour Notes on Sweet Songs," *New Republic*, L (February 23, 1927), 19, 20.

OSGOOD, HENRY OSBORNE. "The Blues," *Modern Music*, IV (November–December, 1926), 25–28.

————. "The Jazz Bugaboo," *American Mercury*, VI (November, 1925), 328–30.

O'STEEN, ALTON. "Swing in the Classroom?" *Music Educator's Journal*, XXV (February, 1939), 25–27.

PATTERSON, FRANK. "An Afternoon of Jazz," *Musical Courier*, LXXXVIII (February 14, 1924), 38.

————. "Jazz — The National Anthem?" *Musical Courier*, LXXXIV (May 4, 1922), 18; (May 11, 1922), 6.

PERKINS, FRANCIS D. "Jazz Breaks into Society," *Independent*, CXIV (January 3, 1925), 23.

PICKERING, RUTH. "The Economic Interpretation of Jazz," *New Republic*, XXVI (May 11, 1921), 323–24.

PITTS, LILLA BELLE. "Modern Youth and His Musical Environment," *Music Educators' National Yearbook*, XXX (1939–40), 69–73. Reprinted: *Music Educators' Journal*, XXVI (October, 1939), 18–19, 67–68.

RIESENFELD, HUGO. "New Forms for Old Music," *Modern Music*, I (June, 1924), 25–26.

RIESMAN, DAVID. "Enter Popular Music," *American Quarterly*, II (Winter, 1950), 359–71.

ROGERS, B. "Capacity House Fervently Applauds as Jazz Invades Realm of Serious Music," *Musical America*, XXXIX (February 23, 1924), 32.

SCHIA, TITO. "Win Success in Singing," *Musician*, XXIX (December, 1924), 11, 28.

SAENGER, GUSTAV, "The Ambitions of Jazz in Artistic Form," *Musical Observer*, XXV (January, 1926), 5.

————. "The Musical Possibilities of Ragtime," *Metronome*, XIX (March, 1903), 11; (April, 1903), 8.

SANDOR, ARPAD. "American Music and Its Future," *Musical Courier*, CX (January, 26, 1935), 6.

SCHAAF, EDWARD. "Jazz and the Picture House," *Musical Advance*, XVI (May, 1929), 3.

SCHILLINGER, JOSEPH. "At Long Last – Here It is – An Explanation of 'Swing'," *Metronome*, LVIII (July, 1942), 19, 23.

SCOGGINS, CHARLES H. "The Ragtime Menace," *Musical Progress*, II (April, 1913), 3–4.

SEBASTIAN, JOHN. "From Spirituals to Swing," *New Masses*, XXX (January 3, 1939), 28.

SEEGER, CHARLES. "Music and Class Structure in the United States," *American Quarterly*, IX (Fall, 1957), 281–94.

SELDES, GILBERT. "Jazz and Ballad," *New Republic*, XLIII (August 5, 1925), 293–94.

———. "Jazz Music Not Such an 'Enfant Terrible' after All but Clever Adaptation in Current Style, Says Seldes," *Musical America*, XL (July 19, 1924), 13.

———. "Jazz Opera or Ballet?" *Modern Music*, III (January–February, 1926), 10–16.

———. "No More Swing?" *Scribner's*, C (November, 1936), 70–71.

———. "Position of Jazz in American Musical Development," *Arts and Decoration*, XX (April, 1924), 21.

———. "What Happened to Jazz?" *Saturday Evening Post*, CXCIX (January 22, 1927), 25, 102, 107.

SIMON, HENRY. "Benny Goodman Grows Long Hair," *PM*, XIII (December 13, 1940), 1–2.

SISSON, KENN. "Modern Masters of Music: The Arrangers," *Metronome*, LII (February, 1936), 36; (March, 1936), 37; (April, 1936), 34; (May, 1936), 31–32; (June, 1936), 27; (August, 1936), 22; (September, 1936), 47–48; (October, 1936), 24.

SCHULTZ, WILLIAM J. "Jazz," *Nation*, CXV (October 25, 1922), 438–39.

SLONIMSKY, NICHOLAS. "Our Jazzing, Their Jazzing, Reasons Why," *Boston Evening Transcript* (April 21, 1929), Sec. III, pp. 12, 15.

SLOTKIN, J. S. "Jazz and Its Forerunners as an Example of Acculturation," *American Sociological Review*, VIII (October, 1943), 570–75.

SMITH, CHARLES EDWARD. "Blues Stanzas," *New Republic*, XCVI (September 21, 1938), 184.

———. "Collecting Hot," *Esquire*, I (February, 1934), 79.

———. "Hard Liquor and Hot Jazz," *Stage*, XIII (March, 1936), 58–59.

———. "Heat Wave," *Stage*, XII (September, 1935), 45–56.

———. "Jazz: Some Little Known Aspects," *Symposium*, I (October, 1930), 502–17.

———. "Some Like It Hot," *Esquire*, V (April, 1936), 42, 186, 188.

———. "Swing," *New Republic*, XCIV (February 16, 1938), 39–41.

———. "Two Ways of Improvising on a Tune," *Down Beat*, V (May, 1938), 5, 27.

SPAETH, SIGMUND. "Dixie, Harlem, and Tin Pan Alley," *Scribner's*, XCIX (January, 1936), 23–26.

———. "Jazz Is Not Music," *Forum*, LXXX (August, 1928), 267–71.

SPERLING, GRACE DICKENSON. "Jazz – Our Race Emotion," *Musical Observer*, XXV (July, 1926), 15, 30–31.

STJERNBERG, LYDIA N. "Finding Merit in Jazz," *New York Times* (October 20, 1934), p. 14.

STONE, JAMES H. "Mid-Nineteenth Century American Beliefs in the Social Value of Music," *Musical Quarterly*, XLIII (January, 1957), 38–49.

STRATE, MARVIN W. "Swing — What Is It?" *Musical America*, LVI (May 25, 1936), 6–7.

STRINGHAM, EDWIN J. "Jazz — An Educational Problem," *Musical Quarterly*, XII (April, 1926), 190–95.

STUDEBAKER, J. W. "The Age of Jazz," *Journal of Education*, CIX (January, 1929), 68.

TAYLOR, DEEMS. "Music," in HAROLD STEARNS (ed.), *Civilization in the United States* (New York, 1922), pp. 199–214.

THOMPSON, OSCAR. "Much-Bruited Jazz Concerto Causes Stir When Given Orchestral Baptism," *Musical America*, XLIII (December 12, 1925), 43.

THOMPSON, VIRGIL. "The Cult of Jazz," *Vanity Fair*, XXIV (June, 1925), 54.

————. "Jazz," *American Mercury*, II (August, 1924), 465–67.

————. "Swing Again," *Modern Music*, XV (March–April, 1938), 160–66.

ULANOV, BARRY. "Critics and Criticism," *Metronome*, LXIII (December, 1947), 19, 32–35.

————. "The Function of the Critic in Jazz," *Metronome*, LXV (August, 1949), 16–17.

————. "The Jukes Take Over Swing," *American Mercury*, LI (October, 1940), 172–77.

VAN VECHTEN, CARL. "George Gershwin: An American Composer Who Is Writing Notable Music in the Jazz Idiom," *Vanity Fair*, XXIV (March, 1925), 40, 78, 84.

————. "Music after the Great War," *Forum*, LIV (September, 1915), 356–67.

————. "The Black Blues," *Vanity Fair*, XXIV (August, 1925), 57, 86, 92.

————. "The Folksongs of the American Negro," *Vanity Fair*, XXIV (July, 1925), 52, 92.

————. "The Great American Composer," *Vanity Fair*, VIII (April, 1917), 75, 140.

WATERMAN, RICHARD ALAN. "African Influence on the Music of the Americas," in SOL TAX (ed.), *Acculturation in the Americas* (Chicago, 1952), pp. 207–18.

————. " 'Hot' Rhythm in Negro Music," *Journal of American Musicological Society*, I (1948), 24–37.

WEBB, H. BROOK. "The Playing of Jazz," *American Speech Magazine*, XII (October, 1937), 179–84.

WELLES, KINGSLEY. "Is the Popularity of Jazz Music Waning?" *Radio Broadcast*, VIII (December, 1925), 177–78.

WEINBERGER, JULIUS. "Economic Aspects of Recreation," *Harvard Business Review*, XV (Summer, 1937), 448–63.

WHITING, ARTHUR. "The Mechanical Player," *Yale Review*, VIII (July, 1919), 828–35.

WHITEMAN, PAUL. "In Defense of Jazz and Its Makers," *New York Times* (March 13, 1927), Sec. IV, pp. 4, 22.
———. "What Jazz Is Doing to American Music," *Etude*, XLII (August, 1924), 523.
WILSON, EDMUND. "The Jazz Problem," *New Republic*, XLV (January 13, 1926), 217–19.

INDEX

Acceptance of jazz: and European opinion, 141–42; factors in, 52–55; and growing respectability of jazz men, 127–32, 145–47; hypothesis concerning, 3–4, 154–57; in schools, 152; and types of people, 54, 69–72, 147–53

Acceptance of refined jazz, 73–78; and dancing, 73–74; and types of supporters, 74–76

Acceptance of symphonic jazz, 75–89; and enthusiasts, 75–76; and enthusiasts' opposition to real jazz, 76–77; and enthusiasts' values, 75–76

Adams, Franklin P., 70

Adams, Hazard, 119

Alda, Frances, 80

American Federation of Musicians, 26, 144

American Jazz Music (Wilder Hobson), 137

American Mercury, 56

American in Paris, An (George Gershwin), 82

American Record Company, 103

American Society of Composers, Authors, and Publishers (ASCAP), 98, 104

Ansermet, Ernest: quoted, 142

Apollo Club (of Chicago), 18

Armory Show (1913), 48

Armstrong, Louis, 11, 12, 13, 57, 61, 68, 95, 102, 125, 135, 139, 141, 145, 149, 168–71; analysis of his lyrics, 110–19, 167–72; *Swing That Music*, 137; quoted, 63, 64, 71, 107, 121, 126, 127

Artist-audience gap, 4–5, 147

"Ash Can School," 49

Austin High Gang, 14, 56

Aux Frontières du Jazz (Robert Goffin), 141

Avakian, George, 167

Aylesworth, M. H., 105

Bach, Johann Sebastian, 21, 25, 146, 151; *Second Brandenburg Concerto*, 142

Bach Society of New Jersey, 100

Bailey, Buster: quoted, 39

Barnum, P. T., 20